W9-AQQ-438

CNN REPORTS

KATRINA
State of Emergency

Introduction by Ivor van Heerden

Andrews McMeel
Publishing

Kansas City

05 06 07 08 09 BBL 10 9 8 7 6 5 4 3 2 1
Library of Congress Control Number: 2005935404

ISBN-13: 978-0-7407-5844-7
ISBN-10: 0-7407-5844-6

www.andrewsmcmeel.com

Editorial Cartoons
pp. 37 and 91 Auth © 2005 by the *Philadelphia Inquirer*.
p. 55 Oliphant © 2005 by Universal Press Syndicate.
p. 77 Carlson © 2005 by the *Milwaukee Journal Sentinel*.
pp. 91 and 155 Sargent © 2005 by the *Austin American Statesman*.
p. 117 Higgins © 2005 by the *Chicago Sun-Times*.
p. 117 Toles © 2005 by the *Washington Post*.
All reprinted by permission of Universal Press Syndicate. All rights reserved.

p. 55 © 2005 Don Wright, *Palm Beach Post*, distributed by Tribune Media Services Inc.

p. 77 By permission of Chip Bok and Creators Syndicate, Inc.

Additional Photo Credits
Title page–Willie J. Allen Jr./*St. Petersburg Times*/WpN
p. 42 Clockwise from top–James Neilsen/AFP/Getty Images;
AP Photo/Steve Senne, CNN; AP Photo/Eric Gay; AP Photo/Eric Gay

p. 43 Clockwise from top–Rick Wilking/Reuters/Landov; Mario Tama/Getty Images;
AP Photo/Rob Carr; Joe Skipper/Reuters/Landov; AP Photo/Eric Gay; Mario Tama/Getty Images;
Alex Brandon/Newhouse News Service /Landov

Reprint Permissions
p. 6 Thomas Lynch © 2005, "Local Heroes."

p. 7 Ivor van Heerden, "A Hurricane Night in Louisiana," Reprinted by permission.

p. 93 Abraham Verghese © 2005, "Close Encounter of the Human Kind," *New York Times*, Reprinted by permission.

CNN Reports: Katrina—State of Emergency was produced by Lionheart Books, Ltd.,
5105 Peachtree Industrial Boulevard, Atlanta, Georgia 30341.

Michael Reagan: Editor-in-Chief/Designer
Gina Webb: Senior Editor and Lead Writer
Caroline Harkleroad: Associate Editor and Lead Researcher
Carley Brown: Associate Designer and Photo Researcher
Lisa Reagan: Research and Copyediting
Deb Murphy: Research and Copyediting
Researchers: Jonelle Celluci, John Christenson,
Carol Clark, and Elana Maxwell

The American Red Cross name and emblem are used with its permission, which in no way constitutes an endorsement, express or implied, of any product, service, company, or individual.

The Voices of CNN

CNN Personnel Who Are Represented in
CNN Reports: KATRINA—State of Emergency

Christiane Amanpour, Chief International Correspondent
Mark Biello, Photojournalist
Wolf Blitzer, Anchor, *The Situation Room*
Donna Brazile, *Political Contributor*
Aaron Brown, Anchor, *NewsNight With Aaron Brown*
Jack Cafferty, Anchor, *In the Money*
Sean Callebs, Correspondent, Washington, D.C.
James Carville, Political Analyst
Sophia Choi, Anchor, *Headline News*
Anderson Cooper, Anchor, *Anderson Cooper 360°*
Carol Costello, Anchor, *CNN Daybreak*
Pat D'Amuro, Security Analyst
Deb Feyerick, Correspondent, New York
Tom Foreman, Correspondent, Washington D.C.
Jonathan Freed, Correspondent, Chicago
Jeff Greenfield, Senior Analyst
Drew Griffin, Correspondent, Investigative Unit
Dr. Sanjay Gupta, Senior Medical Correspondent
Tony Harris, Anchor
Ed Henry, Correspondent, Washington, D.C.
Brad Huffines, Meteorologist
Chris Huntington, Correspondent, *Business News*
Daryn Kagan, Anchor
Larry King, Host, *Larry King Live*

Kathleen Koch, Correspondent, Washington, D.C.
Jeff Koinange, Correspondent, Africa
Ed Lavandera, Correspondent, Dallas
Chris Lawrence, Correspondent, Chicago
Rob Marciano, News and Weather Anchor
David Mattingly, Correspondent, Atlanta
Jeanne Meserve, Correspondent, Washington, D.C.
Chad Myers, News and Weather Anchor
Beth Nissen, Senior Correspondent
Miles O'Brien, Anchor, *American Morning*
Soledad O'Brien, Anchor, *American Morning*
Kyra Phillips, Anchor, *Live From*
Christine Romans, Correspondent, *Lou Dobbs Tonight*
Ted Rowlands, Correspondent, Los Angeles
Rick Sanchez, Contributor, *Anderson Cooper 360°*
Bonnie Schneider, Meteorologist
Jim Spellman, Producer
Barbara Starr, Pentagon Correspondent
Brian Todd, Producer
Gary Tuchman, National Correspondent, Atlanta
Adaora Udoji, Correspondent, New York
Paula Zahn, Anchor, *Paula Zahn Now*
John Zarrella, Correspondent, Miami

Hundreds of dedicated CNN employees contributed to the network's coverage of Hurricane Katrina, including those on the ground throughout the Gulf Coast and those working from numerous bureaus around the country. Our appreciation extends to all of those who made this book possible, and we regret that due to the limitations of space, we cannot include them all.

"The reporters of CNN are my heroes. They were and are
true saints in covering Katrina and Rita. They risked their lives
to keep the nation focused on these unspeakable disasters."

—*Anne Rice, author, New Orleans native*

Preface

Our mission to cover news as and where it happens frequently puts the men and women of CNN at the center of transforming events. In August 2005, that center was, literally, the eye of a hurricane that changed profoundly and perhaps permanently the geographic, social, economic, and political landscape of three southern U.S. states, and, to varying degrees, the 47 others. Months later, we continue to experience, explore, and respond to the dimensions of this epic story as journalists, but also as people who were there.

This book collects the facts we know about Hurricane Katrina—the science of the event and the physical devastation in its wake—and what we saw across Louisiana, Mississippi, and Alabama: suffering and heroism; good intentions and mixed results; the end of something, and beginnings. The words and pictures that follow include those of CNN personnel who weathered the storm to tell these stories.

It is our wish that this project and all proceeds from it support recovery and rebuilding efforts in affected areas. I am proud to dedicate this book to the millions of lives touched by Hurricane Katrina, and to direct our material gain from its publication to the American Red Cross. This pledge is made possible by the professionalism, commitment, compassion, and journalistic integrity of my colleagues at CNN. Their excellence defines our organization and inspires my gratitude and respect.

—*Jim Walton, president, CNN News Group*

Local Heroes

Some days the worst that can happen happens.
The sky falls or weather overwhelms or
The world as we have come to know it turns
Towards the eventual apocalypse
Long prefigured in all the holy books —
The end times of floods and conflagrations
That bring us to the edge of our oblivions.
Still, maybe this is not the end at all,
Nor even the beginning of the end.
Rather, one more in a long list of sorrows,
To be added to the ones thus far endured,
Through what we have come to call our history:
Another in that bitter litany
That we will, if we survive it, have survived.
Lord, send us in our peril, local heroes,
Someone to listen, someone to watch,
Some one to search and wait and keep the careful count
Of the dead and missing, the dead and gone
But not forgotten. Sometimes all that can be done
Is to salvage one sadness from the mass of sadnesses,
To bear one body home, to lay the dead out
Among their people, organize the flowers
And casseroles, write the obits, meet the mourners at the door,
Drive the dark procession down through town
Toll the bell, dig the hole, tend the pyre.
It's what we do. The daylong news is dire—
Full of true believers and politicos
Old talk of race and blame and photo ops.
But here brave men and women pick the pieces up.
They serve the living tending to the dead.
They bring them home, the missing and adrift,
They give them back to let them go again.
Like politics, all funerals are local.

—Thomas Lynch

Introduction

Low lying, marshy, and swampy coastal Louisiana has always been very susceptible to the ravages of hurricane storm surges. Hurricane Betsy in 1965 revealed New Orleans' weaknesses all too plainly, when large parts of the city flooded and 75 folks drowned. However, since Betsy there had been no other major surge flooding event, and some thought New Orleans would always be safe, "after all there were the new levees the Corps had built." In the early 1990s I and others started to suspect that Louisiana was far more vulnerable to severe hurricane surge devastation than the average citizen realized. Scientists also realized that restoring the coastal wetlands was the key to long-term surge mitigation, but politics determined that this was not a national priority. A chance meeting with a very dynamic wind engineer, Dr. Marc Levitan, resulted in the establishment of the LSU Hurricane Center, which in turn presented a platform to assemble a group of dedicated scientists, from multiple fields, to really understand all aspects of a major hurricane hit on southeast Louisiana. Early in 1999, while developing a proposal for funding from the Louisiana Board of Regents, I penned the following passage. Little did I know how prophetic these words would be.

A Hurricane Night in Louisiana

"It is 3:00 in the morning, and the wind suddenly dies. You guess that the eye of hurricane 'Big One' must be passing overhead. You look at your watch again, three hours since the levees must have broken. Boy, the water came up quickly. You change your position, scrape your knees again, you did not know how rough asphalt roof tiles could be on your bare skin; you only have on summer pajamas. Just then you realize your children are crying, they are thirsty, they want their pets. You are glad they are not asking about Grandma. You prefer not to think of her. She was an invalid. The water rose up so quickly you could not get her out in time. Your heart aches. She must have drowned.

"Just then you become aware of screams from your neighbor's house. You realize they went up into the attic, as you went up onto your roof. They are trapped in the attic. Oh my God, what can you do? In the mad rush from the house you forgot the cellular phone. Then, you become aware of screams from the large oak tree in your other neighbor's yard. Dim as it is, you realize their trailer home is demolished—gone. They are in the big oak tree; so are all the fire ants, it seems. You told him many times to kill the mounds.

"Your kids scream and whimper at the same time. They are thirsty, hungry, and scared. All you have is your flashlight. You decide to scramble down the roof, dip your pajama top in the water, and then to squeeze that liquid down their throats. But as you clamber down the roof, you realize the water smells of gasoline and chemicals. In the flashlight you see garbage everywhere. Oh my, what is happening? Then with horror, you remember the old landfill down near the bayou! The garbage is coming from there; it was also an industrial landfill. Oh, will this nightmare never end? Then, there is an enormous explosion. It is from the vicinity of the local gas station. Oh no, gasoline floats on water. You see the flames spread very quickly. As you scramble up the roof again, you pray, please don't let the fire come this way."

Our hurricane public health research center was funded and the research proved to be enormously applicable in all phases of the Katrina tragedy. However, these successes pale when compared to the actual event.

Hurricane Katrina's indisputable facts are over 1,000 U.S. citizens gave up their lives; about 100,000 families are homeless; irrespective if it was the "Act of God" flood of eastern New Orleans, or the "man-made" flood of the city proper, the levee systems failed dismally; although scientists have sounded the alarm for 20 years about the need for coastal restoration, land loss continues at an alarming rate and our nation has suffered a major embarrassment—a tragedy that will be remembered for eons.

So now is the time to put politics, egos, turf wars, and profit agendas aside; now is the time to effectively reconstruct New Orleans, engineer proper levees, and restore the coast. Now, because nature will not give us a second chance. We owe it to the 1,000 who died; we owe it to their survivors. Maybe more importantly we owe it to future generations.

*Ivor van Heerden, Ph.D.,
director, Center for the Study of
Public Health Impacts of Hurricanes,
Louisiana State University*

Prologue

A small easterly wave, forming off the coast of Africa, disappears back into the mid Atlantic. It resurfaces 11 days later as a nameless disturbance over the central Bahamas, where the ocean has become a paradise of tropical storm ingredients.

It's late August, peak hurricane season, and conditions offer a nearly perfect breeding ground for storms. Ocean surface temperatures have risen to an ideal 82°F or warmer. Clashing equatorial winds have arrived, providing the necessary energy and spin to motor the storm toward land. The warm moist air evaporates, rising, its water condensing into storm clouds and rain. In turn, the cooler air above rises, replaced by more warm, humid air. The rotating winds converge, circulating around the warm center. Heat powers the vortex, and the storm continues to grow as long as it encounters warm air and water, which it converts into raw energy as it crosses the ocean. Wind speeds increase.

The embryonic disturbance without a name encounters no obstacles to starve it back into a wave. As it moves westward, it begins to organize, gathering strength. On August 23, 2005, the National Weather Service labels the now larger system Tropical Depression 12. Traveling through the warm waters of the Caribbean, its cycle intensifies, until by the afternoon of August 24 its winds clock at 35 mph. It is moving slowly, unsteadily, at 7 mph, giving it plenty of time to churn up moisture and heat into its hungry center. Satellite reports indicate the depression is "getting better organized."

With nothing in its path to weaken it, the storm continues to move erratically west-northwest. When its winds reach 45 mph, it is no longer a Tropical Depression, and earns a name, Tropical Storm Katrina. It is now about 135 miles east of the Florida coast as it continues to feed off the sultry Caribbean waters. Tropical storm-force winds extend out 70 miles, and its power is rapidly increasing. On the morning of August 25, a hurricane watch replaces the already issued tropical storm watch and includes Florida's southeast coast and west coast, and the Florida Keys.

By 5 p.m., with sustained winds of 75 mph extending outward for 15 miles, Katrina explodes into a full-fledged Category 1 hurricane. It takes the storm another hour and a half to reach the Florida coast, where it hits between Hallandale and North Miami Beaches with 80 mph winds and a storm surge of two to four feet.

Katrina cuts a wide swath of destruction as it moves southwest across Florida. Weakening slightly over land, it drops back to tropical storm status before breaking out into the Gulf of Mexico, where it is expected to hug the coastline while moving northward toward the Florida panhandle. Forecasters, however, do not expect it to weaken. Within hours, the storm rebounds and regains hurricane strength, then veers off to the northwest—into the balmy, open waters of the Gulf of Mexico. In perhaps a foreshadowing of what is to come, it slowly passes directly over the "loop current," a great deep patch of tropically hot seawater, which feed Katrina's fire like high octane fuel.

A horrified nation watches as Katrina quickly mushrooms into a Category 4 hurricane with sustained winds of 145 mph, and by Sunday, August 28, it is an unbelievable Category 5 hurricane packing winds up to 175 mph. It is now a massive storm, some 1,000 miles across, with a storm surge predicted up to 28 feet.

Within 72 hours, Katrina had become the "Monster Storm," an indiscriminate killer capable of unimaginable destruction, on a collision course with the coasts of Mississippi and Louisiana. A near direct hit is predicted for New Orleans, a city built below sea level, whose aging levee system and massive loss of protective wetlands make it, and the surrounding coastline, extremely vulnerable to the approaching monster: a potentially catastrophic vulnerability that had been documented at great length, and the dire consequences predicted in eerie detail.

—Michael Reagan and Gina Webb

DAY 1

Sunday, August 28, 2005

> "I told him, 'This is going to be a defining moment for a lot of people.'"
>
> —*National Hurricane Center Director Max Mayfield, recalling his conversation with New Orleans Mayor Ray Nagin the evening of August 27.*

As the day dawns, thousands in Florida are cleaning up damage from Thursday's storm, many without power and standing in line for drinking water and gas.

But Katrina is still motoring up through the Gulf, and residents from southeastern Louisiana through Alabama and as far as Pensacola, Fla. brace for the storm

AP Photo/Andy Newman

Dr. Max Mayfield, director of the National Hurricane Center, was so concerned about the storm, he did something he had never done before in 33 years at the center. He personally called the governors of Mississippi and Louisiana as well as the mayor of New Orleans to make sure they understood the severity of the situation. "I wanted to be able to sleep at night, knowing that I had done everything that I could do."

even in inland counties, which authorities promise will be affected by the storm surge. Forecasters warn that Katrina's impact will be greater than any hurricane in recent history.

Evacuees clog the freeways, deserting southeastern Louisiana and Mississippi; some stay behind, determined to ride it out; and some, unable to leave, some with not transport wait for shelters to open, for help to come.

Dr. Jeffrey Halverston, NASA: "*This is one of the worst-case scenarios. It's kind of a doomsday scenario. Very rarely have we ever seen nature conjure a storm this powerful in the past 100 years. It ranks right up there with storms such as Camille and Andrew and Galveston. [There] is no way to soften the blow of this storm what-soever. It's packing the worst possible energy in terms of ocean atmosphere, and all unimaginable energy.*"

Brad Huffines, CNN meteorologist: "*This storm is stronger than Ivan. This storm is right now stronger than Hurricane Camille, back when the shoreline was much less populated. . . . This hurricane can cause not just trees to be blown down and mobile homes and things like that, that you expect. This storm . . . can cause some catastrophic structural damage, from not just homes along the shorelines, but homes inland. It's a giant F-3 tornado. . . . This is massive.*"

Hurricane Category	Surge and waves at low tide*	Effect on New Orleans
①	7 feet	Lake Pontchartrain's levees stop the low-level surge
②	9 feet	Levees stop the surge, but some waves could find their way over
③	14 feet	Levees stop bulk of surge, but waves could cause considerable flooding
④	19 feet	Levees topped, causing catastrophic flooding
⑤	24 feet	Entire city submerged including Mississippi River levees

A City Under Water

This graphic was published by the New Orleans *Times-Picayune* in June of 2002 as part of a five-part series entitled "Washing Away."

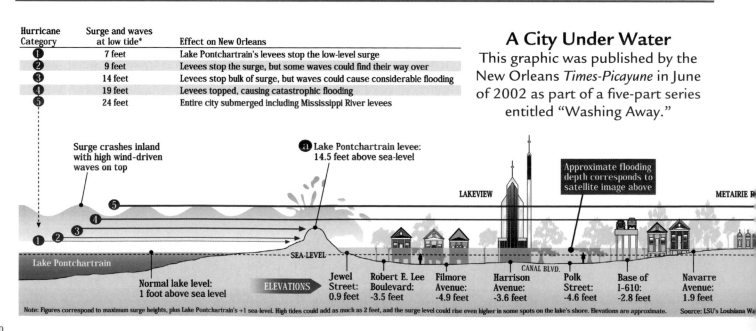

Note: Figures correspond to maximum surge heights, plus Lake Pontchartrain's +1 sea-level. High tides could add as much as 2 feet, and the surge level could rise even higher in some spots on the lake's shore. Elevations are approximate.   Source: LSU's Louisiana Wa

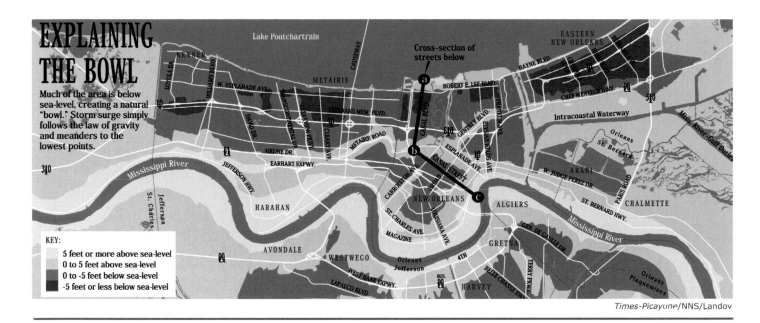

EXPLAINING THE BOWL

Much of the area is below sea-level, creating a natural "bowl." Storm surge simply follows the law of gravity and meanders to the lowest points.

Cross-section of streets below

KEY:
- 5 feet or more above sea-level
- 0 to 5 feet above sea-level
- 0 to -5 feet below sea-level
- -5 feet or less below sea-level

Times-Picayune/NNS/Landov

States of emergency have already been declared in advance of the storm's arrival: Louisiana Governor Kathleen Blanco on the 26th and Mississippi Governor Haley Barbour on the 27th. Blanco asks President George W. Bush to declare a federal state of emergency, which the President does on the 27th retroactive to the 26th. Alabama Governor Bob Riley declares a state of emergency on the 28th as forecasts upgrade Katrina to a Category 5 hurricane.

At 10 a.m., New Orleans Mayor Ray Nagin orders a mandatory evacuation, the first for the endangered city of 485,000 residents. Governor Blanco tries to paint a less catastrophic picture, while simultaneously preparing for the worst. President Bush, still on vacation at his

> **"The problem we have with this storm, if those storm surges are that high, they will top our levees and there will be lots of water in the city of New Orleans."** —*Mayor Ray Nagin*

ranch in Texas, advises Gulf Coast residents to obey the advice of local authorities: Get out. But with some of the poorest communities sitting in the path of the storm,

tens of thousands of the residents are unable to buy a bus or train ticket to leave; many of them have never owned a car. Mayor Nagin opens ten shelters, including the Superdome, to thousands of unfortunate residents, who stand in line for hours waiting to get inside; 36 hours of food is all they have, many with much less.

Fifteen hundred National Guardsmen stand ready to be deployed. Still, these are damage control forces, preparing only for the aftermath; nothing can be done to protect the city.

The National Weather Service catalogs Katrina's potentially catastrophic effects in detail, especially with concern for New Orleans' vulnerable position— surrounded by water on three sides, 70 percent of it below sea level, and its levees unequal to the predicted storm surge of 25, even 28 feet. Authorities predict the Category 4 storm will make landfall anywhere from Galveston, Texas to Alabama.

FEMA representatives assure the press that they are ready and waiting with all available assistance, having practiced and planned for just such a disaster.

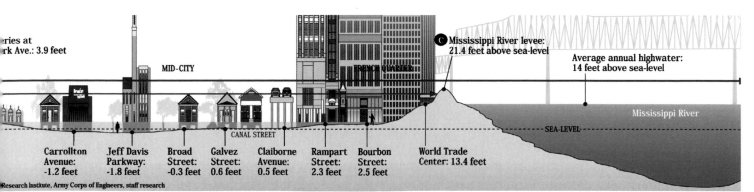

ries at rk Ave.: 3.9 feet

MID-CITY

C Mississippi River levee: 21.4 feet above sea-level

Average annual highwater: 14 feet above sea-level

FRENCH QUARTER

Mississippi River

CANAL STREET

SEA-LEVEL

Carrollton Avenue: -1.2 feet | Jeff Davis Parkway: -1.8 feet | Broad Street: -0.3 feet | Galvez Street: 0.6 feet | Claiborne Avenue: 0.5 feet | Rampart Street: 2.3 feet | Bourbon Street: 2.5 feet | World Trade Center: 13.4 feet

Research Institute, Army Corps of Engineers, staff research

TimesPicayune/NNS/Landov

President Bush is handed a map during a video teleconference with federal and state emergency management organizations to discuss Hurricane Katrina, from Bush's Crawford, Texas ranch on Sunday, August 28, 2005.
EPA/White House/HO/Landov

Below—Workers board up one of the many majestic houses in the Garden District of New Orleans in preparation for Katrina. AP Photo/Bill Haber

Opposite page—Thousands of residents with nowhere else to go wait in a line for hours to take shelter in the Superdome.
UPI Photo/A.J. Sisco/Landov

Drivers and passengers wait outside their vehicles as traffic snarls on the interstate highway leaving downtown New Orleans.
Reuters/Rick Wilking/Landov

A family occupies their time at one of the many shelters in Louisiana, while waiting for Katrina to make landfall.
CNN Photo

URGENT - WEATHER MESSAGE NATIONAL WEATHER SERVICE SLYDELL, LA.

1011 AM CDT SUN AUG 28 2005

...DEVASTATING DAMAGE EXPECTED...

.HURRICANE KATRINA...A MOST POWERFUL HURRICANE WITH UNPRECEDENTED STRENGTH...RIVALING THE INTENSITY OF HURRICANE CAMILLE OF 1969.

MOST OF THE AREA WILL BE UNINHABITABLE FOR WEEKS... PERHAPS LONGER. AT LEAST ONE HALF OF WELL CONSTRUCTED HOMES WILL HAVE ROOF AND WALL FAILURE. ALL GABLED ROOFS WILL FAIL...LEAVING THOSE HOMES SEVERELY DAMAGED OR DESTROYED.

THE MAJORITY OF INDUSTRIAL BUILDINGS WILL BECOME NON FUNCTIONAL. PARTIAL TO COMPLETE WALL AND ROOF FAILURE IS EXPECTED. ALL WOOD FRAMED LOW RISING APARTMENT BUILDINGS WILL BE DESTROYED. CONCRETE BLOCK LOW RISE APARTMENTS WILL SUSTAIN MAJOR DAMAGE...INCLUDING SOME WALL AND ROOF FAILURE.

HIGH RISE OFFICE AND APARTMENT BUILDINGS WILL SWAY DANGEROUSLY...A FEW TO THE POINT OF TOTAL COLLAPSE. ALL WINDOWS WILL BLOW OUT.

AIRBORNE DEBRIS WILL BE WIDESPREAD...AND MAY INCLUDE HEAVY ITEMS SUCH AS HOUSEHOLD APPLIANCES AND EVEN LIGHT VEHICLES. SPORT UTILITY VEHICLES AND LIGHT TRUCKS WILL BE MOVED. THE BLOWN DEBRIS WILL CREATE ADDITIONAL DESTRUCTION. PERSONS...PETS...AND LIVESTOCK EXPOSED TO THE WINDS WILL FACE CERTAIN DEATH IF STRUCK.

POWER OUTAGES WILL LAST FOR WEEKS...AS MOST POWER POLES WILL BE DOWN AND TRANSFORMERS DESTROYED. WATER SHORTAGES WILL MAKE HUMAN SUFFERING INCREDIBLE BY MODERN STANDARDS.

THE VAST MAJORITY OF NATIVE TREES WILL BE SNAPPED OR UPROOTED. ONLY THE HEARTIEST WILL REMAIN STANDING... BUT BE TOTALLY DEFOLIATED. FEW CROPS WILL REMAIN. LIVESTOCK LEFT EXPOSED TO THE WINDS WILL BE KILLED.

AN INLAND HURRICANE WIND WARNING IS ISSUED WHEN SUSTAINED WINDS NEAR HURRICANE FORCE...OR FREQUENT GUSTS AT OR ABOVE HURRICANE FORCE...ARE CERTAIN WITHIN THE NEXT 12 TO 24 HOURS.

ONCE TROPICAL STORM AND HURRICANE FORCE WINDS ONSET...DO NOT VENTURE OUTSIDE!

Michael Brown, director of FEMA: *"We actually started preparing for this about two years ago. We had decided to start doing catastrophic-disaster planning and the first place we picked to do that kind of planning was New Orleans because we knew from experience, based back in the '40s and even in the late 1800s, if a Category 5 hurricane were to strike New Orleans just right, the flooding would be devastating. It could be catastrophic. So we did this planning two years ago. And actually there's a tabletop exercise with the Louisiana officials about a year ago. So the planning's been in place now. We're ready for the storm. . . ."*

Col. Terry Ebert, homeland security director, New Orleans: *speaking of conditions in the Louisiana Superdome on August 28: "It's going to be very unpleasant. We're not in here to feed people. We're in here to see that when Tuesday morning comes, they're alive."*

Jonathan Freed CNN: *"Heading toward Biloxi, traffic is bumper to bumper on I-10. If it wasn't raining, I could be outside walking next to the car more or less and keeping pace with it."*

Hotels stay open for paying guests, many of whom are tourists unable to get transportation out. Massive flooding is expected. Hospitals move their patients and emergency equipment to higher floors. Buses quit running. Airports remain open, and I-10 is designated as the route out, with contraflow in effect and traffic flowing—for a while. Time is running out. Katrina bears down on the city, and more people try to escape. "No Gas" signs appear at the pumps. By 1 p.m., the roads are jammed, airports closed, and the people of New Orleans, trapped in a bowl. Inland, low-lying Slidell mayor's biggest fear is "people drowning in place."

INTERVIEW

Larry King

Ray Nagin,
New Orleans
Mayor

KING: Where are you situated, Mayor?

NAGIN: I'm definitely hunkered down in City Hall waiting for this storm, to kind of decide what it's going to do.

KING: How prepared is the city?

NAGIN: Pretty well prepared. We've gone through out various stages of—excuse me—of our evacuation process. There's a million, two million, three million people in the metropolitan area. We probably evacuated about a million people out of this city and the surrounding parishes.

KING: Are all the hotels, the Superdome, are they safe from these kind of winds?

NAGIN: Well, you know, as safe as you would expect. But this is an unprecedented storm with incredible power—160 mile an hour winds, gusting up close to 200 miles an hour. So, the Superdome is definitely pretty safe, and that's a shelter of last resort. We have about 20,000 to 25,000 people in there right now. And the hotels seem to be holding up OK right now at the moment.

KING: Your city hasn't taken a major, direct hit since Betsy in 1965. It also, the Port of New Orleans, handles much of the nation's oil transportation. Have all those ships moved out?

NAGIN: Most of the ships have moved out. And Larry, you bring up a great point, we probably handle about 25 percent of the nation's domestic oil production. And if that is halted for a significant amount of

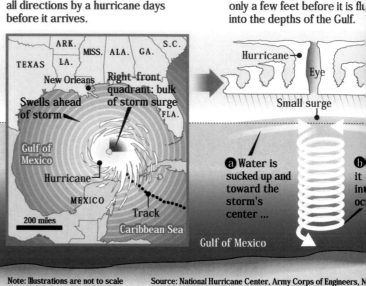

THE SCOURGE OF S

1 CALM BEFORE THE STORM
Clear skies and beautiful weather often mask the choppy, rising waters created by ocean swells spawned in all directions by a hurricane days before it arrives.

2 SURGE IN THE GULF
Over deep Gulf of Mexico wa the hurricane's low air press and high winds pull the water only a few feet before it is flu into the depths of the Gulf.

ARK. MISS. ALA. GA. S.C.
TEXAS LA.
New Orleans
Right-front quadrant: bulk of storm surge
Swells ahead of storm
FLA.
Gulf of Mexico
Hurricane
MEXICO
Track
200 miles
Caribbean Sea

Hurricane→ Eye
Small surge
ⓐ Water is sucked up and toward the storm's center ...
Gulf of Mexico

Note: Illustrations are not to scale   Source: National Hurricane Center, Army Corps of Engineers, N

Times-Picayune/NNS/Landov

time, it could impact prices at the gas pumps.

KING: That's all we need. What about the nightmare scenario that as some are forecasting, as *National Geographic* forecast last year, that this could, if it stays a 5, become a toxic lake of chemicals and oil from the refineries and waste from the septic systems. And you could have a horrendous tragedy?

NAGIN: Well, you know, I think we're going to have an incredible challenge regardless. This storm has a 20-foot storm surge, plus waves. The city of New Orleans is basically designed like a bowl. We're below sea level for the most part, so we most likely will have a significant amount of water and everything associated with that. So it's going to be a tremendous challenge.

KING: What happens in the cemeteries?

NAGIN: Well, the cemeteries, most of them—most of the people are buried above ground, some are below ground. So, with all that water, I'm sure it's going to disrupt several of the cemeteries.

KING: All your police on duty?

NAGIN: Every policeman is on duty. We have the National Guard that has taken control of

RGE

Storm surge is a dome of water accompanying a hurricane when it moves ashore. "The greatest potential for loss of life related to a hurricane is from the storm surge," says the National Hurricane Center's Brian Jarvinen. Louisiana's coastal wetlands and islands create friction that slows surge down, but they're eroding at an alarming rate. That leaves a system of levees as the area's last protection. A look at how storm surge from Category 3 and larger hurricanes can tower over levees.

3 SURGE COMING ASHORE

As the hurricane approaches land, the dome of water – 15 to 25 miles across – rises as high as 30 feet and is topped by violent waves.

4 TOPPING LEVEES

The giant wave moves over the shallow, eroding coastline, threatening the region's last line of defense – levees.

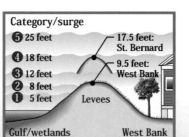

Category/surge	
5 25 feet	17.5 feet: St. Bernard
4 18 feet	9.5 feet: West Bank
3 12 feet	
2 8 feet	Levees
1 5 feet	
Gulf/wetlands	West Bank

5 LAKE BACKLASH

In advance of the hurricane, easterly winds pump water into Lake Pontchartrain through the Chef Menteur and Rigolets passes, raising the lake level.

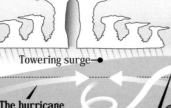

Towering surge

SEA LEVEL

c The hurricane continues to pull water up and toward its center ...

e so it is forced back up.

d but the water can't dissipate in shallows ...

WETLANDS   NEW ORLEANS   LAKE

Lake Pont.   Rigolets

New Orleans   Chef Menteur Pass

As the hurricane passes, its counterclockwise winds can slosh water over lakefront levees.

WILD CARDS

The sponge effect: Every four miles of wetlands can absorb about a foot of storm surge, but Louisiana is losing an acre of wetlands – the equivalent of three football fields – every 24 minutes.

The tidal factor: A high tide can add 2 feet or more to a hurricane's storm surge.

"But the greatest loss of life from this hurricane, I think, will come from the storm surge in the southeastern Louisiana and on the Mississippi and possibly the Alabama coast."—Max Mayfield

the Superdome. I've gotten calls from the White House. There are people standing by ready to help. So, once the storm gets through, the cleanup efforts will commence in haste.

KING: Did you get all the homeless in shelters?

NAGIN: We've got just about everybody in one major shelter, which is the Louisiana Superdome, which is designed to probably sustain the kind of winds that we're going to have. There's probably 20,000 to 25,000 people in the Superdome as we speak.

KING: That can hold 80,000, can't it?

NAGIN: Yes, it can. We've gotten a significant amount of people out of the city, so, fortunately, we didn't have to have it at full capacity.

KING: That doesn't have emergency power, though, does it—the Superdome? It's going to lose its air conditioning, isn't it?

NAGIN: It does have emergency power, but I think for the most part, after the storm hits, the entire city will probably be without power at some point.

KING: Thanks, Mayor. Our prayers are with you.

NAGIN: Thank you, Larry.

The American Red Cross "is prepared for the worst," expecting the relief effort to cost millions of dollars and say it "will probably be the biggest natural disaster relief operation the Red Cross has ever seen."

Hundreds of thousands of people across Alabama, Mississippi, and Louisiana, have evacuated. An estimated one million people have left the greater New Orleans area. Of those who stayed, some still hold out hope that Katrina might shift direction, though meteorologists say it won't. Everyone prays that the levees in New Orleans will hold, despite growing evidence that they will not.

Aaron Brown, CNN Anchor: *"You know, in this business, . . .there is a tendency towards hyperbole at times. This ain't one of those times, folks, . . . The potential for destruction is enormous. And that is not an exaggeration, that's not hype, that's just the way it is. And particularly to a city like New Orleans, which, as we've talked about, is essentially built like a bowl and will collect this enormous amount of water that's going to come ashore over the next 24 hours. It's hard to know precisely what we're going to find tomorrow night when we talk to you again, whether we're going to find a city that is quite literally destroyed, or extraordinarily damaged, when people will be able to come back. Will it be days or weeks or months? And what is it they'll come back to?"*

"A catastrophic hurricane represents 10 or 15 atomic bombs in terms of the energy it releases. Think about it."

—*Joseph Suhayda, LSU engineer*

". . . A stronger storm [than Category 2 Georges,] on a slightly different course . . . could have realized emergency officials' worst-case scenario: hundreds of billions of gallons of lake water pouring over the levees into an area averaging five feet below sea level with no natural means of drainage. . . . Hundreds of thousands would be left homeless, and it would take months to dry out the area and begin to make it livable. But there wouldn't be much for residents to come home to. The local economy would be in ruins.

". . . Amid this maelstrom, the estimated 200,000 or more people left behind in an evacuation will be struggling to survive. Some will be housed at the Superdome, the designated shelter in New Orleans for people too sick or infirm to leave the city. Others will end up in last-minute emergency refuges that will offer minimal safety. But many will simply be on their own, in homes or looking for high ground.

". . . Thousands will drown while trapped in homes or cars by rising water. Others will be washed away or crushed by debris. Survivors will end up trapped on roofs, in buildings, or on high ground surrounded by water, with no means of escape and little food or fresh water, perhaps for several days.

". . . Stranded survivors will have a dangerous wait even after the storm passes. Emergency officials worry that energized electrical wires could pose a threat of electrocution and that the floodwater could become contaminated with sewage and with toxic chemicals from industrial plants and backyard sheds. Gasoline, diesel fuel, and oil leaking from underground storage tanks at service stations may also become a problem, corps officials say."

—*Excerpts from a June 2002,* New Orleans *Times-Picayune, five-part series on the vulnerability of the area to a major hurricane*

"This is a very poor city. Some estimate 140,000 people do not have cars. About a quarter of the residents have no way to get out. I talked to the mayor a couple of days ago. There is not a plan to use city buses to get these people out. He knew they were stuck, and they are stuck."

—*Susan Roesgen, WGNO reporter, responding to a question about why so many have chosen not to evacuate*

"I know they are saying 'get out of town,' but I don't have any way to get out. If you don't have no money, you can't go."

—*Hattie Johns, 74*

"Well, when the exercise was completed it was evident that we were going to lose a lot of people, we changed the name of the storm from Delaney to K-Y-A-G-B.—kiss your ass goodbye . . . because anybody who was here as that Category 5 storm came across . . . was gone."

—*Walter Maestri, director of emergency services for Jefferson Parish, talking about a simulation exercise he participated in with Daniel Zwerdling of American Radio Works in 2002.*

"I have determined that this incident will be of such severity and magnitude that effective response will be beyond the capabilities of the state and the affected local governments."

—*Kathleen Blanco, Louisiana governor*

"FEMA is not going to hesitate at all in this storm. We are not going to sit back and make this a bureaucratic process. We are going to move fast, we are going to move quick, and we are going to do whatever it takes to help disaster victims."

—*Michael Brown, director of FEMA*

"Well, that's not going to be a lot of solace for people in New Orleans because that storm will also flood New Orleans. And what we're concerned about is getting people out of there, 10 miles an hour one way or another is not going to make a big difference. The track is a killer track."

—*Paul Kemp, researcher, LSU Hurricane Center, when asked if the reduction in wind speed of Hurricane Katrina was good.*

". . . Our code is built to handle 150 mile-an-hour winds. That's what our code says. Now, whether they can do that or not, we'll see. But we're looking at a probable forecast of a 15- to 20-foot tidal surge. So this will be a real test on our infrastructure here for those casinos and hotels."

—*A.J. Holloway, mayor of Biloxi, Miss.*

"The security is very high for this. They have been searching every person, every bag. Successfully, they've confiscated several guns, all alcohol and drugs, any weapons, because they're very concerned that this could turn into a very tense environment as the next 36 hours go on."

—*Ben Blake, CNN, reporting from the Superdome*

"It's that calm before the storm, that eerie feeling. . . . a light, light breeze, the wind barely—barely moving. A little bit of a drizzle."
—*John Zarrella, CNN 10 p.m., August 28, 2005, reporting from the French Quarter*

DAY 2

Monday, August 29, 2005

> **"Let me tell you something, folks. I've been out there. It's complete devastation."**
>
> —*Gulfport, Miss., Fire Chief Pat Sullivan, who ventured into the hurricane to check threatened areas*

New Orleans. Just after midnight, traffic on Interstate 10 is bumper to bumper as the threatened city makes a run for it. Hurricane Katrina is 160 miles away—the leading edge only 90 miles off the coast, heading directly for the Big Easy. Forty mph gale force winds have reached Gulfport, Miss., where Mayor Brent Warr estimates that 25,000–30,000 people have evacuated. Water has rushed over the Orange Beach highway in Alabama, where power is already out. In New Orleans, 63 people have been transferred from the Superdome to Tulane University Hospital.

In Katrina's eye wall, wave heights now reach 60 feet. As the storm churns through the Gulf, water temperatures in the mid-90s supply it with "high octane" that ensures its survival, and there is no wind shear to break up its highly organized upper clouds. Nevertheless, as it moves closer to landfall, there's a slight weakening, and the storm downgrades to a Category 4. Forecasters are uncertain whether it will intensify before it hits.

As the storm makes a beeline for New Orleans, it shifts slightly, the eye moving east, fixing in its sights Gulfport, Biloxi, and Mobile; the western eye wall is predicted to have 120–125 mph winds, the eastern more like 155 mph. If it wobbles at all to the right, New Orleans will avoid a direct hit, and it appears to be wobbling.

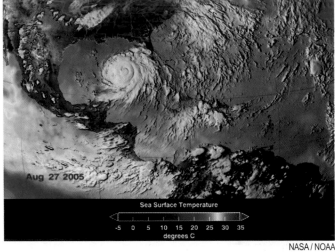

Aug 27 2005

Sea Surface Temperature

-5 0 5 10 15 20 25 30 35
degrees C

NASA / NOAA

"Really warm, deep water ignited Katrina. We were predicting this would likely occur, even on Saturday when the storm was a Category 3. Very deep warm water. It comes in from the Caribbean and the Straits of the Yucatan. You get this warm, deep water sweeping into the Gulf, what we call a loop current. . . .That warm water really can provide the fuel to the fire when a hurricane passes over it." —*Bonnie Schneider, CNN meteorologist, 1a.m.*

"It's like watching a slow-moving bomb approach." —*Candace Watkins, mayor of Covington, La.*

Oil rigs in the central and eastern Gulf of Mexico are evacuated. All refineries in the Gulf Coast region are evacuated. Reports say oil prices have, for the first time, climbed to $70 a barrel.

FACTOID: There are 4,000 rigs and platforms that drill for and produce oil in the Gulf Coast. The Louisiana offshore oil port is responsible for 11 percent of all the oil that is imported into the U.S. All told, the Gulf has a refining capacity of about a million barrels a day. One-third of all the oil that the U.S. produces is produced in the Gulf.

Waves crash against a boat washed onto Highway 90 as Katrina slams into Gulfport, Miss.

AP Photo/John Bazemore

In New Orleans police are hunkered down, and most locals have battened their hatches. But some people—many of them tourists who couldn't get out—are still partying in the bars that never close. Those who could leave are on their way north; those who could not are scattered between hotels, hospitals, shelters, and the Superdome—and there is no way of knowing how many are holed up in their houses, determined to ride it out. These are the diehards, who, it has been said grimly, may die hard.

Carol Costello, CNN: interviews Lt. Kevin Cowan of the Louisiana National Guard. *He is also the spokesman for the Louisiana office of Homeland Security and Emergency Preparedness. From Baton Rouge he assures her that the guard is "prepared and waiting . . . the last time I checked, we had about 3,000 troops that are currently on standby at strategic locations." Costello asks if he knows how things are inside the Superdome, and Cowan admits he has no real idea: "Well, I haven't actually been inside the Superdome." Nor is he sure how many people are inside; he guesses about 30,000. He assures Carol that "there's plenty of water, and we actually have more water staged and ready to go . . . we have the military meals ready to eat, the prepackaged food that the Army guys eat. It's healthy and tasty, and . . . easy to transport." When asked what will happen if the electricity fails and the temperatures tops 100 degrees . . . if it becomes too unbearable inside? "It's not going to be the Hilton," Cowan says, "but at least it's a safe place that they can stay."*

About 9,000 people have spent the night at the Superdome. Power fails at around 5 a.m. There is emergency lighting but

Floodwaters whipped by the wind created a life-and-death situation for those who stayed in thier homes. The floodwaters came up very rapidly along the whole Gulf Coast driven by enormous storm surges. It takes just six inches of moving water to knock you off your feet. Two feet of water can float an SUV.

Below—Arnold James tries to keep on his feet in the strong winds and flowing water as he tries to make his way to the Superdome. The roof of his home blew off, forcing him to flee.

the generators are not capable of powering the air conditioning. By 6 a.m., reports say there are between 12,000 and 20,000 people packed in to ride out the hurricane. As no press are allowed into the "refuge of last resort," these reports continue to vary wildly. Jeanne Meserve reports from an adjacent parking lot. "Periodically we hear huge roars, and you look to the sky and you think, my gosh, is something flying up there? Of course, there aren't any aircraft at all. What you're hearing is the wind just howling through the skyscrapers here."

At 6:10 a.m., Katrina makes landfall near Grand Isle, La., as a Category 4 storm, tearing into the Gulf Coast with winds of 140 mph and massive 24-foot storm surges. In Biloxi, the eye wall approaches. The heaviest part of the storm is east of New Orleans, scheduled to plow into the Mississippi and Alabama coastline in about four hours. "This is not a coastal storm," Mississippi Governor Haley Barbour warns. "We are talking about a 30-foot wall of water. Take this seriously."

Rob Marciano, CNN, Biloxi, Miss.: *"CNN meteorologist Chad Myers tells me he's got winds of possibly 110 mph, possibly 120 mph, and that's totally, totally believable. I can't imagine actually standing out in the middle of this thing. Any winds of over 90 or 100 mph are not fit for humans, that's for sure."*

Two unidentified men help a disabled girl to safety after the home she was staying in was flooded in Pascagoula, Miss., after Hurricane Katrina passed over the Gulf Coast.

In Biloxi, the situation worsens, with frequent squalls of 50 mph winds. In Pascagoula, 113 mph gusts come through. White caps appear on the Mississippi River. There are "reports of boats . . . floating down Highway 90." In New Orleans, as the howling winds of one of the heaviest bands of the storm approaches and relentlessly pound its roof, the Superdome—supposed to be stronger than the Roman Coliseum—springs a leak. Pieces begin peeling off "like aluminum foil." Inside, water sprinkles, then pours. Wind follows. People move out of the way, remaining calm. It's still a two-hour wait before the eye wall of the hurricane gets to New Orleans. Water gushes down the streets like waves on the ocean, coming up through the manhole covers.

Gov. Kathleen Blanco: *"We know that we'll still suffer considerable damage. There will be a tremendous amount of property damage. There will be some light flooding in some areas. . . . We appreciate the president's call to us, giving us all the resources with Mike Brown and all his team of people. It's critical for us at this time that we have that knowledge, and that security that our people will be taken care of."*

Most of downtown Mobile is flooded. Police, fire, and rescue units are necessarily on hold. In Biloxi, the surf is six miles inland. Up to 12 feet of water covers downtown Gulfport. In New Orleans, "entire neighborhoods are submerged up to the rooflines" in many areas, including the Ninth Ward. Downtown, reporter Jeanne Meserve reports not more than two feet of water, which she says has already begun to recede.

President Bush, speaking to the nation from El Mirage, Ariz., where he delivered a speech on Social Security, urges everyone to listen to the local authorities, to stay in the shelters, to take precautions. He promises that when the storm passes, the federal government will be there to help. "In the meantime," he says, "America will pray. Pray for the health and safety of all our citizens."

A vehicle makes its way through a flooded street from the overflowing Grande Lagoon in Pensacola, Fla., as Hurricane Katrina passes through the area.

Katrina now spreads out over 1,300 miles north to south, with winds extending out 400 miles from the center. The eye wall moves up to Hattiesburg, Miss. with winds at 105 mph. Gulfport is "hell on earth," hit by a 20-foot surge. Winds bump up in New Orleans to 120 mph.

In New Orleans, those who expected the worst, and those who thought it couldn't happen, watch as the Big Easy gets hit. The 120 mph winds shriek through the city for hours, tearing roofs off, shattering windows in the hotels, shredding houses, businesses and clubs, hurling appliances out into the street: air conditioners, refrigerators, stoves—all of which then break into pieces. Signs hurtle through the air along with shingles, pieces of siding, corrugated roofing, and gutters. Buildings topple into chunks of debris. Houses and businesses that have withstood hurricanes for decades succumb to Katrina's massive attack. Falling trees rip down power lines. Twelve hours and then, finally, it's gone.

Kyra Phillips, CNN: *"Katrina's lethal spiral snarls across the Gulf and slams into shores. Centuries of proud history, years of hard work, blown literally out of the window or buried in avalanches of debris."*

Gary Tuchman, CNN: *"The winds were at least 100 mph in Gulfport for seven hours, between 7 a.m. and 2 p.m. For another five or six hours on each side of that, we had hurricane-force winds, over 75 mph. Much of the city of 71,000 is under water. We were on U.S. 90 earlier this morning and it was up to my shins, then past my knees. Thirty minutes later, an hour later, it got to 10 and 12 feet."*

As the cautious emerge onto the streets, they're relieved to find that the Big Easy doesn't seem to have been hit as hard as expected. There's damage, of course, but now all eyes are on Biloxi and Gulfport, which were directly in the path of Katrina's eye. There is much talk of how New Orleans dodged a bullet, and people turn around in their cars, ready to come home—if they still have one. Gov. Blanco says things could have been much worse. Talk turns busily to oil and gas prices, and how Wall Street is reflecting the hurricane's toll.

Flooding, assumed to be the result of the storm surge, now takes over, becoming the main cause of damage in New Orleans. Reporters begin to hear that bodies are floating in the water. Police cannot reach their rescue boats, which are in flooded areas, in order to use them for search and rescue, leaving the populace largely on its own. Looting begins as residents try to forage for anything and everything needed for who knows how long. In other areas, the rising water traps holdouts in their homes, where they move upward, sometimes into attics without any means of getting onto the roof. People who are told they cannot be rescued with their pets decline to be rescued at all. The water continues to rise. The Ninth Ward is up to its rooftops. Streets are turning into rivers.

Adeline Perkins carries her dog, Princess and Lynell Batiste carries Timmy, as Kewanda Batiste and Ulysses Batiste swim through the flood waters from their Lacombe, La., home.

BLOGS

Posted 5:06 p.m. ET
CNN's Gary Tuchman, Biloxi, Miss.

Gulfport is basically, at this time, closed off from the rest of the world. There's no cellular service, there's no phone service. There's really no way to communicate from there. That's why we had to leave Gulfport and take a drive. It was quite a trying 18-mile drive from Biloxi. It was like going in a covered wagon. Interstate 10, heading east from Gulfport to Biloxi, is covered with more refuse than you can ever imagine you've ever seen before. There are stoves, there are refrigerators, there are basketballs, there are sinks, there are toys, I mean, literally, the kitchen sink.

In this town of Gulfport . . . miles of the town are underwater.

It's very devastating.

Clockwise from top left—Bay St. Louis, Miss., Emergency Management Agency volunteer crews rescue the Taylor family from the roof of their Suburban, which became trapped on U.S. 90.

Troy Lee, left, embraces his friend Bay St. Louis, Miss, police officer Joel Wallace after discovering he had survived Hurricane Katrina in Waveland, Miss.

Colleen Schneider searches what is left of her home on Ocean Blvd. in Biloxi, Miss. Colleen's partner of 20 years died in the storm and is still buried beneath the rubble.

David Diaz looks at the area where he and his brother used to live in the Sadler Apartments on the waterfront in Biloxi, Miss.

Sam Miller, 10, left, is consoled by a neighbor after viewing the destruction of his home along Beach Boulevard in Pascagoula, Miss.

AP Photo/Ben Sklar

AP Photo/*Mississippi Press-Register*/ William Colgin

REUTERS/Landov/Mark Wallheiser

AP Photo/Ben Sklar

NNS /Landov/Michael Falco

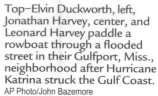

Top—Elvin Duckworth, left, Jonathan Harvey, center, and Leonard Harvey paddle a rowboat through a flooded street in their Gulfport, Miss., neighborhood after Hurricane Katrina struck the Gulf Coast.
AP Photo/John Bazemore

Center—Looters make off with merchandise from several downtown businesses in New Orleans.
AP Photo/Eric Gay

Bottom—Sammuel Dunn, center, is helped to safety by friends when he was rescued by a boat after his home flooded in New Orleans.
AP Photo/Eric Gay

Unbeknownst to almost everyone, the levees had been breached earlier in the day. The 17th Street Canal breach had been confirmed around 2 p.m. by the Corps of Engineers, according to New Orleans project manager Al Naomi. "It [the breach information] was disseminated. It went to our OEP in Baton Rouge, to the state, FEMA, and the Corps," Naomi said. "The people in the field knew it. The people here [in Corps offices] in Louisiana and Mississippi knew it. I don't know how communication worked in those agencies." Naomi also believes the other levees and flood walls that were breached began to fail around the same time.

As almost total darkness settles over the powerless city, most people are unaware of the levee collapses, though there have been persistent reports that the water is rising—not going down. The final blow that will send the Big Easy spiraling into chaos is being delivered in the dead of night.

In an interview on Sept. 9 with Stone Philips on NBC's *Primetime*, Ivor van Heerden, a hurricane expert working at LSU, recalls when he first heard about the rising water. "At eight o'clock, the hammer dropped. Somebody came to us at the LSU desk and said 'There is

"We saw people sticking their hands outside through the rafters, waving little tin pans, aluminum pans, to signal, you know, some kind of reflection. . . . they are chopping through with axes on the rooftops to pull people that are literally just breathing the last air in their homes." —*Mark Biello, CNN*

a nursing home that's just phoned in. The water is rising half a foot an hour.'" Phillips asks what van Heerden thought when he realized it was the levees that had failed. "My God, it's nighttime. The water is going to rise, slowly, quietly, and the next thing, they are going to climb out of their beds and step in water. And the panic is going to set in. So what do a lot of them do? They are probably forced to go up into the attic. You know, I just had the worst chill. . . . Imagine the chill that went through those people."

The Superdome late on the evening of Day Two is pandemonium, as every rescue victim is dropped off and more hospitals try to evacuate their patients by moving them there. There is no power. The lighting is dim, the bathrooms are dark. The toilets won't flush anymore. Many move outside onto the walkway, to smoke, release tension, get some fresh air. Emergency workers say the situation can't last much longer, that the special-needs patients won't survive. There is no plan, as yet, to move any of the Dome's inhabitants anywhere else.

News of the levees hasn't yet been made public. Nevertheless, there's no doubt New Orleans' situation is much, much worse. At 11 p.m., the only sight is the occasional flare as the Coast Guard drops them to mark survivors. The only sound are the cries of people in the darkness, yelling for help. And the dogs, stranded and helpless, barking throughout the night. It is a day that felt like it would never end. The powerful Katrina returns to tropical storm status on the way out, turning an indifferent back on a city in shambles and the absolute chaos soon to ensue.

Top—Two people yell to rescuers as they launch the boats to save people in the lower Ninth Ward of New Orleans.
Times-Picayune/NNS /Landov/Alex Brandon

Center—NOPD SWAT officers Lt. Cris Mandry, left, and Sgt. Todd Morrell, right, help Henry Winter out of the water in his home at Forstall and N. Rampart Streets in the lower Ninth Ward.
Times-Picayune/NNS /Landov/Alex Brandon

Bottom—A dead body floats in front of a house on the east side of New Orleans in the aftermath of Hurricane Katrina.
AP Photo/Phil Coale

INTERVIEW

Aaron Brown

Jeanne Meserve,
CNN
Correspondent

BROWN: It's been quite a—we don't use this word lightly, but quite a dramatic and difficult night down there, hasn't it?

MESERVE: It's been horrible. As I left tonight, darkness, of course, had fallen. And you can hear people yelling for help. You can hear the dogs yelping, all of them stranded, all of them hoping someone will come. But for tonight, they've had to suspend the rescue efforts. It's just too hazardous for them to be out on the boats. There are electrical lines that are still alive. There are gas lines that are still spewing gas. There are cars that are submerged. There are other large objects. The boats can't operate. So they had to suspend operations and leave those people in the homes.

As we were driving back, we passed scores of boats, Fish and Wildlife boats that they brought in. They're flat bottomed. They've obviously going to put them in the water just as soon as they possibly can and go out and reach the people who are out there who desperately need help. We watched them, some of them, come in. They were in horrible shape, some of them. We watched one woman whose leg had been severed. Mark Biello, one of our cameramen, went out in one of the boats to help shoot. He ended up being out for hours and told horrific tales. He saw bodies. He saw where—he saw other, just unfathomable things.

Dogs wrapped in electrical—electrical lines that were still alive that were being electrocuted.

The police are having radio problems. At least they were earlier this evening. They didn't have enough boats. They put out an appeal to various police who had personal boats to bring them to the scene. But the problem was the people who had the boats couldn't get to the boats to bring them to the scene to go out and rescue the people. People are out there tonight. One of the EMS workers told us that the water is rising, and I can tell you that when we came back into the city tonight, it certainly was higher here. Whether it's rising in that neighborhood as much as it has here, I don't know, Aaron.

BROWN: Jeanne, let me walk you through a couple of things. Are they able—are authorities able to, in any way, communicate with these people who are stranded and scared and hungry and cold and desperate?

MESERVE: They aren't tonight. When the boats were in the water, as the boats went around through the neighborhood, they yelled. And people yelled back. But Mark, when he came back, told me that—that some of the people, they just couldn't get to. They just couldn't get to them. They couldn't maneuver the boats in there. Because this had happened before in Hurricane Betsy, there were many people who kept axes in their homes and had them in the attic in preparation for this. Some people were able to use those axes and make holes in their roof and stick their head out or their body out or climb up completely. But many others clearly didn't have that. Most of the rescuers appeared to be carrying axes, and they were trying to hack them out as best they could to provide access and haul them out.

Alex Brandon/NNS /Landov

Michael Falso/NNS /Landov

Left—Legendary musician Fats Domino, center, is helped off a boat by NOPD SWAT officer Trevor Reeves. Right—NOPD SWAT officers Sgt. Todd Morrell and Lt. Cris Mandry help an unidentified man in the lower Ninth Ward out of his attic into a waiting boat.

BROWN: I'm sorry. What . . .

MESERVE: There were also Coast Guard helicopters involved in it, Aaron . . . flying overhead. It appears that when they saw someone on a rooftop, they were dropping flares, to try to signal the boats to get there.

BROWN: Is there any sense of—that there is triage, that they're looking to see who needs help the worst? Or they're just—they were just getting to whomever they could get to and get them out of there?

MESERVE: I had the distinct impression they were just getting to whoever they could get to. I talked to one fire captain who'd been out in his personal boat. He said he worked an area probably 10 square blocks. He'd rescued 75 people. He said in one instance there were something like 18 people in one house, some of them young. One, he said, appeared to be a newborn. And he said other boats were working the same area at the same time, also picking up large numbers of people. And he doesn't believe they got all of them. And that's just one 10-block area. I don't know how big the area is. I haven't been able to see any footage from the air, but it appears to go on forever. It's hard for me to comprehend how many people might be out there and how many people's lives are in jeopardy or how many people may already be dead.

BROWN: It's—it's—just stay with me for a bit, OK? It's what is—for everybody now, what's very difficult is there isn't what we refer to in the business as a wide shot. We can't get—authorities can't get, we can't get, we can't give to those of you who are watching tonight that wide picture of what these scenes are like. Can you—what kind of neighborhoods are we talking about? Are these middle-class neighborhoods? Are they—the homes structurally sound? What are we talking about?

MESERVE: Well, the area where I was, and I don't know what the other neighborhoods are like, but this was a poor neighborhood. These were very humble homes. Most of them appeared to be only one story high with, then, some small attic space above them. These people are people of not much means. Some of them, I would guess, do not have cars and didn't have the option of driving away from here. Some of them, I would guess, did not have the money that would have bought them a hotel room.

BROWN: Yes.

MESERVE: Clearly, there were many warnings to evacuate, and people were told there was shelter downtown. And I can tell you that the rescuers tell me that everybody they picked up regretted their decision to stay where they were. But clearly, getting out of their homes would not have been easy for these people.

BROWN: How far from downtown or the center of New Orleans were you working?

MESERVE: It's a little hard for me to judge, because we were traveling in such peculiar circumstances and very low rate of speed, having to maneuver around the boats that are on the—that are on the highway. And I might mention that the—the exit ramps and the entrance ramps to the highway are now going to be used as boat ramps to get those boats into the water to get out and rescue people. It's a little difficult for me to judge. I would guess, you know, somewhere between maybe five miles, I would say, to the east of the city.

BROWN: You talked about all the water there and the boats there. Do you have any sense of how deep that water is?

MESERVE: Well, I can tell you that in the vicinity where I was, the water came up to the eaves of the house. And I was told by several rescue workers that we were not seeing the worst of it, that we were at one end of the Ward 9 part of the city and that there's another part, inaccessible by road at this point, where the road—where the houses were covered to their rooftops. And they were having a great deal of problem gaining access down there. The rescue workers also told me that they saw bodies in that part.

BROWN: Any—you mentioned earlier that the water seemed to get progressively deeper. The walkway from this, if you don't know, is just a question of tide moving in and tide moving out?

MESERVE: Well, I can tell you that the people who were rescued with whom I had a chance to speak told me that the water came up very suddenly on them. They said most of the storm had passed and what apparently was the storm surge came. Some of them talked about seeing a little water on their floor, going to the front door, seeing a lot of water, going to the back door, seeing more water, and then barely having time to get up the stairs. One man I talked to was barefoot. He hadn't had time to put on shoes. Another woman was in her housedress and flip-flops.

As for the water tonight and how fast it may be going up and down, and you know, I may not have the most current information about the tides, but I can tell you that downtown here the water seemed to be,

I'd say, six inches or so deeper than it was when I left earlier this afternoon. It may be a totally . . . different situation . . .

BROWN: Sure.

MESERVE: . . . out where those houses are. But I can tell you, the water certainly did not appear to be going down. And one thing we saw that—that was, oh, I just couldn't imagine being in this situation, one of the boats had managed to pick up a fairly large group of people. And it brought them in, and the only—the only land that was above ground were some railroad tracks. And they put them there and then they had to sit there for what seemed to me to be a couple of hours before another boat could pick them up and bring them in to the highway. And then when they got to the highway, there was no truck to bring them in to the city, and they set off on foot into the city, Aaron.

BROWN: If you mentioned this, I apologize. . . . You're working with a crew of people, a photographer and others. Do you have a sense of how many people may be stranded tonight?

MESERVE: Yes. Nobody has a sense of that. And may I say that the crew was extraordinary. We've had very difficult situations. Our cameraman, Mark Biello, is working with a broken foot since 9 a.m. this morning to try and get this story to you. Big words of praise for them and for Mark, who went out and ended up in that water, trying to get the rescue boats over partially submerged railroad tracks.

BROWN: Our thanks to you for your efforts. It—you don't need to hear this from me, but you know, people sometimes think that we're a bunch of kind of wacky thrill seekers doing this work, sometimes, and no one who has listened to the words you've spoken or the tone of your voice could possibly think that now. We appreciate your work.

MESERVE: Aaron, thank you. We are sometimes wacky thrill seekers. But when you stand in the dark, and you hear people yelling for help and no one can get to them, it's a totally different experience.

BROWN: Jeanne, thank you. We'll talk later tonight. Thank you. Jeanne Meserve, been on the team for almost 15 years, I think. She is a very tough, capable, strong reporter, and she met her match on a story tonight.

Rescued from the flooding in New Orleans lower Ninth Ward, survivors must wonder what future awaits them.

"Mr. President, we need your help. We need everything you've got."

—Louisiana Governor Kathleen Blanco
in a phone call to the president, who
assures her "help is on the way."

"We've been here for over 300 years. We've continued to say, invest in our levee systems. We've said, invest in our coast. So this will be some picture and some hopefully unfortunate tragedy that will get the country to recognize investment up front could save us all not only money, but a lot of pain and lives in the long run."

—Sen. Mary Landrieu (D-La.)

"To this day [FEMA] coordinates to make sure local agencies, state agencies, federal agencies, all come together as best they can in circumstances which are trying at best. And by golly, the Gulf Coast is going to find out about that in coming weeks and see how well it works or sometimes doesn't, in the worst case."

—CNN reporter Tom Foreman's observatation after
explaining the history of FEMA

"Closed due to Katrina. Katrina Go Away."

—A flashing sign at the Treasure Bay Casino in Biloxi, Miss.

"We finally cleaned up public housing in New Orleans. We couldn't do it, but God did."

—U.S. Rep. Richard Baker (R-La.)

"God attacked America and the prayers of the oppressed were answered. . . . The wrath of the All-powerful fell upon the nation of oppressors."

—Internet statement attributed to al-Qaeda in Iraq

"You know it's really sad. We're not hearing anything about Mississippi. We're not hearing anything about Alabama. We're hearing about the victims in New Orleans. Those are the only ones we're seeing on television are the scumbags."

—Chris Beck, Clear Channel radio host

"It's our duty as Kuwaitis to stand by our friends to lighten the humanitarian misery and as a payback for the many situations during which Washington helped us through the significant relations between the two friendly countries."

—Kuwait Sheik Ahmed Fahd Al Ahmed Al Sabah on the Persian Gulf
state's donation of $500 million to hurricane relief

"Keep your head up from stuff flying around! It is white-capping in the parking lot! Look at the debris! Look at that! The entire thing is coming apart! I feel real scared!"

—CNN crew member working with Anderson Cooper
during the height of the storm

"It was a day that felt like it was never going to end."

—Gary Tuchman, CNN

"They all ask me, 'Can I use your cell phone? Can you call somebody for me? Can you call my mother? Can you call my father? Last I heard, the water was rising. Can you help?' And I say, 'I can't help. . . . ' I'm in one of the last areas with a functioning phone line. The Verizon tower is down."

—WGNO reporter Susan Roesgen

"I can't say that I feel that sense that we've escaped the worst, I think we don't know what the worst is right now."

—Louisiana Gov. Kathleen Blanco

"I think our government officials are assuming that everyone in New Orleans are idiots. My opinion is you should have the option to stay . . . with the stipulation that if you decide to stay, you are on your own."

—Tom Richards, 50, who stayed behind in a sound house with
electricity from a generator and supplies of food and water

"French Quarter types are pretty hearty types. We're ready to start cleaning up and getting the show back on the road. We want to have the place decent by Labor Day, so everybody can come down and have a good time."

—Unidentified male, 9 p.m.

"Now we are all learning what it's like to reap the whirlwind of fossil fuel dependence which [Mississippi Governor] Barbour and his cronies have encouraged. . . . Katrina is giving our nation a glimpse of the climate chaos we are bequeathing our children."

—Robert Kennedy Jr.

DAY 3

"It's ghostly here. It's absolutely ghostly, the silence, blackness. I'm alone here. All alone. And there's no light. No heat . . . nothing."

—*Jack Fine, 78, in an 8:30 p.m. phone interview with Paula Zahn. He tried to flee the city on Sunday, but returned home because of traffic jams.*

Katrina has moved on, but in its wake, the SOS signals continue. The toll is enormous and still mounting: Millions of people without power from Mississippi to Florida. Untold structural damage in almost 90,000 square miles of wreckage, an area roughly equivalent to the size of Great Britain. Oil rigs adrift and missing. Bodies floating in the floodwaters. Survivors invisible in attics and on rooftops. Search and rescue units are now deploying to hard-hit areas in Mississippi and Alabama, efforts made far more dangerous by being conducted in the dead of night along flooded streets.

"There's a total of eight people stranded in my family, ages one to 75. Some are on the roof, some in the attic. It is pitch-dark. There are no streetlights or anything. There's a lady in a tree across the street. They have been in the attic since about 10 or 10:30 Monday morning. My nephew said off in the distance he saw something like a flashlight. He yelled and had a flashlight he could wave. Then the flashlight, or whatever it was, just went away."

—Cathleen Whitelow-Twitty, midnight phone call to CNN

In New Orleans, answering calls for help, the rescue workers make their way slowly, painstakingly, along roads not designed for boats, through treacherously deep water beneath which lie piles of debris, stop signs, fences, huge chunks of wood with nails jutting out. Power lines. Submerged cars. Spewing gas lines. And help can't come fast enough. In some areas, houses are all but submerged. People yell from attics for help. They call on their cellphones, but reception is bad. If they can, they hack their way from the attic to the roof. They stand on their roofs but no one can see them. In some places, the water has actually receded—downtown New Orleans, for instance. In others, it is still rising, and no one in charge seems to know why.

From the French Quarter to St. Bernard Parish, everything is under water. In St. Bernard's alone, 40,000 houses lie submerged—miles and miles of homes, small one-story houses with small attics. An estimated 300

NNS/Landov/Ted Jackson

Members of the Texas Task Force 1, FEMA search and rescue team, call to a man who was calling for help from his attic all night. When they found him, he had already died.
Below—One of many dogs stranded on an island of debris.

to 500 people are still trapped in their houses. Some of them have been there since the previous morning. Some of them have been sitting in trees for hours, waiting for help. An unexpected heartbreak is the plight of the animals of New Orleans, trapped by the floods, stranded in houses or trees, caught in power lines, scared and hungry. Police, firemen, and the Wildlife and Fishery first responders are out in boats, returning with loads of people. Mayor Nagin estimates that casualties could be anywhere from 2,000 to 10,000.

NNS/Landov/Alex Brandon

In Biloxi, police patrol the streets as the body counts rise. The mayor calls Katrina "our tsunami." Gov. Barbour is unable to get rescue operations running in Gulfport and Bay St. Louis, ground zero for Mississippi. Alabama, though reeling from the worst flooding it has experienced in 90 years, offers to lend a helping hand; Gov. Riley offers to send 800 National Guardsmen to help Louisiana and Mississippi, where at last count, an estimated 50 people have died in five counties. The floodwaters in New Orleans are six, eight, ten feet deep; in some sections, as high as 20 feet. The mayor tells the press that 80 percent of the city is underwater.

In response to the rising water in New Orleans, Charity Hospital is working with FEMA and the National Guard to evacuate their 90 patients by air. Tulane University Hospital, housing 1,000 patients directly across the street, confirms that they will need to evacuate. They have been on emergency backup generators since 2 a.m. on August 29, and the water is rising an inch every five minutes, which by their calculations will drown the generators that power the ventilators of patients on life support.

Sometime after 2 a.m., in the course of a discussion about how FEMA will evacuate the patients, Tulane University Hospital's vice president, Karen Troyer-Caraway, tells CNN's Rick Sanchez she has confirmed reports that there is a breach in the 17th Street Canal levee that holds back Lake Pontchartrain. It is 200 feet wide. Millions of gallons have been pouring into the city throughout the day and night. As CNN reports the news, the rising floodwaters start to make sense: Lake Pontchartrain is draining hour by hour into the city of New Orleans. Pouring in. And the breaches—soon it will also become clear there is more than just one—are widening.

FACTOID: Lake Pontchartrain is the second largest saltwater lake in the country. It's about four miles wide east to west, 24 miles from north to south. The Lake Pontchartrain Causeway, which connects New Orleans to Mandeville, is considered the longest bridge in the world.

"I mean, from the top of our buildings we have white caps on Canal Street, the water is moving so fast."—Karen Troyer-Caraway, 2 a.m.

With first light comes the first sense of devastation. Estimates of Katrina's costs to insurers are up to $26 billion. Oil prices are climbing above $68 after their record high of nearly $71. Gas prices are predicted to soar. Biloxi's huge Grand Casino lies a quarter mile off its moorings, smashed in two. Across three states, the Red Cross begins to mobilize the largest relief effort in its history.

A neighborhood is destroyed in Gulf Shores, Ala.

"A large section of the vital 17th Street Canal levee, where it connects to the brand-new 'hurricane proof' Old Hammond Highway Bridge, gave way late Monday morning in Bucktown after Katrina's fiercest winds were well north. The breach sent a churning sea of water from Lake Pontchartrain coursing across Lakeview and into Mid-City, Carrollton, Gentilly, City Park, and neighborhoods farther south and east."

—Times-Picayune, *August 30*

Daybreak also brings an end to the rain and to the screams in the dark in New Orleans. A false calm settles over many drier parts of the city, where broken windows and doors on storefronts create a haven for looters. A giant new Wal-Mart in the Garden District is looted when a limited distribution of supplies broke down into chaos. Some take what they need. Others take what they want. There are reports of armed gangs moving around the city. Shootings are reported. In the Second District, many police fail to report for duty, and the numbers of those who do, will dwindle throughout the day. People appear in stores with bags, filling them up "like Santa Claus." Vigilantism replaces law and order in pockets of the city and signs appear: "You loot, we shoot."

"Put this in your paper. They told us nothing. We were unprepared. We are completely on our own."
—*Police officer on Canal Street to a* Times-Picayune *reporter*

The morning sun also brings its warmth to the Superdome, whose inhabitants—on their second day of water and food, with one left to go, and with sweltering heat pouring through the open roof—have swelled to a reported 20,000. Crime increases, despite approximately 6,000 National Guard units that have arrived. The Army Corps of Engineers struggles with the difficult task of how to repair the "football field"–sized breach in the 17th Street levee. Attempts to shore it fail, and the pumps are overwhelmed. Water is rising at the rate of three inches per hour: Rainfall from Katrina that filled north shore rivers and streams is continuously flowing into Lake Pontchartrain, which is already six feet above sea level.

Two more breaches are reported along the Industrial Canal, explaining the intense flooding in the lower Ninth Ward on Monday. The water spreads south towards the French Quarter. The state Department of Transportation and Development and the Army Corps of Engineers work around the clock to stem the flooding. The plans include 108 15,000 lb. concrete barriers and fifty 3,000 lb. sandbags, which will be helicoptered in and dropped into place. If that doesn't work, they aren't sure what will. Mayor Nagin estimates the water could reach three feet above sea level, or 12 to 15 feet high in places. But experts warn that if it reaches the height of the levees along the lakefront, the floodgates designed to keep the lake out, and which would be needed to allow it to leave, would be blocked. By now, it's clear that the worst possible scenario has been set in motion: The city is, indeed, a soup bowl filling up with water. Lots of it. Hundreds of thousands of gallons of lake water per second. In an oddly discordant statement at a 4 p.m. press conference Sen. David Vitter (R-La.), tries to assure the public. "I don't want to alarm everybody that, you know, New Orleans is filling up like a bowl. That's just not happening."

Times-Picayune/NNS/Landov

President Bush announces that he will cut short his vacation and return to Washington to deal with the crisis. He assures the public that "teams and equipment are in place" and that the federal, state, and local governments are "beginning to move in the help that people need."

Buses scheduled to arrive at the Superdome never arrive; in a tangle of red tape, the state was to provide them, then FEMA would handle it, then FEMA's buses would take too long, so the buses would come from the state. Rumors of violence and chaos at the Superdome abound—a man is reported to have calmly leaped from the second-level bleachers to his death—but reports vary, and some say the atmosphere is "not too horrific." Toilets have been overflowing for two days. The heat is intolerable. Many are ill and in need of medical attention. There is no drinking water. Reporters who manage to get in or near the Dome are approached by people begging for reassurance: "Tell President Bush we need some help," they plead. "Do you know when FEMA's coming? When are the supplies coming?" Ray Bias, an emergency worker who answered a radio signal to come help, establishes a small first-aid station inside the Dome, trying to assist those who need dialysis, and to help with cuts, falls, weakness. But it's not enough. The population inside now reaches around 30,000, as search-and-rescue drops off more and more people.

Far left–Stranded survivors wait on a roadway turned island to be rescued.

Top–The interior of one of the few houses in Waveland, Miss., still standing.

Left–Flood victims take shelter near ticket windows at the Superdome in New Orleans.

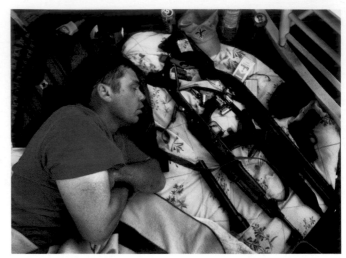

Chris Granger/NNS/Landov

Meanwhile, Katrina travels into Tennessee, Georgia, Kentucky, and the Carolinas. It unleashes tornadoes that rip through Carroll County west of Atlanta, destroying 30 buildings. Part of West Virginia and western Virginia are expected to see its still considerable power. Towns and cities as far away as Pittsburgh may see tornadoes before the storm dissipates.

The Coast Guard's heroic efforts throughout the day result in at least 1,200 people being rescued. Police, firefighters, EMTs, Fish and Wildlife personnel, and other "first responders," as well as individual volunteers, are "angels in the storm" and save many lives, acting on their own with no official instruction or authorization.

The water is still rising and neither the levees nor the pumps can be repaired in order to drain it out of the city. It is a unique New Orleans blend of chemical

AP Photo/*San Antonio Express News*/Nicole Fruge

Top left—People walk along flooded railroad tracks near the Superdome.

Top—A New Orleans man grabs a couple hours of sleep next to an arsenal of guns. He and several friends rode out Hurricane Katrina. Sleeping outdoors on a balcony they heard gunfire on their streets every night following the storm. The guns were donated to them by out-of-town residents so they could protect everyone's property.

Left—Joann Moriarity (with her dog) and her brother get boat-lifted from Canal Street. Many of those who did not evacuate were unwilling to leave their pets.

Right—Rhonda Braden walks through the destruction in her childhood neighborhood in Long Beach, Miss.

Alex Brandon/NSS/Landov

BLOGS

Posted 2:20 p.m. ET
Anderson Cooper on his way to Gulfport, Miss.

We're trying to find a way to Gulfport, Miss., from Meridian. We luckily just found some gas at the Wal-Mart. Got some beef jerky, too. We were nearly out of gas last night. Down to about a gallon, if that.

We finally got a place to stay around 1:30 a.m. last night. We stayed in this Choctaw Native American casino in Philadelphia, Miss. It was kind of strange to see people playing slot machines at 7 a.m. this morning. They were serving biscuits and gravy and keeping the slot machines going.

At the gas station we were in line for about a half an hour. Hardly any of the gas stations are open. After a storm like this everyone is swapping information in line at Wal-Mart about where to find gas or food.

The main roads have been shut down. Right now we are trying to find out what road is open. We're trying to move our big truck. We wanted to go down Highway 59 but we heard it was closed.

We're in the midst of what everyone else is facing in terms of trying to get gas and food and ice. The Wal-Mart was really the only place open. We stocked up on a lot of jerky and Gatorade. Strip malls are closed. No restaurants are open. Along these back roads in Mississippi, you have local residents who are coming out with chainsaws and clearing the roads with their neighbors.

People came out in Meridian and helped clear the road for a CNN crew. My dad was born just south of Meridian. Turns out it was my cousins who helped clear the road. That was a bizarre incident. When we were stuck last night I thought about trying to track one of my cousins down to give us some lodging.

waste, gasoline, and the inevitable coffins from the city's above-ground cemeteries: Toxic Gumbo, it's called. By evening, with most authorities involved with search-and-rescue efforts, looting becomes widespread in all parts of the city.

Night falls again in New Orleans, and Coast Guard helicopters and boats continue searching for survivors. In the darkness, the beams of hundreds of flashlights suddenly appear, waved from attics, windows, roof-tops—signals that there are still people out there, waiting, praying to be seen.

AP Photo/Rob Carr

Hardy Jackson Jr.,12, stands in the area where his home previously stood in Biloxi, Miss.
Though Hardy, his siblings, and his father survived the blow of the hurricane, his mother met a different fate.
She was ripped from her husband's grip when the water rushed in.

BILOXI FLOOD SURVIVOR HARDY JACKSON'S STORY

Hardy Jackson's house was literally split in two by the force of the storm. Jackson and his wife, Toni, managed to get onto the roof of their house. At first, it seemed safe enough. But the force of the water tore the house in two. He and his wife were in the separate halves. And even though they tried holding onto each other, they were swept apart. She was lost.

Jennifer Mayerle, for WKRG-TV, spoke to Harvey within hours after it happened, asking how he was doing. "I'm not doing good," he admitted simply. At first, all he could tell Mayerle was that the house had "just split in half." Pressed for details, he said, "We got up in the roof, all the way to the roof, and the water came." He tried desperately to hang onto his wife when the house began to split in half.

Mayerle asked him who was with him on the roof, and Jackson said simply, "My wife." But when asked where she was now, Jackson told the simple, devastating truth. "Can't find her body. She's gone. . . . " Mayerle, in disbelief, asked again if he had found his wife. "I was holding her hand tight as I could. And she told me you can't hold me." The two had been married for 29 years.

"No," he said, "she told—I tried. I hold her hand tight as I could. And she told me, 'You can't hold me.' She said, 'Take care of the kids and the grandkids.' "

"It was a knock of death, doom, doom, doom, doom, doom. I said, 'Oh, babe, things don't look good, they don't look good.' I said, 'Baby, please don't let go, please don't let go.' Nobody ran to help. Nobody. Just me and her." And she said, 'Hardy.' She said, 'Let go. You can't hold me.' I said 'Please, baby, don't say that. I'll save you. Please, don't leave me.' She said, 'Take care of them kids and take care of them grandkids.' She looked at my eyes just like I'm looking into your eyes, man, and let go. And she went back to the north, man. That water, man, took her back, I didn't see, somewhere."

Mayerle asked his wife's full name, Tonette Jackson, in case she might be recovered during rescue efforts. She asked Jackson where he was going. "We ain't got nowhere to go," he said. "I'm lost. That's all I had. That's all I had. This is all a horrible joke."

" It is not a simple natural disaster tonight. It is becoming a disaster caused by humans. New Orleans is no longer safe to live in. It is that simple and that stark."

—Aaron Brown

"My brother is trapped in an attic at his home in New Orleans. And I'm trying to get someone out there to rescue him. He don't know how to swim. He was calling us yesterday morning, when the storm hit. He got trapped in the home, and the water was coming up and he was calling us on his cell phone, and he was saying that he's trying to get into the attic. And the attic, he has no [inaudible] in the attic, as far as something, you know, to break through the attic. He was just so worried about getting up there, because he has—he can't swim. And I think he dropped his cell phone and we lost contact. And we've been worried ever since, and we're scared."

—Caller to Larry King Live, 9:30 p.m.

"While many people carried out food and essential supplies, others cleared out jewelry racks and carted out computers, TVs, and appliances on handtrucks. Some officers joined in taking whatever they could, including one New Orleans cop who loaded a shopping cart with a compact computer and a 27-inch flat-screen television.

"Officers claimed there was nothing they could do to contain the anarchy, saying their radio communications had broken down and they had no direction from commanders. 'We don't have enough cops to stop it,' an officer said. 'A mass riot would break out if you tried.'

". . . Throughout the store and parking lot, looters pushed carts and loaded trucks and vans alongside officers. One man said police directed him to Wal-Mart from Robert's Grocery, where a similar scene was taking place.

"A crowd in the electronics section said one officer broke the glass DVD case so people wouldn't cut themselves. 'The police got all the best stuff. They're crookeder than us,' one man said.

"Most officers, though, simply stood by powerless against the tide of lawbreakers. One veteran officer said, 'It's like this everywhere in the city. This tiny number of cops can't do anything about this. It's wide open.'"

—Times-Picayune report: "Looters leave nothing behind in storm's wake"

"I do not think the water is toxic. It's just, you know, water."

—Louisiana Gov. Kathleen Blanco

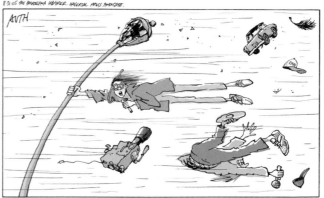

"THIS IS CNN REPORTING ON THE FOOLISHNESS OF OUR SPECIES... ...FOR INSTANCE, THERE GOES THE WEATHER CHANNEL GUY..."

"Many people are doing good deeds. Yesterday, when I was out on I-10, watching that horrible flooding and the people trapped in their houses, there was one family who wouldn't evacuate until the elderly woman who lived next door was taken out. And they inflated an air mattress and put her on that to try to keep her afloat. I saw people who were disabled being hauled through the streets by other younger, healthier people.

"Hundreds and hundreds of people taking whatever they like . . . from stores. It's chaos here. New jeans, Nikes are very popular. People trying stuff on right in the street, making sure they get the best fit.

"As we walked, we saw people, refugees, literally refugees, walking toward the Superdome. That's what they've all been told to do. They are lugging plastic bags. They are pushing bins. Many of them are carrying children."

—Jeanne Meserve

"You do live with the belief that some day the big one's going to get you. You're almost fatalistic, which is part of the reason New Orleans has that mixture of frivolity and fatalism. Living in a soup bowl will do it to you, like Romans dancing while Nero fiddled and the city burned."

— Patricia McDonald Gomez, general manager of Aunt Sally's Original Creole Pralines, in an interview after Hurricane Andrew missed hitting New Orleans directly

"We'll rebuild, of course. But what made New Orleans is the polyglot, the tapestry, the mosaic, the gumbo. So the French Quarter get most of the attention, but the Quarter feeds from the arteries of the neighborhoods."

—Marc Morial, former mayor of New Orleans

DAY 4

Wednesday, August 31, 2005

HOUSES WALK AND THE DEAD RISE UP
—Washington Post *headline*

Rising waters. Rising fears. As the sun illuminates cities wiped out by Hurricane Katrina, New Orleans this morning is the Big Uneasy. It's decision time, but no one knows where to start.

Plug the levees. Save the living. Dispose of the dead. Restore civil order. Officials scramble to set priorities as the floodwaters keep rising. The plan yesterday was for helicopters to drop 1,500 lb. concrete blocks and 3,000 lb. sandbags, reported to be filled with gravel, into the massive breach in the 17th Street Canal levee. When the drop is scrapped in favor of a rescue in a church, Mayor Nagin explodes in frustration. If the levee repair had been done earlier, he insists, much less flooding would have taken place. However, with so many different agencies trying to coordinate, and with communications down—even most of the batteries have run out on the radios—things aren't getting done. Not yesterday, not today.

"There's way too many freakin'—excuse me—cooks in the kitchen. We had this implementation plan going. They should have done these sandbag operations first thing this morning and it didn't get done. I'm very upset about it."—*Mayor Ray Nagin*

In nearby Slidell, just across Lake Pontchartrain, many stuck it out for the same reason many stayed in New Orleans: They simply didn't have the finances to leave. Says the mayor, "It's absolutely awful. Everything is broken. . . . I'm anticipating 15,000 homeless people. . . . I am one." A conservative estimate of the number of large trees the town has lost is somewhere between 10,000 and 15,000.

In Biloxi, rescue teams search the rubble in 24-hour shifts. Teams of mortuary specialists have arrived to identify and process the bodies. Gov. Barbour compares the aftermath to another site of unfathomable loss: "I can only imagine this is what Hiroshima looked like 60 years ago." Mississippi is losing $500 thousand a day in tax revenues due to the loss of its waterfront casinos, most of which were obliterated. Barbour tells the press that 90 percent of the structures between the beach and the railroad in Biloxi, Gulfport, Long Beach, and Pass Christian are destroyed.

Allen Fredrickson/Reuters /Landov

Justin Sullivan/Getty Images

Top–A Chinook helicopter drops a 3,000 lb. sandbag to shore up a broken levee wall north of downtown New Orleans.

Left–A coffin floats in a cemetery in New Orleans.

Top Right–All of the Biloxi casinos were destroyed, which in addition to generating $500 million a day in taxes, are also the largest employer in the region.

Washington Post/Panoramic Composite–John W. Poole

President Bush sends in the Navy and plans to do an aerial survey of the Gulf Coast in Air Force One. In Norfolk, the USS *Iwo Jima*, the USS *Shreveport*, the USS *Tortuga*, and the USS *Grapple* prepare to head toward the Gulf Coast, loaded with supplies and six disaster-relief teams onboard. Asked if the ships could accommodate hurricane victims, the answer is yes.

Parts of Interstate I-10 are destroyed, the twinspan bridge is wiped out. The city, slowly turning into Lake Pontchartrain. Looting is on the rise along with the water. Shootings, carjackings. Looters break into businesses and homes alike, taking supplies—and too often, much more. The National Guard moves in to try to stem the looting, and they join police in patrolling the downtown streets. The police force is overwhelmed, trying to maintain order and conduct search-and-rescue missions. Gov. Blanco says she tries to call President Bush to again to request more help for her state, and is transferred around the White House until finally ending up on the phone with Homeland Security Advisor Fran Townsend. Their conversation is inconclusive, and Blanco is worried.

The Superdome, where conditions are not only deplorable but unsafe, is Blanco's other priority—it must be evacuated. The "refuge of last resort" simmers in the broiling sun. The people there have been given fresh water and food, but water is lapping at the ramps, filling with waste, corpses, and chemical contaminants, which experts warn may contain E-coli and other harmful bacteria. The Dome is filling with waste, the result of overflowing toilets. There are dead bodies covered with blankets, some still sitting upright in chairs. The stench is horrendous. Thirty thousand people, their numbers are growing. Local, state, and federal communications are in chaos. Sen. Mary Landrieu, standing outside the Superdome, asks to borrow a FEMA official's phone to call her office in Washington. "It didn't work," she said. "I thought to myself, 'This isn't going to be pretty.'"

A WALL, AND A CITY, TUMBLE DOWN
Here's what Army Corps of Engineers officials believe happened at the 17th Street Canal that caused the cataclysm

1. Under normal operating conditions, the levee along the canal is augmented by a concrete seawall embedded in the levee.

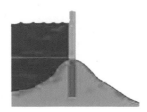

2. Under the awesome force of Katrina, the water in Lake Pontchartrain rises high enough to top the seawall.

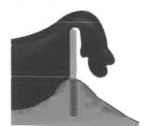

3. Water coursing down like a powerful waterfall at the base of the dry side of the levee begins eroding the dirt.

4. Eventually, the weakened levee can no longer support the concrete wall, and it collapses, sending lake water pouring into the city

Times-Picayune/NNS/Landov

Hours later, Blanco calls President Bush again demanding to speak with him directly, and asks for whatever he has: 40,000 troops, she says, later admitting she "pulled a number out of the sky." He agrees to send troops and more aid.

The unanswered question everyone is asking, however, is why military transport planes can't come and airlift people out—out of the drowning city, out of the stifling Superdome, out and away to shelters in neighboring states. Again, carefully coordinating preparations and staging seem to doom any timely results. Still, Nagin soon shifts into a more political gear, insisting that the federal government is doing all it can. But the tradeoff on the levee repair is costly: Another 10 to 15 feet of water could accumulate as a result.

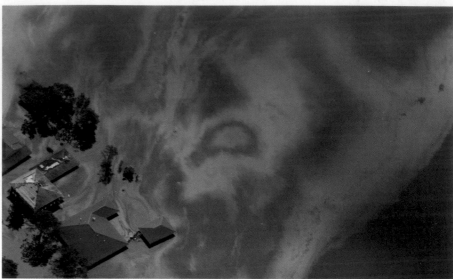

Dave Einsel/Getty Images

A toxic film spreads over the water near a flooded home in the Lakeside area.

In the Gulfport/Biloxi area, Kathleen Koch, CNN, reports: *"We talked to someone from the coroner's office, describing people bringing bodies to their office in the backs of cars, in the backs of trucks. Bodies of loved ones, bodies of neighbors. And then when the phones were still functioning—they don't work anymore—telling the coroner's office, 'You could find a body on this corner, on that corner, we marked it, please come and get it.'"*

President Bush makes the decision to release oil from the strategic petroleum reserve. In San Diego giving a speech, the president will return to Washington today.

AP Photo/Eric Gay

Evelyn Turner cries alongside the body of her common-law husband, Xavier Bowie, who had been ill with lung cancer. He died on Tuesday afternoon, August 30, when he ran out of oxygen.

INTERVIEW

Soledad O'Brien

Sidney Barthelemy,
Former Mayor of
New Orleans

O'BRIEN: Let's get right to Sidney Barthelemy. He was the mayor of New Orleans from 1986 until 1994. He's in Atlanta this morning. Thank you for talking with us. We certainly appreciate it. You know, we've been asking a lot of people this morning this question: Why was there no plan in place? New Orleans has been below sea level forever. And clearly, it's in the path of hurricanes. So why no plan?

BARTHELEMY: I think, Soledad, everyone thought there was a plan. Everyone thought that we could handle most of the problems that would come due to a hurricane. No one ever dreamed that it would take—be such devastation. We really need the president of the United States to make this a priority. We have to stop the breaches in the levee. We have to, or we're going to lose New Orleans and lose thousands of people there. . . .

O'BRIEN: But the Army Corps of Engineers—we spoke to them this morning—they're working on it. It seems that they're doing what they can do. What more should they be doing? What else could the president do?

BARTHELEMY: Well, then, the president can send the Army to help and resolve this. Three thousand new troops are coming in. That's not enough. We did everything possible to help the people who were suffering from the tsunami. We have to make this a priority. We have to send the Army to stop this, or we will lose New Orleans, and we will lose 80,000 people, I believe.

O'BRIEN: Mayor Nagin we heard earlier. I guess he was doing an interview earlier, and he said there are too many cooks in the kitchen, essentially. It sounds like a lot of the elected officials are frustrated, and a lot of lack of coordination, in addition to the fact that, clearly, you know, no cell phones. It's just difficult, but it also seems like on that front there was no plan either. I mean, who's really in charge?

BARTHELEMY: Soledad, I think it's just overwhelming. I have to believe the officials now are doing all that they can do, using as many resources that they have. That's not enough. The president of the United States is the only person who has the resources to coordinate, to bring in the troops, to make this city a safe place, and solve the problems, particularly the breach in the levee. They're losing hope. Everything they're doing, the problem is not getting better. It's getting worse.

O'BRIEN: The president would say, listen, we declared a disaster area before the storm even hit, I'm coming on Friday to take a look at the devastation in the region. What more do you want?

BARTHELEMY: Friday may be too late, Soledad. We don't have that time to wait. We need him now—to send the troops now. If we can spend the money that we are spending to help the people in Iraq, then we can do the same thing for New Orleans.

This is a great country, we have tremendous resources. We have to make this a resolve, because if New Orleans goes, it's going to have a devastating impact not just on the people who live there, but on the rest of this nation.

O'BRIEN: Can we take a moment and talk a little bit about the Superdome? You've got 20,000 angry, hot, tired, underfed people in really disgusting conditions, I think it's fair to say. What should be done with them? The governor says we need to get them out now, but the plan seems to be buses. I don't know where—how the buses would get out of the city. What do you do with them?

BARTHELEMY: Again, Soledad, I think we have to send the resources in. The governor, she wants to do the best thing. She wants to evacuate. The mayor wants to evacuate.

They do not have the resources. I don't know how you say to the federal government, this is a national disaster. We must save those people and save that city. That means sending the military in right now. We can't wait. We've got to send the military in now who have the resources to save this city and save those people down there that are trapped.

O'BRIEN: Thank you for talking with us. And I'm sure this is just devastating to you to be watching this.

BARTHELEMY: I've lost everything, Soledad. And I want to thank you for trying to get our story out. It is—it is such a disaster. We need the help. We need the president to focus on what's happening in New Orleans right now.

O'BRIEN: Thank you, sir.

HEROES:
The First Responders

Many come from faraway places to lend their professionalism in the midst of a crisis. Those already there are survivors themselves with families who have suffered. The Coast Guard, police and fire rescue units, emergency medical personnel, FEMA teams, and many others—most are nameless, they seek no credit or rewards. If pressed they will tell you it is their job, but we know it is more than that. Others are just ordinary people who come to do whatever, volunteers whose only reward is helping. Still others are just in the wrong place at the wrong time and rise up to do extraordinary things. In the worst of times, they are the best of us. They are the heroes.

(Photo credits can be found on page 2.)

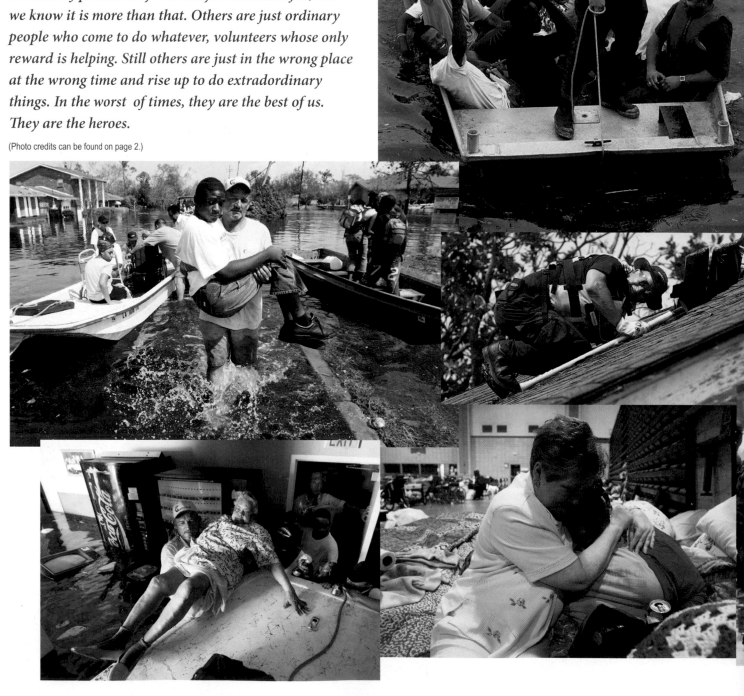

Thousands of Hurricane Katrina survivors wait to be evacuated from the Louisiana Superdome in New Orleans.

Tom Foreman, CNN: *"This is a major American city. We haven't had anything like this—I can't recall, in modern history, a major American city being shut down in this way. I think we're going to see, in coming days, discussion at the highest federal levels of even things like public works programs. Because they're going to say what do we do with all these people who are now wandering the South and the Midwest with their families, their children, their grandparents, saying what do we do now? They have no jobs. They may not be able to access their banking at the moment. We don't know about that. We don't know what's going to happen with insurance. They don't even know if they've lost their homes. This is going to be enormous."*

By 1 p.m., a decision is made to evacuate 23,000 from the squalid, sweltering Superdome to the Astrodome in Houston. Buses to ferry them more than 300 miles to the rarely used, air-conditioned center are supposed to arrive any minute.

Many people are still being rescued. The Coast Guard alone has brought more than 1,260 to safety. Unfortunately, the only place to bring them is the Superdome. Reporters are banned from inside, and rumors of lawlessness and crime continue to surface—gangs terrorizing the weak, elderly, and the children. Outside, it is not much different: There are reports of looters cleaning out the gun department in a newly opened Wal-Mart and New Orleans' Homeland Security chief warns there are armed gangs roaming the city. The local police are overwhelmed and outnumbered. With limited radio communication organizing reinforcements was difficult at best.

Despite the crisis situation, emergency management officials assure everyone that the water is not rising. "The good news here is that we've restabilized. Water is not rising in the city." Supplies—sandbags, sheet piling, rock and concrete bars—are being airlifted in by helicopter to close up the breaches in the levees. But worries about acre after acre of filthy standing water have begun to cause real concern about sanitation, especially a problem with mosquitoes and West Nile fever.

Looters drive off with a trunk full of beer after raiding a Rite Aid Drug Store in New Orleans.

AP Photo/Christopher Morris/VII

Air Force One flies over New Orleans and the Gulf Coast hovering for 35 minutes at 1,700 feet. President Bush is able to see the Superdome and the flooded neighborhoods. "It's devastating," he remarks. "It's got to be doubly devastating on the ground." Passing over Mississippi, he comments that it is "totally wiped out."

BLOGS

Posted: 1:03 p.m. ET, John Zarrella in New Orleans

We are part of a convoy of CNN personnel who left the city. We left the hotel this morning. As we did so, we helped evacuate people from it.

We drove on the sidewalks to stay high enough out of the water so the cars would not bog down, until we made it over to Canal Street. Canal Street was dry in the middle. We stopped where the police were and I told one of the officers that we had these evacuees from the hotel and that we were told to drop them off there with him. He said, "Well, we're not going anywhere. We're only here because we can't get back to our station. Everything's flooded under water." So they're sitting in the middle of Canal Street. We took the evacuees to another area by another hotel and dropped them off there.

We wound our way through the city this morning through back streets and side streets, downed power lines, around downed industries. We were driving on the wrong side of the road periodically, up along the Mississippi bank, along the levee. and finally made it over the Huey P. Long Bridge on Highway 90. We are making our way up to Baton Rouge now. Highway 90 is a steady stream of traffic.

In New Orleans, there's no sanitation any longer. The knee-deep water in the hotel lobby is just full of stench. It is a miserable, deteriorating situation in the city and it is growing worse by the hour and the water is rising.

The fact of the matter is this bowl, as they call it, is filling up. The estimates of time that it's going to take to get the water out of the bowl are three to six months. You could be sitting there in absolutely untenable conditions, in water that is filled with disease and germs, for months to come, walking through it, slogging through it.

With the looting that's going on and with the deteriorating sanitation conditions, it is a situation where you can't cover the story because you can't venture out from the hotel. It's so dangerous, one, because the water is getting higher, and two, because of the disease factor that is beginning. There's no food, there's no water.

Kyra Phillips

Dr. David Satcher,
Former Director of the CDC and former U.S. Surgeon General

PHILLIPS: I've just got to ask you, sir, from your experience. . . . Have you ever seen anything like this in the United States?

SATCHER: Kyra, I don't think any of us has ever seen anything like this… I don't remember anything that compares with this. I think this is sort of beyond our imagination. . . .

Let me just say a few things that are critical. Water safety is critical. And people need to be aware of the fact that water can be very dangerous, after and during a flood. So it's very important to limit consumption to bottled water, to treated water, and to boiled water if that's possible.

It's also important to be careful with food at a time like this. And to make sure that contaminated food is not consumed, food that has been contaminated by floodwater. But also food spoils if it's not maintained in refrigeration.

You mentioned the mosquitoes and the concern about the West Nile fever. That's a real threat here with standing water, so people need to be aware of that. That probably will come a little later. Injuries can lead to tetanus if people get puncture wounds. So we're dealing with all of these things. We're dealing with the danger of people going back into buildings prematurely. That's very dangerous. Dangerous, acutely, because the buildings are unstable.

An enormous gathering of Homeland Security, Health and Human Services, Energy, and EPA officials, including Michael Chertoff, Homeland Security secretary—"along with almost every other secretary that leads this country"—convenes in New Orleans for a press conference to reassure the public that everything in their power is being done to alleviate the human suffering and dangerous conditions. A laundry list of supplies is again announced, and there are promises to restore "at least minimal transportation infrastructure in the region." Roads will be cleared, bridges inspected, airport services reestablished, pipelines restored. The Department of Defense will provide a 500-bed mobile hospital, 50 helicopters, and eight ships, including a hospital ship. So far, 11,000 National Guardsmen have been

AP Photo/Bill Haber

A New Orleans resident walks through floodwaters that are rapidly turning into a "toxic gumbo" in the flooded downtown area.

deployed "in and around the affected area." In coordination with the governor, it's the Guard who will have to restore civil order: All told, 31,500 National Guardsmen from Louisiana, Mississippi, Alabama, and Florida are providing support to civil authorities—though whether they're trained to deal with civil disorder is the question of the day. Regardless, many in New Orleans were hoping for more—they want the cavalry to arrive.

"We are extremely pleased with the response that every element of the federal government, all of our federal partners, have made to this terrible tragedy."

—Michael Chertoff, Homeland Security secretary, at a 1:30 p.m. press conference

Question to Chertoff at press conference: *"As far as the chain of command in this first use of the law, are you in charge of local and state officials? And if there is any conflict between you and the locals of the state, how does that get worked out?"*

A: "We come in to assist local and state authorities. Under the constitution, state and local authorities have the principal first line of response obligation. DHS has the coordinating role, or the managing role. The president has, of course, the ultimate responsibility for all the federal effort here. I want to emphasize the federal government does not supersede the state and local government. We fit . . . in a comprehensive response plan."

By mid-afternoon, Mayor Ray Nagin tells the Associated Press that there are "hundreds, perhaps thousands," dead in New Orleans. Although the Red Cross says it has raised $22 million in the last two days, supplies aren't getting into the beleaguered city. Downtown hospitals are barely functioning, and the Coast Guard begins to drop off patients at the Louis Armstrong New Orleans International airport, one of 40 field hospitals set up around the region. Pharmacies are set up inside FedEx trucks, and there are disaster medical teams made up of professionals from all over the country. For the four Florida hurricanes last year, there were never more than five of these teams dispatched to any one of the hurricanes. For Katrina, they've set up 40.

A nurse at Baptist Hospital says the backup generators that care for the bone marrow patients are gone. There's no ventilation, no running water, no food, and they're using portable oxygen. The nurse walks outside to get a breath of fresh air and says she is held up at gunpoint. At nearby Charity Hospital staffers have ripped doors off their hinges to serve as carriers to move the seriously ill to the ninth floor, just out of reach of the angry waters. Charity houses 250 patients, 50 of whom are critical and for whom time is running out. Without water, workers cannot run the dialysis machines. The generators they're using are diesel powered, and will soon run out of fuel. Despite the deployment of thousands of National Guardsmen and Air National Guardsmen, Charity has only been able to evacuate five patients in two days.

INTERVIEW

Kyra Phillips

Richard Zuschlag,
CEO Acadian
Ambulance Service

(Acadian is the largest private ambulance and EMS company in Louisiana)

PHILLIPS: So, Richard, tell me right now, what you are doing. What type of resources do you have and how are you responding with your service?

ZUSCHLAG: We're involved in evacuating patients from hospitals. We just received a urgent call from Touro Infirmary. They're asking us to get 100 babies out of their unit by dark this evening. Part of the reason they're asking for that is the unrest in New Orleans. We definitely need the president to send the military troops in to regain control of the city. The site of this disaster and this flood is very unsafe for anybody that's left behind.

We have about 120 ambulances that can get in on

the interstate so far. And we're using wildlife and refuge boats and the National Guard. . . . to get patients from the hospital over to the interstate and bring them back up to Baton Rouge. The military has sent us in an extra 25 helicopters. The problem is some hospitals can't handle the heavy military helicopters and they can't land down on the ground because there's too much water. We're hoping that we can get most of the 2,000 patients left in the hospitals out of New Orleans this evening before dark. But it's going to be a close call. . . . If we do not, the federal presence in New Orleans tonight at dark—it will no longer be safe to be there, hospital or no hospital.

PHILLIPS: What about infants, what about women giving birth? Is this an issue with regard to babies and . . .

ZUSCHLAG: This is all happening in an environment without electricity, without water. It is very primitive. It's very difficult. I think people do not realize how bad things have gotten in New Orleans.

PHILLIPS: Let me ask you about the law and order. As you are treating those individuals medically? What about the criminal aspects of things and the looting? Is that hampering efforts for you to do what you need to do?

ZUSCHLAG: It certainly is. My people are in harm's way. They are scared. Our command station about an hour ago had the generator stolen off the back of it. We've had an ambulance turned over. Things are not good in New Orleans. It's very serious right now. I did not think it could come to this. These people are frustrated, they are hungry, they're trying to get to higher ground. They're taking over some hospitals. We're getting calls from nurses, on cell phones, begging us to send help.

The problem is the military's so busy rescuing all these other people that they think we're taking care of all the patients from the hospitals, and we have a congressman in our control room right now, trying to get more help, to get the Coast Guard to help us start getting patients out of these hospitals because of the dangerous situation.

PHILLIPS: We sure appreciate your time. And, boy, we extend our heartfelt wishes to you as you continue to work one of the biggest and most important operations underway right now in the city of New Orleans, and that's finding and rescuing survivors and treating those that desperately need your help. Richard, thanks you.

ZUSCHLAG: Please keep us in your prayers.

Top–Medical workers and patients ride in the back of a military vehicle as they are evacuated from New Orleans.
Bottom–Residents wait on a rooftop to be rescued from floodwaters in New Orleans.

Dr. Jeffery Williams, Charity Hospital ICU: *"We're just not getting information. We hear a lot of conjecture: National Guard is coming. Air National Guard is supposed to be coming. But even yesterday, we were told to get patients ready to evacuate and nothing has happened. And you know we just had another announcement that they would be trying to bus some of the less critical patients. But we have a number of patients here that won't tolerate a bus. We need to get them helicoptered out. We don't have water. We have at least 42 critical patients as of early this morning. A couple have died and a couple of people have gotten worse."*

An official report now confirms that two of the canals—the Industrial and the 17th Street canals—on the south side of Lake Pontchartrain have holes in them, allowing the lake to drain backward into the city. The Army Corp of Engineers speculate a three-to-six-month period before the water can be completely drained. Normally, barges would transport the sandbags needed to close the gaps, but with bridges out and trees down, maneuvering is impossible

At the Superdome, thousands of people are walking away from the injured structure, literally trying to walk out of the city. They stream out of the city, seeking shelter on highway overpasses. Buses filled with prisoners drive by, but there are no buses for the citizens. The water is everywhere, but undrinkable, and with the temperature is in the 90s, dehydration is inevitable, especially among the elderly and the children.

Leo Dollide, 59, far left, leads a group of residents waiting to board a U.S. Coast Guard helicopter to take them to the New Orleans airport. Dollide said he rode out Hurricane Katrina because he didn't have the money to leave.

AP Photo/Rob Carr

BLOGS

Posted: 3:46 p.m. ET, Jim Spellman in New Orleans

New Orleans has fast become a refugee city. Thousands and thousands of people are seeking shelter on the highway overpasses looking for some sort of help, some sort of information.

They are screaming out to us and anybody around for water and for help. They are looking for information and for a way to get out.

On the highway overpasses and underneath the highways as well, people are trying to find a spot for themselves. Prison buses are streaming by to evacuate prisoners and a lot of people are very, very upset that they aren't getting help, but the prisoners are.

We have seen looting all day long. We actually went right up to a Walgreens where people were trying on shoes to get the correct size. They were picking out whatever it is they wanted—televisions, just anything they could get. The police have definitely been trying to keep it to a minimum. The police are in boats but there's really nothing they can do. I don't know where they would even take anybody. They are taking all the looted material and they are trying to keep the chaos to a minimum.

Today is the first day when I think lack of water is starting to become a problem. It's about in the 90s. It's extremely humid here. And people are just baking out on these highways. There is nowhere else for them to go.

Excerpts from President George W. Bush's speech from the Rose Garden, 5 p.m.

"I have directed Secretary of Homeland Security Mike Chertoff to chair a Cabinet-level task force to coordinate all our assistance from Washington. FEMA Director Mike Brown is in charge of all federal response and recovery efforts in the field. I've instructed them to work closely with state and local officials, as well as with the private sector, to ensure that we're helping—not hindering—recovery efforts. This recovery will take a long time. This recovery will take years. . . .
The Department of Transportation has provided more than 400 trucks to move 1,000 truckloads containing:
  • 5.4 million meals ready to eat
  • 13.4 million liters of water
  • 10,400 tarps
  • 3.4 million pounds of ice
  • 144 generators
  • 20 containers of prepositioned disaster supplies
  • 135,000 blankets
  • 11,000 cots
And we're just starting."

The body count in Mississippi hits 110, as many as 100 from Harrison County alone, with 20,000 in shelters. A FEMA official refers to search-and-rescue efforts there as a "bag and tag." In the town of Waveland, west of Bay St. Louis, they're finding bodies every hour. Huge, age-old trees have been uprooted and tossed onto the roads like twigs. Eighteen-wheelers that once trucked fruits and meats out of Gulfport are beached, their contents rotting, like giant whales. Eighty miles of coastline annihilated. No economy, no commerce, no banks. The parallels with the tsunami in Southern Asia are inevitable, while others remark on the similarity to places like Bangladesh—not America.

According to a FEMA representative in Biloxi, "there's a pipeline which slows things down," when it comes to relief aid, so that even though the goods are staged in Alabama, then sent to the states, and then fanned out to the cities and neighborhoods that need them—it would not be unreasonable to allow five or six days for relief aid to arrive. FEMA Director Michael Brown, hearing of the miserable conditions in Biloxi, promises immediate attention, claiming that relief will be sped up.

Joseph Gibson, a Biloxi resident, says he rode 25-foot waves from his first-floor apartment to safety upstairs. A diabetic running out of medication, all he's eaten for three days is potato chips. "My next-door neighbors drowned. I saw the bodies floating in the water. One lay exposed in the street for two days. This is taking too long. . . ."

> **"You can tell them, you've talked with the FEMA director and it's going to happen."**
> —*FEMA Director Michael Brown, to Anderson Cooper, 7 p.m.*

Getty Images/Joe Raedle

Landov/Lykson

Top—I-90 in front of the Grand Casino in Gulfport is littered with Dole Fruit trucks. The casino barge was tossed onto the highway.
Bottom—People gather what belongings they can find from their Biloxi neighborhood after Hurricane Katrina leveled it.

Fires break out, dotting New Orleans' festering landscape. The National Guard beefs up to 22,000 reservists, pulled in from 12 states. Warships stream out of Norfolk, Va. Blackhawk and Chinook helicopters rip noisily through the sky. Of the dozens of rescue helicopters scheduled to arrive, many are on ships that won't arrive until next week.

Chris Lawrence, CNN, 8 pm: *(talking about the Convention Center)* *"These people are hungry. They're tired. They've got nowhere to go. They've got no answers, and they've got no communication whatsoever. And the officers said, when night comes—I'm watching the sun dip behind the buildings right now, he was very afraid—he said, I don't know which night it's going to break, but these people have a breaking point. And I'm scared to see what happens when they reach that point. Because they just have no answers. They're wandering. And they're hungry. They're hungry and they're thirsty. And they've got kids with them. And like any of us, you do what you can to try to eat, and to drink water, and help your family. And he felt like these were very, very desperate times down here.*

At the Superdome, the National Guard is losing control. Ten dead bodies covered with blankets lie in and outside of the vast center. Evacuation finally begins just in time, sparing 27,000 of the desperate inhabitants another night without lights, bathrooms, or the slightest relief from the heat and stench. It's a seven-hour drive from New Orleans to Houston under the best of circumstances. The logistics of getting out of the city will be a nightmare and will add more time to the trip for those crowded together on buses. But the buses will be clean, air-conditioned, and safe.

The supplies promised in President Bush's speech earlier in the evening are still hours away. The police are pulled off search-and-rescue to maintain order in the city. The word "refugee" is becoming commonplace in news reports. It's estimated that at least 80,000 people cannot escape the floodwaters. At approximately midnight, the first bus arrives at the Astrodome. It is the faintest ray of hope for a city of lost souls who are beginning to think that, for them, none exists.

Aaron Brown: *"It became clear today that the Gulf Coast is facing the type of crisis we expect to see in a developing country, not the richest country in the world."*

AP Photo/*San Antonio Express-News*/John Davenport

A man carries an ice chest into the water as a building burns out of control in downtown New Orleans near the Superdome.

Aaron Brown

Michael Brown,
Director of FEMA

A. BROWN: And Mr. Brown joins us now from Baton Rouge.... I know you're hearing the same kinds of things from people that we're hearing today. So it won't surprise you when I ask you if you underestimated, particularly Monday, the gravity of the situation in New Orleans and the area?

M. BROWN: You know, Aaron, I anticipated that would be the question you asked. And during the break I was thinking about it, and I was just asking my staff, reminding me about when we came down here. I remember we started ramping up last Friday. And then during Saturday, I started getting the reports in from the National Hurricane Center. Sunday we made the decision to get in here and preposition assets.

And I remember waking up Monday morning and having just this gut feeling that it was going to be worse than we even anticipated. I remember calling Max Mayfield that morning and talking about what kind of reports he was getting. And I just knew in my gut and my heart Monday morning this thing would continue to grow, even after it made landfall. . . .

Unfortunately, I was right. So all of those things that we had prepositioned to move in for a normal disaster response was not enough. And we needed to move more equipment and more teams in. So we started doing that immediately. We then found out, unfortunately, that we were having as much of a difficult time getting in, as the people were getting out. And that's why today, the president said all hands on deck. Every Cabinet department, every agency, the military. We're going to do whatever it takes. I've got the resources that I need now. And we're moving full steam ahead.

A. BROWN: Let's work through some of that. I heard you say earlier that you ran, I think a couple of years ago, computer models on what a Cat 5 hurricane would do. That you exercised this problem over the last year. Did you anticipate that 20,000, 25,000 people would be, essentially, refugees in the Superdome? That there wouldn't be power there for them? That there wouldn't be facilities there for them? That you'd have to move them out of the area? Were you that specific in the way you worked these problems?

M. BROWN: We went from the absolutely very worst, down to what we thought would be the absolute very

best conditions for a hurricane. And we did recognize that there would be people that would not evacuate, that there would be people that could not evacuate. And that we would have to deal with that. I think what we did not anticipate was that there would be quite the numbers that we are dealing with. And that we would have the logistical problems that we're having getting those people evacuated. And in addition to the levee breaks—the levee breaks have been much more widespread than we anticipated, spreading the flooding throughout the metropolitan area, so that in essence the mayor is right, we have to, literally, shut down the city of New Orleans.

A. BROWN: Was it a mistake not to send in the National Guard and military police? There actually have been—in fairness, and all of this is with the clarity of 20/20 hindsight—there were National Guard people in, mostly doing civilian-affairs kinds of work, not law enforcement kind of work. In hindsight, [does] that seem to have been a mistake?

M. BROWN: Well, it may have been. But you know what? Tonight's not the night that we're going to deal with that. That's what we'll deal with in the aftermath, when we start doing our studies of how we can do things better. We're still focused right now on making certain that we save every life that we can that's still out there. That those people that have been rescued, that we get them to places.

And as I heard you during your introduction, talking about now we have the issues of schools. We have the issue of housing. We have all of those issues. Those are the things that we're focused on right now. And, you know, I'd be happy to come back to you later sometime, next year, whatever, and talk about what we learned and what we're going to do different. And it's getting my teams in place to do that long-term recovery that we're going to have to do to rebuild New Orleans.

A. BROWN: That's fair enough. So, I'll put it in my date book. And we'll get back to you on the other stuff. Let's look ahead to other problems that clearly need to be solved. Basically, a major American city needs to be evacuated. Which means these people have to go live somewhere. How do we pay for that? Where do we put them? You're really going to have people living in the Astrodome for three, four months?

M. BROWN: No. I'm not going to have people in the Astrodome for three or four months. We are putting together, with not only government officials but with the private sector also, of doing a massive housing project. And that's going to be—as I think the president said this morning on the conference call that I was on with him, that there's no idea that's too crazy to not consider right now. So I'm looking at every possible idea of how to do this. And, I suppose in the media, I don't want to tell you some of the crazy ideas I've heard, because I may actually end up using some of those crazy ideas.

A. BROWN: Believe me. My e-mail box, sir, is full of them. Some don't sound so crazy on Wednesday, as . . . they sounded on Monday. And people talk about cruise ships, using cruise ships to house people. That doesn't sound like a terrible idea.

M. BROWN: Well, in fact, I will tell you that that's one of the ideas that this very evening that we're working on. And we're talking to the cruise ship lines. And we may have something to announce in the next couple of days about that.

A. BROWN: . . . Are we going to see tent cities sprouting up?

M. BROWN: Well if we do see tent cities, that's going to be a very short-term, temporary affair. Because I just do not want tent cities out there for any length of time. But we have to be realistic. This is a catastrophic disaster. This is not your run-of-the-mill disaster, where you have a small population, where you have what's not, I mean, let's face it we have a major disaster, in a major American city that's covered 80 to 90 percent of this city. So we may have to put people in tents, temporarily. But I, personally, don't want to see that last very long.

A. BROWN: We've only got you for a couple more minutes. Let me run some other things by you. Do you have any sense of an emerging public health problem?

M. BROWN: Not yet. But we have teams that are out there doing that. And I've heard the reports in the media about, you know, the contamination. And why aren't we picking up bodies right now? That's going to be a health issue. We recognize that. But our primary, and, Aaron, I just can't emphasize this enough, our primary response right now in New Orleans, in the other parishes outside New Orleans, in Mississippi, we can't forget Mississippi, and some of those areas of Alabama, is to save lives. That's the first thing we have to do. We'll start cleaning up the water. We will retrieve those bodies, treat them with the respect they deserve, get them back to their families, and deal with the contamination issues, once we get through this life-saving mission that we're in right now.

A. BROWN: Do you think by, just a final question, sir, do you think by this weekend we will look at this and it will be a much more stable situation than it is right now?

M. BROWN: Well that's my objective. I mean, every disaster has a cyberspace. And we're going through the second or third stage of this particular disaster. And I've now got the teams. I've got the equipment. I've got the oomph behind me right now to get this done. And so you're going to start seeing, I mean, there will always be complaints, always be concerns. But we'll see a stabilizing effect. And I think that's what the American people want. That's what they expect. I need the American people to recognize how catastrophic this is, to be patient and to work with this. We're going to start putting out calls eventually for certain types of volunteers and donations and that sort of thing. But in the meantime, recognize we're doing lifesaving and life-sustaining efforts. That next phase is just about to start.

The city of New Orleans is inundated with water.

Times-Picayune, August 31, 2005
Desperation, Death on Road to Safety
Wednesday, 11:09 p.m.

By Keith Spera, staff writer

At 91 years old, Booker Harris ended his days propped on a lawn chair, covered by a yellow quilt and abandoned, dead, in front of the Ernest N. Morial Convention Center.

Mr. Harris died in the back of a Ryder panel truck Wednesday afternoon as he and his 93-year-old wife, Allie, were evacuated from eastern New Orleans. The truck's driver deposited Allie and her husband's body on the Convention Center Boulevard neutral ground.

And there it remained.

With 3,000 or more evacuees stranded at the Convention Center—and with no apparent contingency plan or authority to deal with them—collecting a body was no one's priority. It was just another casualty in Hurricane Katrina's wake.

A steady stream of often angry or despondent people, many from flooded Central City, trickled first toward Lee Circle and then to the Convention Center, hoping to be saved from increasingly desperate straits. Food, water, and options had dwindled across Uptown and Central City, where looters seemed to rage almost at will, clearing out boutique clothing shops and drugstores alike. Hospitals would no longer accept emergencies, as staffers prepared to evacuate with patients.

"If you get shot," said a security guard at Touro Infirmary, "you've got to go somewhere else."

As a blazing sun and stifling humidity took their toll, 65-year-old Faye Taplin rested alone on the steps of the Christ Cathedral in the 2900 block of St. Charles Avenue. Rising water had finally chased her from her Central City home. She clutched two plastic bags containing bedding, a little food and water and insulin to treat her diabetes.

She needed help but was unsure where to find it. She wanted to walk more than 15 blocks to a rumored evacuation pickup point beneath the Pontchartrain Expressway, but she doubted that was possible.

"I'm tired," she said. "My feet have swollen up on me. I can't walk that far."

The church custodian, Ken Elder, hoped to free his car from the parking lot behind the church as soon as the water went down. He rode out Katrina on the Episcopal church's altar steps and was well stocked with food. But he feared the marauding looters that roamed St. Charles Avenue after dark.

"I lived in Los Angeles during the Rodney King riots," Elder said. "That was a piece of cake compared to this."

Clara Wallace pushed her brother in a wheelchair down St. Charles from Fourth Street to the Pontchartrain Expressway. Suffering from diabetes and the after effects of a stroke, he wore only a hospital robe and endured part of the journey through standing water.

"Nobody has a bathroom he can use," Wallace, 59, said of her brother. "Nobody would even stop to tell us if we were at the right place. What are we supposed to do?"

A man in a passing pickup truck from the State Department of Wildlife and Fisheries finally directed Wallace and the 50 other evacuees under the overpass to the Convention Center.

But they would find little relief there.

New evacuees were being dropped off after being pulled from inundated eastern New Orleans and Carrollton, pooling with those who arrived on foot. Some had been at the Convention Center since Tuesday morning but had received no food, water, or instructions. They waited both inside and outside the cavernous building.

The influx overwhelmed the few staffers and Louisiana National Guardsmen on hand.

With so much need and so few resources, the weakest and frailest were bound to suffer the most. Seated next to her husband's body on the neutral ground beneath the St. Joseph Street sign, Allie Harris munched on crackers, seemingly unaware of all the tragedy unfolding around her. Eventually, guardsmen loaded her into a truck and hauled her off with other elderly evacuees.

Mr. Harris's body was left behind.

Such a breakdown did not bode well for other evacuees. As the afternoon wore on, hope faded, replaced by anger.

"This is 2005," John Murray shouted, standing in the street near Mr. Harris's body. "It should not be like this for no catastrophe. This is pathetic."

Lykson/Landov

" It looked like the dust bowl. You've seen the pictures of the dust bowl, of people piled onto the backs of tracks and moving their lives. That's what is happening here."—*Jeanne Meserve*

"We've lost our city, I fear it's potentially like Pompeii."

—*Marc Morial, former mayor of New Orleans, now serving as president of the National Urban League*

"We're not even dealing with dead bodies, they're just pushing them on the side."

—*Mayor Ray Nagin*

"It makes no sense to spend billions of dollars to rebuild a city that's seven feet under sea level. . . . It looks like a lot of that place could be bulldozed."

–*U.S. House of Representatives Speaker Dennis Hastert (R-Ill.)*

"That's like saying we should shut down Los Angeles because it's built in an earthquake zone."

—*former Sen. John Breaux (D-La.)responding to Rep. Hastert's remark*

"It appears that the money has been moved in the president's budget to handle homeland security and the war in Iraq, and I suppose that's the price we pay. Nobody locally is happy that the levees can't be finished, and we are doing everything we can to make the case that this is a security issue for us."

—*Walter Maestri, emergency management chief for Jefferson Parish, Louisiana;* New Orleans Times-Picayune, *June 8, 2004*

"You can smell there is death around there."

—*Barbara Petway of Brewton, Ala., talking about her neighborhood*

"Someone said Armageddon instead of Apocalypse. What's the difference at this point?"

—*Wolf Blitzer*

"It's downtown Baghdad."

—*Denise Bollinger, a tourist from Philadelphia who witnessed the looting*

Cafferty Question: How should authorities handle the lawlessness in the city of New Orleans?

R. writes, "Regarding the looters, the law enforcement personnel should photograph or otherwise identify them and after order is restored hunt them down and make them clear debris or help rebuild the infrastructure of New Orleans for a minimum of one year to pay for their crimes."

Peter in Houston writes, "The emphasis has to be on violent crime. The looting is irrelevant. The whole city has become a write-off. Resources first should be focused on the mandatory evacuation. Get the people out. The crime goes away."

Marion in Enfield, Conn., writes, "The looting pales in comparison to what else is going on. By the way, if this had been an act of terrorism, I'm glad to know Homeland Security has things well in hand. Don't you feel safer now?"

And Anita in Indiana, "Dear Jack, if there were ever a job for our National Guard, this is it. You know, National Guard. Oh, wait, they're all in Iraq."

"You want to cry, you want to just tear up and do that, but you know life goes on and you take the good with the bad. We're alive, we're happy to be alive."

—*Gulfport resident Billy Barrett to CBS Early Show co anchor Harry Smith as Barrett looked at the wreckage of his home*

DAY 5

> "I have not heard a report of thousands of people in the Convention Center who don't have food and water." —*Secretary of Homeland Security Michael Chertoff*

Although it feels like one, this is no dream: It's a nightmare, and it's far from over. Residents of the Gulf Coast awaken to the tragic reality of Hurricane Katrina's aftermath—many of them in shelters, but many of them still trapped in attics, waiting on roofs for rescue, or lined up outside the hellish Superdome, hoping to board buses heading to Houston's Astrodome.

New Orleans Mayor Ray Nagin has reassigned officers from search-and-rescue missions to patrol the increasingly unsafe streets. Gov. Blanco has commandeered yet another 5,000 National Guardsmen for the city, which join more troops fanning out across coastal Mississippi. The hospitals have been evacuated, and officials say help is on the way. It is the same thing they've been saying since Monday.

Ted Rowlands reports from Biloxi, where it's been four days since Hurricane Katrina made landfall; water, food, sleep, and medical supplies are still just a hair's breadth away from nonexistent. Mississippi residents are desperate, saying they have not received any relief, despite reports that FEMA has set up makeshift hospitals in Biloxi. The death toll now approaches 185 in Mississippi, and 20,000 people are in shelters across the state. Waveland, Miss., a town of 7,000, has been entirely wiped out, not a single house left standing—just the shell-shocked survivors wandering in the wreckage. Gov. Haley Barbour, asked if he thinks federal response was sufficient, strongly defends the federal government, insisting that Katrina did not give anyone enough advance warning.

Buses have begun to liberate survivors from the New Orleans Superdome, but it's slow-going, taking 50 to 60 people out at a time, loading them onto a bus, then driving 330 miles to Houston's Reliant Astrodome. At around midnight, people fleeing the city begin arriving in Houston and in other cities around the country. Before long, worried Houston officials will start turning away the buses, explaining that it can't hold the promised numbers after all, and diverting them to other cities, other shelters. Worse, the long journey has not been quite as refreshing as hoped: Some buses had no air-conditioning throughout the 12-hour ride.

The lucky will find lodging next door at the adjacent Reliant Center. Others head on to Dallas, Huntsville,

A view of the Superdome after the thousands of storm victims who had been sheltered there were evacuated.

and San Antonio, cities who agree to take another 25,000 evacuees. Details for where they'll be housed are not yet clear. Texas says its schools will take in all the children from the three affected states. Tennessee reaches out to students whose plans to attend college in the Gulf Coast area are "now uncertain at best." Nearly 300 students from Tulane University transfer to Georgia Tech in Atlanta. Others are sent to Dallas.

Back in New Orleans, amid scrambled reports that shots have been fired at a Chinook helicopter that was transporting some of the people out of the Dome, Judge Robert Eckels, an official in charge of coordinating the evacuation, announces that the evacuation is temporarily unsafe. The helicopter transports are suspended, but the buses continue to roll. It is later reported that some of the gunshots were fired by frustrated survivors, trying to get the attention of rescuers.

In the outside world, gas prices are still soaring, despite word that the two main gas pipelines that have been down due to lack of electricity are running again, with one safely restarted and the other partially open. Driven by rumors that the pipes are down and stations will soon run out of their ten-day supply, hordes of panicked Americans race to the pumps. In Atlanta, lines form at the stations, with gas at a record $3.30, even $5.57 a gallon. Traffic is disrupted and scrawled "OUT OF GAS" signs appear. Georgia Gov. Sonny Purdue signs an executive order authorizing sanctions against retailers gouging consumers; everyone is urged to report offenders and reassures Georgians that gas will continue to be available.

Thousands of New Orleans residents gather at a staging area along Interstate 10 in Metairie, La. There was a severe shortage of buses and many who had been waiting for days were still stranded at the Convention Center and other locations.

Miles O'Brien

Haley Barbour,
Governor of
Mississippi

O'BRIEN: Let's talk about the response and what was put into position in advance of this storm. We knew about Katrina. We knew it was a strong storm developing for several days before it ever made landfall. Do you have the sense—because it's quite clear that state and local officials cannot handle this on their own. This is too overwhelming. Do you have the sense that the federal government has dropped the ball here, sir?

BARBOUR: I really don't. And I think it's very unfair for the federal government, for you to say we knew this was a great powerful storm. This was a Category 1 hurricane when it hit Florida. Now that's the truth.

O'BRIEN: Governor, it was a Category 5 storm.

BARBOUR: The federal government . . .

O'BRIEN: A Category 5 storm when it was . . .

BARBOUR: No, it was a Category 1—it was a Category 1 storm when it hit Florida. It was a Category 5 storm a few hours before it came ashore. The federal government have been tremendous partners in this. They have helped . . .

O'BRIEN: Governor Barbour, surely there was enough knowledge in advance that this was a huge killer storm a matter of days, not hours, before it ever struck landfall. And it seems to me the military. . . .

BARBOUR: Now, Miles, if this is an interview or an argument, I don't care. But if you want to let me tell you what I think, I will.

O'BRIEN: OK, go ahead.

BARBOUR: And what I think is this storm strengthened in the Gulf. We begged the people to leave, and thousands of people left. Thousands of people left New Orleans. The federal government came in here from the first minute—in fact, in advance. They have been tremendously helpful, whether it's the Coast Guard, the Corps of Engineers, FEMA . . .

O'BRIEN: But conspicuously absent from that short list you just gave us was the military, the Pentagon. This is a type of situation that cries out for the kind of support, the kind of logistics, the kind of coordination the military is ideally suited for. Why weren't more military assets pre-positioned and ready for the possibility here?

BARBOUR: We pre-positioned more than 1,000 National Guard, 175 on the coastal counties, 1,000 more 60 miles inland, so that they wouldn't be swept away in the storm. And as soon as it became clear where the storm was going to hit, even Alabama had sent us National Guard. Pennsylvania has offered us and is sending us 2,500 National Guard.

Would I have liked to have had 5,000 National Guard on the ground on Tuesday morning? Yes, that's not—other states are not going to give up their National Guard until they see what's happening to them. I don't blame them.

O'BRIEN: But I'm talking about assets, like, you know, amphibious vehicles that the Navy has. It has helicopter support, hospital support, the ability to generate power, that sort of thing. We haven't seen that kind of thing, the kind of thing we saw, incidentally, in the wake of the tsunami.

BARBOUR: Well, I'm not going to be critical of what the federal government has done. We're very grateful for it. You know, it's easy to go back and pick the bones, but we feel like they have tried very hard. This is the worst natural disaster that's ever struck the United States. Everybody down here is trying hard. Everybody is tired and fractious. So, I don't want to argue with you about it. But a lot of people from all over the country are helping us, and we really appreciate them, because we're making progress. And we're going to recover from what has been a grievous blow to our state, not just the coast. And we're going to rebuild, and it's going to be bigger and better than ever. But we're not going to do it by nitpicking.

Around the globe, countries pledge aid and money. Russia. France. Mexico. Singapore. Afghanistan. From the smallest to the largest, they offer supplies, manpower, money. According to the *Chronicle of Philanthropy*, which tracks charitable giving, American dollars reach $27 million. Presidents Clinton and George H. W. Bush join together to head up an international relief effort similar to their tsunami fund of 2004. Donations are pour in from around the world. New Orleans native Wynton Marsalis performs a benefit concert on Thursday, Sept. 1.

When asked why help has yet to arrive in New Orleans, Secretary of Homeland Security Michael Chertoff explains that efforts to deliver aid after the hurricane were interrupted by the levees breaching, and that efforts to truck and drop in aid after the levees broke were interrupted by the flooding. Since that is ongoing, it's the explanation for why things are still staged and prepositioned rather than on the ground. Officials, he insists, have never had sufficient time to get the help from the staging areas to the affected ones. Rivers are full of debris, unnavigable. Streets are blocked by trees. But the longer they hold back, waiting for a safer environment, the more dangerous the situation grows.

The IRS grants extensions for quarterly taxes; Fannie Mae and Freddie Mac are urging lenders to suspend payments. "The big three" car companies—Ford, DaimlerChrysler, and GM—are allowing deferred payments for those whose cars and homes have been destroyed. Corporate America jumps in to donate cash, phone cards, Similac, Nutrigrain bars, Tylenol, Keebler cookies. But whether any of it will get through is another question.

Relief efforts continue to be plagued by stops and starts. In particular, the evacuation of the Superdome is moving at a snail's pace—60 buses in Houston and 400 yet to go—due to the fact that some of the buses have been rerouted to Metairie, where about 3,000 people have collected. Now, though, more buses are en route to the Superdome. Unfortunately, in appreciation of its being an evacuation point with transportation, more hopefuls have arrived hoping to be picked up. Inside, spilling out, sleeping on the streets, they wait: An estimated 50–60,000 people now expecting a ride out of the city.

Tom Foreman: *"Look, all of this can be fixed and all of this will be fixed and all of this has to be fixed. If this were Chicago or Brooklyn or San Francisco, people wouldn't be saying should we rebuild it? Even though all of those cities have their own natural potential problems they've faced over the years. There's no question this has to be fixed and it can be fixed.*

Why there has not been a steady parade of buses, help, and helicopters in and out—with deference to my old friend Marc Morial, the former mayor— I really do find myself baffled that this is not moving any faster. And frankly, I think if it doesn't start moving, people of New Orleans are going to start stacking up bureaucrats and walking out over them, because I think they're baffled themselves why this isn't happening. And when you say 'We'll delay the buses because it's dangerous'—you know, if it weren't dangerous, we could all do it. That's why we have emergency management people."

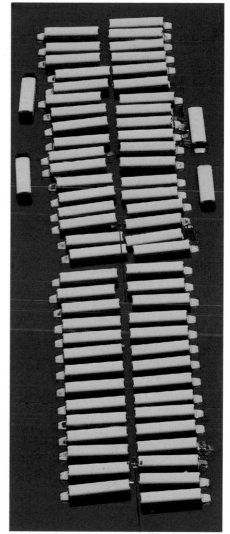

AP Photo/David J. Phillip

Robert Sullivan/AFP/Getty Images

Top–A row of school buses sit in floodwaters east of New Orleans—buses that were desperately needed to move people out of the city.

Left–Hurricane Katrina evacuees cross a bridge on US 90 in a downpour as they walk out of New Orleans.

"I don't think anybody anticipated the breach of the levees."
—*President Bush*

(Both Images) Mark Wilson/Getty Images

Left—People ride in a military vehicle after being rescued from high water on Canal Street in New Orleans.
Right—People walk through high water to reach the Superdome.

INTERVIEW

Soledad O'Brien

Michael Chertoff,
Secretary of
Homeland Security

O'BRIEN: Secretary Chertoff . . . The president this morning in a live interview said that a lot of help is coming. Many people would say, why is it coming? Why three days after the disaster is it not there already?

CHERTOFF: Well, Soledad, we've, in fact, been putting a lot of help into the area. What's made this a very unusual disaster is it's really been a double disaster. We had the hurricane. And even as the hurricane was leaving New Orleans, we started to send the first wave of supplies and the first wave of people in. And then on top of that, we had a flood when the levee broke. And so, as we've been conducting rescue operations and supply operations, we've been contending with an ongoing disaster. That creates, you know, real physical constraints. We have to worry about impassible roads, flooded areas that we can't move in. And so, it's not a question of not having enough assistance there. It's a question of dealing with a very real, an ongoing natural disaster as we are conducting rescue operations.

O'BRIEN: But both of these things, with all due respect, sir, were predicted. They knew it was a Category 3 hurricane hitting the area 48 hours before it struck. People had been writing about the potential disastrous conditions of the levee system for a really long time, years and years and years. There is a sense that everyone knew a disaster could happen, and no one was really prepared.

CHERTOFF: Well, I don't think that's correct, Soledad.

I think people were prepared. But I think a natural disaster has certain physical realities about it. The critical thing was to get people out of there before the disaster. Quite rightly, the officials—local and state officials—called for a mandatory evacuation. Some people chose not to obey that order. That was a mistake on their part. Once the water is there, the physical reality is something that you have to contend with no matter how well prepared you are.

And I think there has been a magnificent job, the courage and ingenuity of all of the forces that we've deployed has been remarkable. But remember, you have to wait until the hurricane passes. You can't fly helicopters in a hurricane. You can't drive trucks through a hurricane.

I have to tell you, one FEMA employee lost his life trying to get a truckload of supplies down to the area. We didn't want to have more of that happening. So, we've had to make sure that as we conduct our rescue operations, we do it in a way that preserves the safety of those people who are engaged in the rescue activities.

O'BRIEN: Let's talk a little bit about the communications problems. It's obviously a huge issue. And in many ways, to me at least, it's very reminiscent of the communication problems during 9/11 four years ago. So what's been learned? Why hasn't the response been improved?

CHERTOFF: Well, actually, it's somewhat different. I mean, this is not an issue of lack of interoperability, where you had fire and police on different channels. This has to do with, again, the physical reality. The wireless towers are down. The land lines are flooded. That leaves only one other kind of communications method, and that's by satellite phone or by walkie-talkie.

O'BRIEN: May I interrupt you there, sir?

CHERTOFF: Yes.

O'BRIEN: Because all of those things, though, are expected when a hurricane passes through.

CHERTOFF: Well, that's right, and . . .

O'BRIEN: The wireless towers are going to go down, and you're not going to be able to communicate with cell phones.

CHERTOFF: That's right. And so, we have people equipped with satellite phones. We have the military in there with walkie-talkies. However, people who have cell phones are not going to have cellphone service. It's not a question of preparedness. It's a question of the physical reality that when the towers are down there's no cellphone service.

So, the responders, the National Guard, have their walkie-talkies. We have emergency communications vehicles in New Orleans. We have satellite phones with the first responders. But in terms of people's ordinary phone and communication service, I've got to tell you, Soledad, no amount of preparedness is going to eliminate the physical reality that without wireless towers, there's no cellphone service.

O'BRIEN: Sir, why has there been no immediate efforts at an online registry? There are so many people that I personally know—and I'm not from the area at all—who are trying to track their family members, and there is no sense of who is where. In this day and age when everybody has access to a computer, you would think that that would be among the first things people would . . .

CHERTOFF: Well, actually we are in the process of putting together an online registry. Remember, there are several elements to this. First of all, we need to have a list of people that are recovered. Many people evacuated on their own. We've got to locate those people. They would have to register in, people who are in shelters.

O'BRIEN: But are the 25,000 people in the Superdome, is there a registry of them?

CHERTOFF: Let me finish. Soledad, let me finish.

O'BRIEN: Sure, excuse me.

CHERTOFF: Well, the people in the Superdome in very difficult conditions were not in a position to start to fill out paperwork. What we will do as people come into our official shelters at the Red Cross, at the Astrodome, we are registering those people. As we get those names and data in place, we will then feed that into databases. We're setting up a call center. We're setting up an online registry.

But, again, you know, in the middle of an ongoing disaster, this is not merely a response to recovery after a disaster. This is a response to recovery while the disaster is raging, while the flood is going on. In the middle of that, the first priority is to save people. And I think it's important to remember that we've got to get through that initial stage. Then we've got to pull the data together, and then we're going to have that registry up and running.

Excerpt from Miles O'Brien Interview with Berna Brown, a New Orleans Evacuee

Berna Brown has just arrived on one of the buses in Houston at the Astrodome:

O'BRIEN: Just describe for me what it's like around the Superdome right now in the wake of all of this.

BROWN: Everybody is going absolutely insane. Sad faces. People who need help, bread, water, clothes. You know water is everywhere, water is everywhere. Then you were talking about something about opening up the levee to the surrounding, you know, areas, and everything. But I really and truly didn't believe that would happen, you know. So now this is what happened. Everything is just gone. Nothing is there. To me it feels like a different time. It doesn't feel like these modern days, you know? Things like I look at on television in slavery days, or in the—I mean, Africa and days, no, the look, the look is look—it just looks horrible.

O'BRIEN: Well it's—you know it's kind of like before there was civilization or something. Civil order has broken down.

BROWN: That's right. That's right.

O'BRIEN: You must have feared for your life.

BROWN: That's right. That's right.

O'BRIEN: Were you afraid?

BROWN: That's right. That's right. That's exactly right. That's what happened to me. And I really and truly haven't—I don't believe that this is really happening to me in these times. You know what I'm saying? It's confusing to me because more people is supposed to pay a lot of attention to things like this that is happening. Because that's just like, what, a bad sickness, or what have you, would just wipe out the human race instead of just try to fight back with it, try to work with it, try to understand what is happening, you know.

More buses arrive at the Superdome, yet there are clearly not enough to deal with the swarming crowds that have converged there, desperate, hungry, without water for their children, angry, sad, and begging for help. There are bodies lying by the side of the street, bloating in the sun. Some have been covered with blankets. Former Mayor Marc Morial puts it succinctly: "There needs to be a massive effort by every available resource, military resources and civilian resources, to evacuate the people, buses, helicopters, airport—or military cargo planes . . . We're dealing with a crisis of Biblical proportions."

While Morial pleads for "the highest levels of government to do everything within their power" to get the people out of New Orleans, news of thousands more stranded at the New Orleans Convention Center begin to trickle out, and reports say conditions there are worse, far worse, than the Superdome.

FEMA officially suspends its search-and-rescue efforts, claiming it's too dangerous and that some of the victims have become violent in their attempts to get into the boats. It's a Catch-22: The longer they wait, the more the craziness escalates. A National Guardsman is wounded inside the Dome. Opportunistic crime intensifies, with looters breaking into stores, even private homes. Gunfire erupts. The city streets are getting too dangerous to even set foot on.

Shannon Stapleton/Reuters /Landov

"Everything is just gone. Nothing is there. To me it feels like a different time. It doesn't feel like these modern days, you know? Things like I look at on television in slavery days, or in the—I mean, Africa . . ."

—*Berna Brown, who was evacuated from the Superdome*

Clockwise from top left—A woman stands among debris outside the Superdome as stranded evacuees wait in lines to evacuate New Orleans.

A woman and her child wait with hundreds of other flood survivors at the Convention Center in New Orleans.

Dorothy Divic, 89, is surrounded by fellow flood victims who are trying to keep her alive on a street outside the Convention Center.

A covered corpse lies in the street as evacuees remain stranded outside the Convention Center in New Orleans.

The president announces another visit to the area, with stops planned in Mobile, parts of Mississippi, and New Orleans. He'll conduct aerial tours of the Alabama–Mississippi coast, and of New Orleans, an area of 90,000 square miles, all of it now under the disaster declaration. The president also waives the state cost-share requirements for emergency response activities, bringing the federal government coverage from 75 percent to 100 percent of the funding for 60 days, retroactive to the date of the declaration. He appears on ABC's *Good Morning America*, and during an interview with Diane Sawyer, claims, "I don't think anybody anticipated the breach of the levees" that protected New Orleans from flooding. Sawyer does not challenge the president's claim.

Excerpt from Soledad O'Brien Interview with James Carville

Carville is a CNN political analyst. He's also a Louisiana native. Some of his family members were forced to evacuate the New Orleans area. His own sister lost her house, we are told, in Slidell.

O'BRIEN: You know, my question is, to an outside perspective, and I'm not from there, it looks like it was very disorganized and very unprepared for a scenario that people will tell you people have been expecting. People have written books about it.

CARVILLE: Right.

O'BRIEN: People have done documentaries on what if a big hurricane hit.

CARVILLE: Look, we knew this. You're exactly right. This shouldn't have been a surprise to anyone. And we knew that those levees were compromised. There was report after report after report. The *Times-Picayune* did a five-part series on that. And somebody is going to have to go back and look at this. This wasn't a surprise.

Last year, I believe, they did an operation, I think they called it Hurricane Pam, I'm told, where they tried to coordinate all of this. So there's going to be plenty of—we're going to learn a lot from what we could have done here.

But you know when the levee breaks, it just—there are some things that you just can't do in a hurricane. And when some people don't evacuate, and the mayor couldn't have been any more forceful and the governor couldn't have been any more forceful before the storm came for people to get out of town. Unfortunately, and we knew this going in that New Orleans is a poor American city and half the people don't have cars. So there's going to be plenty of time to learn a lot from what we could have done about this.

Posted: 10:02 a.m. ET, Jim Spellman in New Orleans

I don't think I really have the vocabulary for this situation.

We just heard a couple of gunshots go off. There's a building smoldering a block away. People are picking through whatever is left in the stores right now. They are walking the streets because they have nowhere else to go.

Right now, I'm a few blocks away from the New Orleans Convention Center area. We drove through there earlier, and it was unbelievable. Thousands and thousands and thousands of people spent the night sleeping on the street, on the sidewalk, on the median.

The Convention Center is a place that people were told to go to because it would be safe. In fact, it is a scene of anarchy. There is absolutely nobody in control. There is no National Guard, no police, no information to be had.

The Convention Center is next to the Mississippi River. Many people who are sleeping there feel that a boat is going to come and get them. Or they think a bus is going to come. But no buses have come. No boats have come. They think water is going to come. No water has come. And they have no food.

As we drove by, people screamed out to us—"Do you have water? Do you have food? Do you have any information for us?"

We had none of those.

Probably the most disturbing thing is that people at the Convention Center are starting to pass away and there is simply nothing to do with their bodies. There is nowhere to put them. There is no one who can do anything with them.

This is making everybody very, very upset.

Excerpt from a White House press briefing, by Press Secretary Scott McClellan, 12 noon

QUESTION: People on the ground, though, Scott, are questioning why it's taken three days or more for federal help to arrive notwithstanding all of the preparations. There's considerable bitterness in some places. We had one woman ask on camera last night, "Where's the cavalry?" And then there's been editorial criticism across the country of the president for not acting sooner or not coming back sooner. What do you say to all that?

McCLELLAN: I can understand how frustrated people are in the region who have been affected by this. There are some immediate priorities that we must remain focused on. First and foremost, that is saving lives. And second, right along with that, is sustaining lives. That's why the federal government is working in close partnership with state and local authorities. This is a massive undertaking by the federal government. It is unprecedented. Remember, we prepositioned assets in the region prior to the storm hitting. You have more than 50 disaster medical

A military helicopter makes a food and water drop to flood victims near the Convention Center in New Orleans, but it's not nearly enough for those trapped there.

assistance teams in the region. You have some 28-plus search-and-rescue teams deployed in the region.

Those efforts are ongoing. I can understand people who have not received the help they need being frustrated at this point. It's going to take time to get help to some people. We've got to prioritize what the needs are. That's exactly what the federal government is doing. And we are going to continue moving resources and assets into the region to help those who are in need.

If you look at what the Department of Transportation, for instance, has done, they have moved, I think, approximately 1,000 truckloads containing more than nearly 7 million meals-ready-to-eat to the region. They have moved millions of gallons of water, 15,000-plus tarps, 10,000-plus rolls of plastic sheeting, 3.4 million pounds of ice that they have helped to transport to those who are in need of those supplies.

QUESTION: But none of that means anything to somebody who's been living on an interstate overpass for the last three days without food or water or any kind of assistance . . .

McCLELLAN: As we were passing over the region yesterday, we saw people that were standing on those highways, those highways that just disappeared into the water. We saw people that were on rooftops. We saw helicopters in the distance engaged in search-and-rescue operations . . .

Our concern, first and foremost, is with the people who have been displaced or affected otherwise by this major catastrophe. It is a major catastrophe, and there is a major response to this catastrophe. And the federal government will continue working to do everything in our power to get help to those in need.

But we certainly understand frustration coming from people on the ground who are in need of help. And we will continue working to get them the assistance that they need. And we appreciate the efforts of all those in the region who are working around the clock to make sure that they are getting help.

QUESTION: Without getting into finger-pointing or partisan politics or anything, would you concede, given the difficult reality on the ground there now, that more could have or should have been done to have resources available to move quickly or to be there? Or is it your position that this is simply the nature of responding to disasters of this scale, that it's going to take . . .

McCLELLAN: That's a very good and legitimate question, and I think that that's something that over time will be able to be addressed and looked at. You're still right now trying to assess all the damage and destruction that's been done. Now is the time to remain focused on the response and recovery efforts, and that's what we're doing. There'll be a time for politics later. There'll be a time to look at all these other issues and do more of a critique or assessment of the response efforts . . .

Chris Lawrence at the Convention Center, 12 noon:

"These people are being forced to live like animals. And we are not talking a few families, or a few hundred families. We are talking thousands and thousands of people just laid out over the entire street. Living in these horrible conditions, trash, feces, dirty food—I mean, in just the worst possible conditions. . . . We saw a man right in front of us literally dying. Going into a seizure on the ground, people trying to prop his head up. They have no medicine, no way to evacuate him . . . these dead bodies. Not one, not two, there are multiple people dying at the convention center. . . . These people are saying, how much longer can we last? Where are the buses? Where is the plan? Where is the help? . . . People are saying, 'We don't have food. We don't have water.' Are you really just going to let us sit here and die like this? Because people are already starting to die, right in downtown New Orleans."

"These people are saying, how much longer can we last? Where are the buses? Where is the plan? Where is the help? . . . People are saying, We don't have food. We don't have water. Are you really just going to let us sit here and die like this? Because people are already starting to die, right in downtown New Orleans."
—*Chris Lawrence*

Right—Displaced flood survivor Michael Ventry (first left), covers his face with his shirt while looking at an unidentified body lying in the kitchen storage space of the Convention Center.

Below—Thousands of refugees wait at the Convention Center for food, water, medicine, and evacuation.

Opposite page: Clockwise from top left—Milvertha Hendricks, 84 (center), waits in the rain with other flood victims outside the Convention Center.

A man covers the body of a fellow flood victim who died at the Convention Center.

Flood victims pile into a truck as hundreds of others wait at the Convention Center.

A man suffering from the heat and dehydration is fanned in front of the Convention Center.

Marko Georgiev/Getty Images

A.J. Sisco/UPI /Landov

AP Photo/Eric Gay

AP Photo/Eric Gay

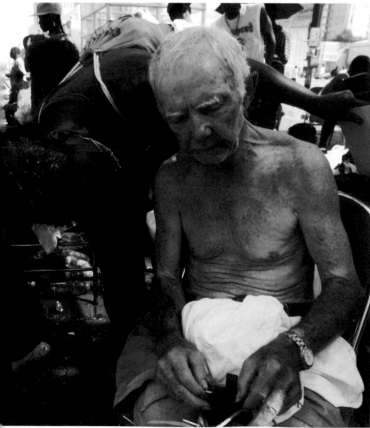

AP Photo/*San Antonio Express-News*/ John Davenport

AP Photo/Eric Gay

The list of military relief is impressive—four ships coming out of Norfolk with 6,000 troops on deck; a brigade of soldiers from Fort Bragg; Blackhawk, Chinook, and MedEvac helicopters; 20,000 National Guard troops at the state level; engineer units; transportation units; water-purification units—but where are they? Even as the officials insist those forces and units are on the ground, the pictures from the Convention Center tell a different story. The footage of people lining the streets outside the Superdome, still awaiting buses, shows them angry, yelling at the cameras, tearful, hot, weeping, in shock. During a 1:30 p.m. press conference, Secretary of Homeland Security Chertoff expands on the available relief aid. But, it begins to be clear, these are what are called "metrics": impressive figures, huge numbers, and large amounts. They represent aid and machinery and manpower deployed to the area, in staging areas, pre-positioned—not necessarily delivered.

Enter U.S. Northern Commander and Lt. Gen. Russel Honore, the newly appointed Joint Task Force commander. A Louisiana native, Honore led the 2nd Infantry Division in Korea from 2000 to 2002, supervising the installation of flood-control measures. Monsoons are his specialty. Mayor Nagin, who originally suggested he be put in charge, champions Honore's take-charge attitude, calling him a "John Wayne dude [who] came off the doggone chopper and he started cussing and people started moving. And he's getting some stuff done." Despite his bluster, everyone warms to Honore, who tells his men to point their weapons down or to sling them over their backs. He tells them, this is not Iraq, you are part of a humanitarian-relief convoy. He is the first sign of the military strength soon to descend on New Orleans.

Meanwhile, people are leaving the modern-day Atlantis on foot, up against seemingly insurmountable odds. Once they get out of New Orleans, it's 40 to 50 miles before any supplies are available. Some can get out of downtown, but even then, with the flooding, the possibility exists of getting trapped again by the water. Trying to walk that far without water or food, in the heat and humidity of summer, compounds the problem. Women carrying their babies have no formula. Some of the babies are infants. A chant rises up in the streets: "We want help! We want help! We want help!" Hundreds of National Guardsmen deployed to the city hold back, obeying orders to wait for this horrific situation to stabilize enough so that they, too, aren't endangered. The death toll is rising.

Lt. Gen. H. Steven Blum, chief, National Guard Bureau: *"We are never in charge. The military is not in charge and not foreseen to be in charge in any respect or manner. The National Guard will be there with what DHS Secretary Chertoff requests from the Department of Defense, the support that is vetted through a vetting*

Times-Picayune/NNS /Landov
Army Lt. Gen. Russel L. Honore (left), commander of all active-duty military forces assigned to the relief effort, lays out mission orders to Maj. Gen. Bill Caldwell (left center), commander of the 82nd Airborne Division, and his staff.

process with the Joint Chief. And I think the greatest thing I can say about this is that before it is over you will see National Guard soldiers and airmen from every state and territory in our nation. I think that sends out a very strong message that when you call out the National Guard, you call out America."

FEMA Deputy Director Patrick Rhode: *"FEMA was in-theater long before this storm arrived, and FEMA will be in-theater well after this early phase of the response has completely gotten under way to its fullest extent. It's important to note, and the Secretary made mention of the fact, that there are massive amounts of commodities in the region. Urban search-and-rescue teams are in the region. Disaster medical assistance teams are in the region. There is no question that, in any sort of a comprehensive response phase, that there are always some little bumps along the road. We recognize that. It's very important that the citizens in these impacted areas exercise—as difficult as it is—exercise as much patience as they possibly can. We understand that you're there. We understand that you're suffering. We're trying to get to you as best as we possibly can. There are massive amounts of FEMA boots—and the entire federal family—that are right now on the ground looking for you, looking to assist you as best as we possibly can."*

At an emergency management conference, Lt. Gen. Russel Honore reels off the numbers of National Guard troops headed for the region: 4,700 in Louisiana on Wednesday night. By the end of today, 7,400. In Mississippi, 2,700, swelling to 6,000 by today. The number will grow over the next three days to 12,000, he says, before the evening of Sept. 4. He goes on to explain the difficulty of actually moving those troops to where they're needed.

The U. S. House and U. S. Senate request an extra $10 billion to keep FEMA operating. The government agrees to send in 250 ConAirs, planes normally used to transport prisoners. Gov. Blanco calls in 250 military police to assist with rescues and also to combat what FEMA director Michael Brown is now calling "urban warfare."

At 3 p.m., a National Guard helicopter drops food to the Convention Center for the first time in four days. Unfortunately, it is only enough for about 25 people. The media expresses its outrage that more can't be done, that the helpless and the dying are still abandoned. It's Thursday, they say, the storm happened four days ago. It's a disgrace. For the first time in those four days, the race issue is mentioned: the fact that most of the victims are poor and balck. And for the first time, reports surface that FEMA is actually blocking rescue efforts by other agencies and private parties. The Ritz-Carlton, for instance, tries to get buses to its French Quarter patrons, only to have FEMA commandeer one of the buses.

Survivors scramble for food outside the Convention Center.   Jason Reed/Reuters /Landov

At Louis Armstrong New Orleans International Airport, commercial airlines have been flying supplies and taking out evacuees since Monday. But on Thursday, after FEMA took over the evacuation, Aviation Director Roy A. Williams complained "We are packed with evacuees and the planes are not being loaded and there are gaps of two or three hours when no planes are arriving." Eventually, he started fielding "calls from the airlines saying, 'Well, we are being told by FEMA that you don't need any planes.' And of course we need planes. I had thousands of people on those concourses." —**Washington Post**

As Charity Hospital evacuates patients into amphibious vehicles in front of the hospital, shots ring out. The evacuation is suspended. A doctor sitting in an airstrip in Baton Rouge waiting for a helicopter scheduled to evacuate premature babies gets a call saying the helicopter is delayed; it is too dangerous to make the trip.

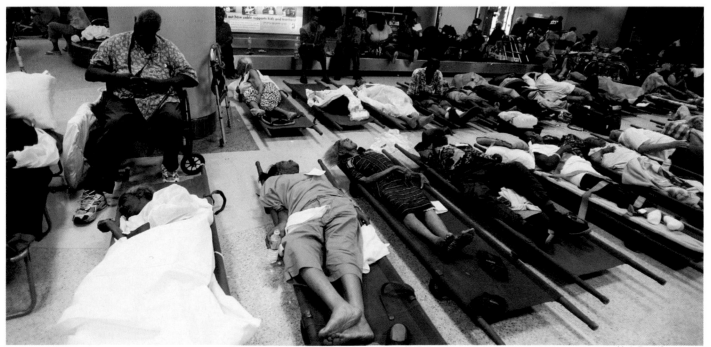

Mario Tama/Getty Images

The sick and wounded lie in the baggage pickup area of Louis Armstrong New Orleans International Airport.

Excerpt from Paula Zahn Interview with Dr. Ruth Berggren at New Orleans' Charity Hospital

ZAHN: How severe are things right now?

BERGGREN: Well, we have just had a major setback, Paula. We waited all day for the sniper situation to get stabilized, so that we could recommence evacuating our patients.

About an hour or so ago, we got the signal to bring down patients who could walk. I came down with my patients all the way from the ninth floor, including people with spinal fractures and people who were in federal custody, and we actually loaded them on to boats. And we just saw a boat come back with some of our patients, and we're being told that all the patients that were just evacuated in the second wave are coming back to the hospital. Because the place of higher ground to which the patients were taken did not have the expected transport for patients to the next phase of the evacuation.

ZAHN: So, Dr. Berggren, what is going to happen to these patients? Are some of them going to die?

BERGGREN: Some of them have died. I—honestly, as I ran back up the stairs from that scene to come and take this phone call, they were bringing a dead body down from the third floor.

One of my patients, whom we worked very, very hard to get on the critical list and to move out as fast as we could, we have been by his bed all day, was sitting on that boat that came back and leaning over the edge and vomiting. And my heart just breaks for him, because I think he just feels terrible.

Michael Brown, director of FEMA: *"I have people out there literally handing out food and water to individuals. We have distribution sites where the Guardsmen are actually forming lines and people are coming through that. We have formed distributions—what I would call kind of retail distribution sites where we bring in large supplies of the food and water and then the guard and volunteers, Boy Scouts and others will come together. And we're trying to do it as efficiently as possible by having cars drive through that can drive through. In New Orleans that's not possible, so we're doing it hand by hand with the Guard. It's every single means of distribution that we can utilize we're utilizing."*

Confronted on National Public Radio with evidence of the horrific scenes at the Convention Center, Homeland Security Secretary Michael Chertoff, insists he is unaware of the thousands stranded at the Convention Center without food or water, and suggests that NPR reporter John Burnette should be careful about "extrapolating" rumors. The disconnect between what the authorities say they're doing and what seems to be happening grows wider.

Excerpt from Robert Sigel Interview with Michael Chertoff on National Public Radio's *All Things Considered*, 3 p.m.

SIGEL: We are hearing from our reporter, and he's on another line right now, thousands of people at the Convention Center in New Orleans with no food. Zero.

CHERTOFF: I am telling you we are getting food and water to areas where people are staging. The one thing about an episode like this is if you talk to someone or you get a rumor or an anecdotal version of something, I think it's dangerous to extrapolate it all over the place. . . . The limitation here on getting food and water to people is the conditions on the ground, and as soon as we can physically move through the ground, with these assets, we're going to do that.

SIGEL: But Mr. Secretary, when you say we shouldn't listen to rumors; these are things coming from reporters who have not only covered many, many other hurricanes, they've covered wars and refugee camps. These aren't rumors. They're seeing thousands of people there.

CHERTOFF: Well, as I say . . . I have not heard a report of thousands of people in the Convention Center who don't have food and water.

Robert Sullivan/AFP/Getty Images

A U.S. soldier carries a box of MREs (meals ready-to-eat) to be distributed to people leaving the Superdome.

At a 5 p.m. press conference, FEMA Director Michael Brown tells a questioner that not only does he have people on the ground handing out supplies, but claims to have "no reports of unrest." He later reiterates to CNN's Paula Zahn that FEMA was unaware of the people in the Convention Center.

Excerpt from Wolf Blitzer Interview with Ray Cooper, an Evacuee

BLITZER: What is it like inside the Convention Center? There are thousands of people inside.

RAY COOPER: Sir, you got about 3,000 people here in this—in the Convention Center right now. They're hungry. Don't have any food. We was told two-and-a-half days ago to make our way to the Superdome or the Convention Center by our mayor. And when we got here, was no one to tell us what to do, no one to direct us, no authority figure. They had a couple of policemen out here, sir, about six or seven policemen told me directly, when I went to tell them, hey, man, you got bodies in there. You got two old ladies that just passed, just had died, people dragging the bodies into little corners. One guy—that's how I found out. The guy had actually, hey, man, anybody sleeping over here? I'm like, no. He dragged two bodies in there. Now you just—I just found out there was a lady and an old man, the lady went to nudge him. He's dead.

BLITZER: Are there any National Guard personnel, any troops on the scene?

COOPER: Yes. There's troops passing by with their weapons like a show of force and stuff, as if I'm in Iraq and stuff. I'm ex-military. I know what they look like. And that's basically what it is.

BLITZER: And what about police? You say there's about six police officers outside?

COOPER: There's six, seven police officers on the corner back off to the side in a garage with their generators going on. They told me, said, hey, it is nothing that we can do.

INTERVIEW

Wolf Blitzer

Michael Brown,
Director of
FEMA

BLITZER: Mr. Brown—you just heard this individual, Raymond Cooper. He's 43 years old, together with 3,000 other people. They're stuck inside that Convention Center and there's no help in sight. What do you say to this individual?

BROWN: Wolf, we just learned today from the state about the Convention Center and the folks there. And the state ordered five truckloads of meals and food, so we started delivering those today. So the mayor should be seeing those just any time.

BLITZER: When do you think that those truckloads will arrive?

BROWN: Well, the request came in from the state about four, five hours ago. So they should be on the way. And I would think literally they should be there any time now.

Jason Reed/Reuters /Landov

Heavily armed police patrol rolls past Hurricane Katrina survivors outside the New Orleans Convention Center.

BLITZER: So help is on the way to those 3,000 people? The mayor in his desperate SOS appeal said if those individuals inside want to start walking away from the Convention Center over to an expressway that's not far away and just start walking, that would be fine with him, given the deteriorating health and security situation inside that Convention Center.

BROWN: If people want to leave and are capable of leaving, I think that's great. That is not a decision—FEMA does not do law enforcement. That's up to state and local authorities. So if someone is able to walk to safety, I would encourage them to do that.

BLITZER: When do you think FEMA will have the resources in New Orleans to save these people? Because we're hearing at hospitals, the situation is getting increasingly dangerous and worse, and elsewhere in the city as well. When do you think you will have the resources you need to secure New Orleans?

BROWN: We have those resources now. I just met with Lt. Gen. Honore, who is our military commander here working in conjunction with FEMA and the Department of Homeland Security. The general assured me that we have 4,700 National Guard troops in New Orleans now. That number is going to go to some 7,000. And over the next two or three days it will increase exponentially where we'll have slightly over 30,000 National Guard troops to do both security work and to help us in the distribution of supplies. We continue to do search-and-rescue missions. I learned today that we just completed or are in the process of completing the evacuation of the hospitals and that those are going very well. So I think that the things—considering the dire circumstances that we have in New Orleans, virtually a city that has been destroyed, that things are going relatively well.

BLITZER: Knowing what you know now, Michael Brown—and obviously all of us are a lot smarter with hindsight—what would FEMA—what should FEMA have done differently in the days leading up to Hurricane Katrina to save people's lives in New Orleans? Because as you know, we're getting reports from the governor, from the mayor, that perhaps the death toll will go into the thousands.

BROWN: Well, I think the death toll may go into the thousands. And unfortunately, that's going to be attributable a lot to people who did not heed the evacuation warnings. And I don't make judgments about why people chose not to evacuate. But, you know, there was a mandatory evacuation of New Orleans. And to find people still there is just heart wrenching to me because the mayor did everything he could to get them out of there. And so we've got to figure out some way to convince people that when evacuation warnings go out, it's for their own good. Now, I don't want to second-guess why they did that. My job now is to get relief to them.

BLITZER: I know you have to run. I'll ask one final question. So many people, especially in New Orleans, are now saying all of this was predictable, that the levees, the flood walls, they could sustain a Category 3 but for days they knew this was going to be potentially either a Category 4 or a Category 5 with winds more than 150 or 160 miles an hour. And they're saying this was predictable, people should have realized the potential danger. Is that a fair criticism?

BROWN: Well, I think it's a fair question to ask. And I know that government officials and engineers will debate that and figure that out. You know, right now, I'm focused on trying to save lives. I'm trying to focus on getting people out of harm's way. And I think we should have that debate, but at the appropriate time.

"Mayor Nagin has put out a desperate SOS. That is what he calls it, a desperate SOS. There are police barricading themselves on the roofs of buildings. There are snipers taking shots at MedEvac helicopters trying to rescue wounded people and evacuate the people of New Orleans. The mayor at one point has told people there are no more buses to evacuate them out. Just get to the highway and start walking out of the city. We have never seen anything like this in the United States of America."
—Anderson Cooper

While the city explodes around them, the Corp of Engineers reports they have closed 50 percent of the breach in the 17th Street Canal. They've sandbagged the hole, then built a road to the breach, dumped rock onto the road, and bulldozed it into the breach. Work is ongoing at the London Avenue Canal, using rubble and other materials to close the entrance.

Hope is in very short supply, but at this late hour, glimmers of it appear: A baby, left behind at a hospital in New Orleans, is found in Ft. Worth. A woman who last saw her four friends on a roof in Waveland, Miss., gets a cell phone call during breakfast: They're alive. The parents of a seven-month-old baby left at a Slidell hospital with pneumonia get a call from a Houston hospital where their baby "is being spoiled terribly," and doing great. A 99-year-old woman and her 87-year-old husband who survived 13-foot floodwaters but lost each other during a hospital evacuation are back together again, even if they don't know where they'll end up in the coming days.

Excerpt from Anderson Cooper Interview with Tad and Helena Breaux, Parents who Had Become Separated from Their Newborn Baby

COOPER: I'm joined by some parents, Tad and Helena Breaux, who had to leave their baby behind in a hospital in New Orleans for the last couple of days. They've been trying to find their baby. Within the last 15 minutes, when they just arrived here, they got some great news. Their baby is alive. It's in Ft. Worth. How you are guys doing? How are you holding up?

HELENA BREAUX, MOTHER: We're great, now.

TAD BREAUX, FATHER: It's just fantastic. . . . Saturday was the last time I had an opportunity to be with my son, Zachary. And the nurse took some pictures of us. And it was Saturday afternoon that the doctor had advised us that it wouldn't be advisable to take him with us, because they didn't have any of the proper medicine, and we couldn't get ahold of a monitor to take him, because all the monitoring companies were closed.

And everybody was leaving for the hurricane. And we knew he was in great hands and everything was fine, as long as we were able to hear from the hospital on a daily basis. And then the phones went out, and things started deteriorating, and then our cellphone went out, we just . . .

H. BREAUX: Didn't know where he was.

T. BREAUX: Didn't know where he was. We got a phone call from the nurse's sister out of San Diego who told us that everything was doing fine, the hospital had been damaged. It had taken in water. They had brought patients to the fifth floor up from the second floor, but the baby was fine. He was healthy. And he is eating like a pig. And that was kind of the last we'd heard of him for a day or two. And then somebody else had called and said they thought he had been evacuated to Charity Hospital. And then, we have been listening to CNN and heard all the terrible stories of everything that went on with Charity, and just been going in circles, calling every hospital in Arkansas, and in Texas, and in Louisiana.

COOPER: So for two days, you haven't known?

H. BREAUX: What's today, Thursday? Four days.

T. BREAUX: Yes, we haven't known he was going to be safe. And today we found out that he had been—

finally, they evacuated Methodist [Hospital] around 11:30. But no one could tell us where he was. We've just been going crazy, calling and getting on the Internet, and looking up hospitals, and just calling I'm sure . . .

H. BREAUX: Everybody.

T. BREAUX: I'm sure all of our friends, and family, and even people and family we don't know who have been calling. And it's just been sort of a snowball that each person we've called empathized with our situation, and gave us a suggestion to call, and said they would call the local chief, and they made phone calls. And, I guess, finally, he just landed somewhere. And somebody had a number and called and found him. So we're just so elated.

T. BREAUX: It's Ft. Worth. So it's just fantastic. We can go get our little boy. And that's basically what it is.

Helena Breaux with husband, Tad, holds a photo of their son, Zachary

---

Excerpt from Paula Zahn Interview with Michael Brown

ZAHN: And what about a situation like you just heard at Charity Hospital tonight, where they were in the process of evacuating patients and they were told, once they got those critically ill patients in a boat, put them on the boat, that the boat had to be sent back because where it was being dispatched to was underwater as well and there wasn't any reasonable place to leave them off?

BROWN: And that is a great example, unfortunately, a great example of how catastrophic this disaster is, that we may have a place that we're going to take critically ill patients and suddenly it's not there, and we have to change plans on the fly. That's how devastating this is. And that's why we're bringing in the National Guard. That's why the Coast Guard will continue to run missions all night with night vision. That's why the First Army is here. That's why the American public needs to understand exactly how catastrophic the situation is in New Orleans.

Joseph Gerdes of New Orleans rides in a boat with an officer armed with a shotgun as he is evacuated from his flooded home. The officer is on the lookout for hostile gangs and snipers. Fear and tension gripped the city as it decended into anarchy and violence.

Aaron Brown: "*Things are so political these days. It seems to us that if you ask why government responded this way or didn't respond that way, one side says you shouldn't ask the question at all. And the other side says you're not asking the question enough. The fact is, reporters ask why.*"

As the city prepares for another long night, it's clear that this tragedy has layers, and when the most obvious one is peeled back, another is revealed: the failure of government to take care of its citizens when they're in dire straits. Was the catastrophe too overwhelming even for the feds to handle? They say it was. Could it have been mitigated by federal aid, perhaps when, as many accounts just now surfacing foretold, authorities knew

that New Orleans "had a big bull's-eye right smack in the middle of the French Quarter?" Should the state and local officials have done things differently?

Chris Lawrence: "*We are right here on top of the roof. And I can see from this point and this vantage point right here, we have a pretty good view of the city. Right now, behind me, I can see smoke rising from across the Mississippi River, where police tell us that a mall is literally burning to the ground. Right here in the city, overhead, helicopters are literally just completely surrounding the city. We have seen some news helicopters, but a lot of Red Cross, police helicopters, a lot of the big Chinooks that the military uses. It is virtually a state of siege here in New Orleans right now and just a*

INTERVIEW

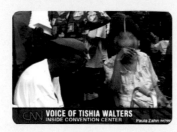

Paula Zahn

Tishia Walters,
Evacuee Inside the
Convention Center

ZAHN: Tishia, describe to us what it's been like there over the last couple of days.

WALTERS: What it has been like, right now, we have dead bodies in the freezer. People are dying. There is no lights, no water. There is no food. . . . They are just—they are looking for a 13-year-old child, but they just—they think she's been raped. They can't find her. There's a child downstairs that's 10 years old that they attempted to rape this morning. And they broke both of her—they broke both of her ankles.

We have people—the police is not doing anything. They are shooting. And the people that has looted the food that was here, they are trying to sell it back to you. They are selling bottles of water for $5. We can't get anything. . . . And there is more and more and more and more and more and more people going to die. And all the police say is, they are coming. They're going to be here.

I have been sitting here since 7:00 this morning. They are telling us that the buses are coming. Get out of the street. And people—six people have died today. And what are we going to do? We need help. I went to the police station around the corner, the (INAUDIBLE) police station. And I asked them—because I have some nursing experience, I asked them for things to help these people, the invalids. They told us that the (INAUDIBLE) we should have got out, and now we have to wait.

ZAHN: Are you seeing, besides the police that are on duty, any soldiers at all?

WALTERS: There's no police around here.

ZAHN: You don't see any police at all?

WALTERS: There's no police. It's total chaos. There is no authority figure in this building. They are taking this building apart. Every—they're kicking in the doors. They're defecating on the carpets. They're (INAUDIBLE) the stairwells. There is nothing.

ZAHN: And, Tishia, the one thing we're really having trouble figuring out is how many people are at the Convention Center. Do you have any idea?

WALTERS: It's about 3,000 people and more of them. There's one man, he can't walk on both of his legs. They look—they are blistering with sores. And he's barely moving. Last night, we spent the night outside on (INAUDIBLE) highway with babies. There was babies laying in the middle of the highway, because they left us there. A lady, we—there was one lady we had to resuscitate, because she was dying. Somebody walked up and left her in the wheelchair.

There are people here that really, seriously need help. There's (INAUDIBLE) cardiac. We have diabetics. We have everybody that needs some help. And, right now, we are searching the building for a 13-year-old child that we think has been raped. But there are so many rooms in the Convention Center that we cannot find her.

ZAHN: Well, Tishia, we have just finished interviewing the head of FEMA. And he said he is just finding out about how difficult things are at the Convention Center and that help is on the way.

---

scene that you never thought you would see in a major American city. Down on the ground, police were telling us when they got us off the street, it's just too dangerous to stay. One officer said, there have literally been groups of young men roaming the city, shooting at people, attempting to rape women. As we were getting hustled out of our location, one of the officers told a group of young ladies, do not go down that street. He ordered them to turn around and head back up another street. He said, the situation is just extremely dangerous on the ground right now."

"This is not the America that I have grown up in."

—David Mattingly

Toward midnight, military helicopters circle the city. A mall burns to the ground. At the International Airport, hundreds of patients lie on the floors, some dying. On the dark streets, rampaging gangs take full advantage of the unguarded city. Anyone venturing outside is in danger of being robbed or even shot. It is a state of siege, where authorities are afraid or unwilling to intervene.

Aaron Brown: "*Four thousand have escaped to the Houston Astrodome, but thousands more remain trapped inside the Convention Center, which if possible, is a lower level of hell than the Superdome. The Lord of the Flies has come to New Orleans.*"

INTERVIEW

Anderson Cooper

Sen. Mary Landrieu,
Louisiana Senator (D)

COOPER: Joining me from Baton Rouge is Louisiana Senator Mary Landrieu. Senator, appreciate you joining us tonight. Does the federal government bear responsibility for what is happening now? Should they apologize for what is happening now?

LANDRIEU: Anderson, there will be plenty of time to discuss all of those issues, about why, and how, and what, and if. But, Anderson, as you understand, and all of the producers and directors of CNN, and the news networks, this situation is very serious and it's going to demand all of our full attention through the hours, through the nights, through the days.

Let me just say a few things. Thank President Clinton and former President Bush for their strong statements of support and comfort today. I thank all the leaders that are coming to Louisiana, and Mississippi, and Alabama to our help and rescue. We are grateful for the military assets that are being brought to bear. I want to thank Sen. Frist and Sen. Reid for their extraordinary efforts. Anderson, tonight, I don't know if you've heard—maybe you all have announced it —but Congress is going to an unprecedented session to pass a $10 billion supplemental bill tonight to keep FEMA and the Red Cross up and operating.

COOPER: Excuse me, Senator, I'm sorry for interrupting. I haven't heard that, because, for the last four days, I've been seeing dead bodies in the streets here in Mississippi. And to listen to politicians thanking each other and complimenting each other, you know, I got to tell you, there are a lot of people here who are very upset, and very angry, and very frustrated.

And when they hear politicians slap—you know, thanking one another, it just, you know, it kind of cuts them the wrong way right now, because literally there was a body on the streets of this town yesterday being eaten by rats because this woman had been laying in the street for 48 hours. And there's not enough facilities to take her up.

Do you get the anger that is out here?

LANDRIEU: Anderson, I have the anger inside of me. Most of the homes in my family have been destroyed. Our homes have been destroyed. I understand what you're saying, and I know all of those details. And the president of the United States knows those details.

COOPER: Well, who are you angry at?

LANDRIEU: I'm not angry at anyone. I'm just expressing that it is so important for everyone in this nation to pull together, for all military assets and all assets to be brought to bare in this situation.

And I have every confidence that this country is as great and as strong as we can be do to that. And that effort is under way.

COOPER: Well, I mean, there are a lot of people here who are kind of ashamed of what is happening in this country right now, what is—ashamed of what is happening in your state, certainly.

And that's not to blame the people who are there. It's a desperate situation. But I guess, you know, who can —I mean, no one seems to be taking responsibility. I mean, I know you say there's a time and a place for, kind of, you know, looking back, but this seems to be the time and the place. I mean, there are people who want answers, and there are people who want someone to stand up and say, "You know what? We should have done more. Are all the assets being brought to bare?"

LANDRIEU: Anderson, Anderson . . .

COOPER: I mean, today, for the first time, I'm seeing National Guard troops in this town.

LANDRIEU: Anderson, I know. And I know where you are. And I know what you're seeing. Believe me, we know it. And we understand, and there will be a time to talk about all of that. Trust me. I know what the people are suffering. The governor knows. The president knows. The military officials know. And they're trying to do the very best they can to stabilize the situation. Senator Vitter, our congressional delegation, all of us understand what is happening. We are doing our very, very best to get the situation under control. But I want to thank the president. He will be here tomorrow, we think. And the military is sending assets as we speak. So, please, I understand. You might say I'm a politician, but I grew up in New Orleans. My father was the mayor of that city. I've represented that city my whole life, and it's just not New Orleans. It's St. Bernard, and St. Tammany, and Plaquemines Parish that have been completely underwater. Our levee system has failed. We need a lot of help. And the Congress has been wonderful to help us, and we need more help. Nobody's perfect, Anderson. Everybody has to stand up here. And I know you understand. So thank you so much for everything you're doing.

> "This is an event of Biblical proportions."
> *—Former New Orleans Mayor Marc Morial*

"I wouldn't say I'm angry, you know. I think I'm tired of hearing the politicians say that, you know, they understand the frustration of people down here. To me, you know, it's not frustration. It's not that people are frustrated. It's that people are dying. I mean there are people dying. They're drowning to death and they drown in their living rooms and their bodies are rotting where they drowned and there are corpses in the street being eaten by rats and this is the United States of America."

—Anderson Cooper, in response to a question by Larry King about why he was angry after he lashed out at Sen. Mary Landrieu [D. La.] for thanking politicians for their hard work

Cafferty Question: How would you rate the response of the federal government to Hurricane Katrina?

"Get the talking heads off the TV. How many times do we need to hear what they're doing? Pictures show clearly what they're not doing."

—Delores in Mt. Ephraim, N.J.

"I think the government is handling the program in a remarkable fashion. Calling back Congress is a brilliant move by the president. What I don't like is the negativism from the media. Maybe they should volunteer to go help with the cleanup instead of being so critical."

— John in Carmel, Ind.

"I sit here in Seattle wishing like hell I could do anything besides give money and send prayers to help those poor souls. This is not my America. This is not my government. I'm ashamed of this administration beyond any shame I have ever felt before. I hope the people of this country can pull together in spite of government ineptitude to help wherever necessary."

—Penny in Renton, Wash.

"Right now, the days seem awfully dark for those affected, and I understand that. But I'm confident that with time, you get your life back in order, new communities will flourish, the great city of New Orleans will be back on its feet, and America will be a stronger place for it. The country stands with you. We'll do all in our power to help you."

—Pres. George W. Bush

"But ironically the failure at the Convention Center would have been fairly easy to put right. Reporters drove there without problems. One took a taxi. What one wonders, was FEMA/the mayor's office/the governor's office doing while all that was played out on live TV? One lesson agencies might want to learn is that someone senior should do nothing but monitor TV."

—Paul Reynolds, BBC World Affairs Correspondent

"I've been a supporter of President Bush, but I just got to come back to the fact that this is a failure of leadership and I'll tell you I'm personally angry . . . and I don't want a president who is taking six-week vacations anywhere when Americans are dying . . . whether they are dying in Iraq or Louisiana."

—Lt. Col. Ralph Peters, on MSNBC

"The dreadful aftermath of Hurricane Katrina has exposed personal and structural failings in America's government, and eroded respect for the country around the world."

—The Economist magazine

AP Photo/Eric Gay

AP Photo/Rick Bowmer

Top–A fire burns on the east side of New Orleans early Friday morning. Bottom–A soldier patrols the street next to a house fire in the Garden District in New Orleans.

Anarchy. All night long, it's been like a scene from *Apocalypse Now*: darkness unrelieved by any light, distant explosions punctuating the silence, smoke billowing up into the sky. Fires break out on the horizon, glowing orange in the blackness. Cars burn. The remaining local police are stretched to the breaking point, one precinct dubbed "Fort Apache" is barricaded in a building after being shot at by snipers. Heavily armed gangs roam the streets. Shots ring out in the night.

But this is no movie. It's America, five o'clock in the morning, New Orleans.

At the Convention Center, chaos has turned to violence and bloodshed. The police say there's no way they can even think about going in without 40 to 50 fully armed men. In addition to those inside, families have now piled up on the streets outside the Center, where they've been waiting for three days for help to come: Having survived Katrina, they wonder if they'll survive the catastrophe left in its wake. In the pitch-black Center, thousands upon thousands of people mill about, try to sleep, some die in corners. The violence is senseless, random.

Firsthand accounts continue to trickle out: people say there's no one in charge, and they feel they are there to kill or be killed. They claim that the "gun-toting thugs" have been their saviors, the ones to organize and provide food,

> **"I think it's gone.
> I think we lost her."**
>
> —*Unidentified New Orleans
> policeman, talking about the city*

with guns, say some people, there wouldn't have been any food or water at all. Other accounts confirm the worst. After five days of unmitigated hell, there is no running water, no toilet facilities, only sick and dying people, armed gangs, and everyone, from small children to the elderly, helpless, terrorized, and terrified. No air conditioning, no food. Five days.

A police officer keeps watch as a building fire burns in downtown New Orleans.

Mario Tama/Getty Images

> *"This is one big family now. We got to help each other because nobody else is helping us. They put us out of our homes. They turned off the water and the gas and literally forced us out of our homes, put us in these places and now they don't want to help us. They keep giving us the runaround—help is coming, help is coming. I mean, it don't take five days to get a bus here."*
>
> —Alan Gould, calling from inside the
> Convention Center, 5:30 a.m.

On a late Thursday-night broadcast from radio station WWL-AM, Mayor Nagin erupts in an explosive interview that seems to speak for all the people of New Orleans trapped in silent helplessness. He lashes out at everyone, including the President, for failing to provide adequate federal support. His remarks, unedited and frank, instantly make headlines and are rebroadcast across the country by morning. The President will be in Biloxi later today and will take part in a briefing in Alabama. There are as yet no plans for him to tour New Orleans on the ground.

**Excerpt from Mayor Nagin's WWL-AM Interview
with Garland Robinette**

NAGIN: I basically told [President Bush] we had an incredible crisis here and that his flying over in Air Force One does not do it justice. And that I have been all around this city, and I am very frustrated because we are not able to marshal resources and we're outmanned in just about every respect. . . . They flew down here one time, two days after the doggone event was over, with TV cameras, AP reporters, all kind of goddamn—excuse my French, everybody in America. But I am pissed.

ROBINETTE: Did you say to the president of the United States, I need the military in here?

NAGIN: I said I need everything. Now, I will tell you this, and I give the president some credit on this. He sent one John Wayne dude down here that can get some stuff done. And his name is Lt. Gen. Honore. And he came off the doggone chopper and he started cussing and people started moving. And he's getting some stuff done.

ROBINETTE: What do you need to get control of this situation?

NAGIN: I need reinforcements. I need troops, man. I need 500 buses, man. What are they talking about, you know, one of the briefings we had they were talking about getting, you know, public school-bus drivers to come down here and bus people out of here. I'm like, You've got to be kidding me. This is a natural disaster. Get every doggone Greyhound bus line in the country and get their asses moving to New Orleans. That's, they're thinking small, man. And this is a major, major, major deal. And I can't emphasize it enough, man. This is crazy. I've got 15,000 to 20,000 people over there at the Convention Center. It's bursting at the seams. . . . It's awful down here, man.

ROBINETTE: Do you believe that the president is seeing this, holding a news conference on it, but can't do anything until Kathleen Blanco requested him to do it? And do you know whether or not she has made that request?

NAGIN: I have no idea what they're doing, but I will tell you this, you know, God is looking down on all this and if they are not doing everything in their power to save people, they are going to pay the price, because every day that we delay, people are dying. . . .

Excerpt from Miles O'Brien Interview with Gov. Kathleen Blanco [D-La.]

O'BRIEN: Let's talk about that request for federal troops, 40,000 federal troops. When did you make that request? Was it on your first phone call to President Bush?

BLANCO: OK. My first phone call—or my first conversation with President Bush—was asking for all federal firepower. I mean, I meant everything. Just send it. Give me planes, give me boats . . .

O'BRIEN: But did you specifically ask—Governor, did you specifically ask for troops? Did you ask that the Pentagon deploy troops? Because that is a very specific request that a governor needs to make of the federal government.

BLANCO: We had troops—we had troops being deployed. We had the first wave of troops being deployed at the level of 12,000. But before we even got to 12,000, I asked for 40,000. So, you know, I saw that we needed to raise capacity . . .

O'BRIEN: When did you make that request, though?

BLANCO: Miles, I'm lost in the days.

O'BRIEN: When did you make that request? OK.

BLANCO: I don't even know what today is.

O'BRIEN: On Wednesday morning . . .

BLANCO: I made that request perhaps Wednesday. . . . But on Tuesday we didn't have the 12,000 that I had asked for. On Tuesday, the day after the hurricane, you know, the ramp-up was not as rapid as we needed.

O'BRIEN: Do you fault yourself for not asking for troops sooner?

BLANCO: Miles, I asked for everything the federal government could possibly deliver. You know, I'm a governor. You know, I think that people in the field were analyzing the situation. It was deteriorating. In the first instance, we didn't have all of the water in the streets. Then the dike broke.

You know, everything has changed so dramatically. You know, I'm not going to stand here and play the blame game. We have a problem. You know, I say let's get to the problems. We'll talk about all of the circumstances later. But, you know, everybody here looks at it, looks in the mirror and says I wish I would have known this an hour earlier. I could of done this an hour earlier or a day earlier. But, you know, we're asking for ramp-up. It has finally arrived or is in the process of arriving. It just takes a while. And I'll tell you something, we are all frustrated. . . .

And then finally, help is not just being promised. It's actually here. Boots, as they say, are on the ground.

A convoy of 50 trucks carrying National Guard MPs, combat-ready military police, are the first wave of what Homeland Security Chief Michael Chertoff says will continue for three days, with an additional 1,400 soldiers arriving every day. Gov. Blanco issues a tough warning about the troops: They are fresh back from Iraq, locked and loaded and know how to shoot.

With helicopters roaring overhead, the troops arrive at the Convention Center to distribute food and water. Cargo trucks carrying long-awaited supplies, hundreds of troops, and thousands of pounds of food and supplies are finally snaking through the rancid waters. CNN dubs New Orleans "Mission Critical." The crowd erupts in cheers when they see soldiers. But many of those who have waited so long and in such drastic conditions for help are disappointed that the Guard hasn't also brought the crucial thing they need: buses to leave. In the next few hours, a thousand people will be evacuated from the Convention Center.

"This is not Iraq, you are part of a humanitarian relief convoy."—Lt. Gen. Russell Honore

Michael Chertoff: *"We have 2,800 National Guard in New Orleans as we speak today. Fourteen hundred additional National Guard military police–trained soldiers will be arriving every day. Fourteen hundred yesterday, 1,400 the next day, 1,400 the next. . . ."*

REUTERS/David J. Phillip/POOL /Landov

Military soldiers patrol the uptown section in New Orleans.

Bottom left–A military convoy drives through floodwaters in downtown New Orleans finally bringing emergency supplies for desperate survivors of Hurricane Katrina after days of delays and broken promises.

Bottom right– Army National Guard soldiers distribute food and water to stranded victims of Hurricane Katrina at the New Orleans Convention Center.

Gen. James "Spider" Marks, military analyst: *"There are restrictions to what soldiers can and cannot do. Soldiers are allowed to walk through procedures. And the procedures could take a nanosecond to go from an arming order that's very benign to one where you may have to shoot to kill. Because . . . yes, they're allowed to shoot to kill. But it's based on very precise circumstances and the threat to the individual soldier and the circumstances on the ground. When a governor activates a National Guard soldier, that National Guard soldier can act as a law enforcement agent. That soldier has the ability to arrest, to pursue and arrest. A federally activated soldier cannot do that. Those are legal prohibitions. So there are some advantages of the governor stepping up saying these are state-activated soldiers versus federally activated soldiers. When the governor activates soldiers [at the state level], they work for the local law enforcement."*

"These are some of the 40,000 extra troops that I have demanded. They have M-16s, and they're locked and loaded. . . . I have one message for these hoodlums: These troops know how to shoot and kill, and they are more than willing to do so if necessary, and I expect they will."

——Gov. Kathleen Blanco

As President Bush prepares to visit the Gulf Coast for his second look at the damage, he remarks that he has reviewed the federal response to Hurricane Katrina and is not happy. "The results are not acceptable," he says. "I'm headed down there right now." Scheduled to be in the area by mid-afternoon, the president will conduct his survey by helicopter, with a stop planned in Mississippi. He's also expected to deliver remarks from the Louis Armstrong New Orleans International Airport, though he has no plans to tour the city. Senator Trent Lott, who lost his Pascagoula home to Hurricane Katrina, accompanies the President. Around noon, Congress passes an emergency measure providing $10.5 billion for rescue and relief efforts, which President Bush will sign following his return to Washington.

Carol Costello: *"Well, you know, one of the things I think that the people still trapped in New Orleans will be disappointed in is that if President Bush makes his speech, you know, and you hear it via television or radio, these people in New Orleans have no electricity. They can't hear him. How will they get the message?"*

In neighboring Mississippi, frustrations are also running high. Biloxi survivors are almost out of water and food, wondering where the federal relief is and when it will arrive. In an area of the city called the Point, ominous black marks on the houses identify where bodies have been found. But people walking through don't need any marks; they can smell the bodies decomposing. Hearing that President Bush plans another flyover, perhaps another stop along the coast, residents are less grateful than indignant: Why have they been forgotten? Isolated, suffering and without adequate security, they're relying on the press as their liaison to the outside world.

Mississippi state senators say the Labor Department will provide some $50 million to try to hire people to help in the cleanup. In Alabama, the governor announces what he calls "Operation Golden Rule" to try to find housing for some 10,000 homeless people. The number of homes and businesses without power is now 135,000. The state government is making up to $25 million available for emergency loans for disaster victims.

In New Orleans, Mayor Nagin issues yet another statement. He says more than 10,000 were evacuated yesterday, but as many as 50,000 survivors remain on rooftops, in shelters, elsewhere. "The people of our city are holding on by a thread. Time has run out. Can we survive another night, and who can we depend on? God only knows."

In fact, there's very little of New Orleans that doesn't resemble a war zone. In some districts, up to 30 percent of New Orleans police have abandoned their jobs. The hospitals are unable to evacuate and their upper floors are scenes of horror, as patients desperately in need of medication and treatment struggle to hang on until something comes along. Charity Hospital has gone from bad to worse, waiting past hope as promised helicopters fail to arrive. The only bright spot is the doctors who managed to get in to help out. The angels of mercy who never left.

Deborah Feyerick: *"Spoke with a police sergeant who described a horrible situation within the city. He had spent 60 straight hours there. He said, 'It is a war zone, and the federal government is not treating it like one.' He described groups of gunmen riding around on trucks. And he compared it to Somalia, saying they were firing at police officers using rifles and AK-47s. He said he saw bodies riddled with bullet holes. The top of one man's head completely shot off. [later turned out to be inaccurate] And a sergeant said, 'No one is coming to help.' The police officers have been working five to six days straight without sleep. When darkness comes, the police hide and simply try to ride out the night. The police are not getting supplies. They're not getting reinforcements. He said they are having to steal trucks and siphon off gas just to get around. The sergeant was telling me, 'If this were a terrorist attack, we would all be dead.' And then he broke down in tears, saying he had to pass by other police officers who had drowned doing their jobs. So the situation inside the city of New Orleans is very, very desperate indeed. The fatigue on the police department is clearly showing through. They are waiting for help and, again, in his words, 'Nobody is coming.'"*

Firefighter Kevin King marks a house as clear after searching in Pass Christian, Miss.

Angela Jenkins screams "Help us, please!" outside the Earnest Morial Convention Center.

Excerpt from Soledad O'Brien Interview with Dr. Sanjay Gupta from Charity Hospital:

GUPTA: I've been hearing varying reports that maybe the hospital had been evacuated as early as this past Tuesday. Still over 200 patients here. We just found our way in through a chopper and had to land at a landing strip across the way here, and then take a boat over to the hospital. And it is exactly in that boat area where the boat was traveling where the snipers actually opened fire yesterday, halting all the evacuations, at least for a while yesterday.

It is really just impossible to take care of patients anymore. Any patients who are critically ill at this point have either died—and there have been a few that have literally died in the parking deck waiting to be taken out by choppers—or they are still having their bags pumped, their air pumped into their lungs by hand, as doctors and nurses and healthcare professionals sit there for hours on end just pumping air into their lungs. So it is truly an impossible situation out there. They're hoping that the evacuations resume today. . . .

O'BRIEN: Sanjay, is it chaotic? Are people panicking? Are they just resolved it's not going to get better any time soon? What's the mood like?

GUPTA: I think the mood is becoming somewhat despondent, not so much chaotic. I think they've probably already gone beyond that stage. I think when patients started dying, it just became very despondent. It became beyond frustrating, beyond angry, to, you know, "Oh my gosh, people are going to die because of this now, and we can't get them out."

And I should remind you, and maybe this is already obvious, that a lot of these patients were already in the hospital. So these weren't patients who were necessarily injured by the hurricane or even affected by it necessarily, but now, they just can't get care that would otherwise be absolutely standard and they're dying as a result of that, and that is frightening. . . .

A lot of these doctors came in because of the hurricane. They knew that they might be needed. They've been here since Saturday. They plan on staying until every patient has been taken out, and they've really—again, I've seen a lot of situations. I was in Sri Lanka for the tsunami. I was in Iraq for the war. I've seen a lot of different situations, where people have to make shift, make do with what they have. This has been as bad as any of those. I mean, no food, no electricity, no water, and surrounded by this cesspool of potential infectious diseases as well. They've been very, very diligent about taking care of these patients, which is remarkable. I think a lot of lives that otherwise would have been lost have been saved by these doctors who have not slept in several days, have very little food and water themselves, and are operating under the most remote conditions really possible.

President Bush flies into Mobile, Ala., then on to Keesler Air Force Base in Biloxi, and for the first time touches ground and actually walks through the devastated neighborhoods. Residents greet the president in tears, obviously distraught. The President meets with people who tell him their personal stories. He assures them, "We're going to clean all this mess up. The federal government will spend money to clean it up. The first down payment will be signed tonight by me as a result of the good work of the Senate and the House, $10.5 billion. But that's just the beginning." He qualifies his earlier comment that the "results are not acceptable" by explaining that the response to the crisis met with his approval. It's rumored that the President is behind schedule, but that he may do a walking tour in New Orleans nonetheless.

Excerpt from President Bush's press briefing in Mobile, Ala.

QUESTION: You talk about fixing what's wrong and you talk about the results not being acceptable, but there are a lot of people wondering why you weren't fixing the problems yesterday or the day before and why the richest country on earth can't get food and water to those people that need it.

PRESIDENT BUSH: The levees broke on Tuesday [sic] in New Orleans. On Wednesday and Thursday we started evacuating people. A lot of people have left that city. A lot of people have been pulled out on buses. I am satisfied with the response. I'm not satisfied with all the results. They started pulling people off of roofs immediately. We started rallying choppers to get people off rooftops, start saving lives. I mean, thousands of peoples' lives have been saved immediately. . . .

Our job as people in positions of responsibility is not to be satisfied until the job is done as good as it can possibly be done. And that's what I was referring to. We're certainly not denigrating the efforts of anybody. But the results can be better in New Orleans. And I intend to work to—with the folks to make it better.

"Brownie, you're doin' a heckuva job."

—President Bush to FEMA Director Michael Brown, press briefing at Mobile Regional Airport, Mobile, Ala.

Louisiana Sen. Mary Landrieu, currently aboard Marine One with the President asks the president today to appoint, within 24 hours, a Cabinet-level official to direct the national response to this tragedy. The suffering has gone on long enough, Landrieu says. Clearly, she's losing confidence in FEMA, and FEMA Director Michael Brown.

The sudden show of force, and the President's visit, raise more and more questions about why help didn't come sooner. Much sooner. Coincidentally, reports surface that make it clear the experts had long predicted

New Orleans would be a vulnerable target for such a catastrophic storm. First to come to light is the eerily prophetic New Orleans *Times-Picayune*'s series from June 2002, a five-part special called "Washing Away," which laid out in painstaking detail the threats New Orleans faced if it were to be hit by a Category 4 or 5 hurricane. The articles foretold exactly what has happened to New Orleans, including the levee breaches, the flooding, and the numbers of people stranded and dead. Washington-based *Times-Picayune* reporter Bill Walsh confirms the fact that politicians have known for decades what would happen to New Orleans.

Excerpt from Kyra Phillips Interview with Bill Walsh about the *Times-Picayune* series "Washing Away"

WALSH: The Louisiana Congressional Delegation in Washington has been beating this drum for years . . . They've been raising concerns about the vulnerability of the city and trying to make their case in Washington, with very limited success.

PHILLIPS: Going on to another part of another article, another quote I want to read. And this one just took my breath away. This was from the director of the New Orleans Office of Emergency Preparedness: "We think we're going to do our people a terrible disservice if we don't tell them the truth, and the truth is that when it happens, a lot of people are going to die. Those who remain should not expect to find safe shelter. Few buildings in the area can withstand the forces of a Category 4 or 5 hurricane. We don't have the structures that can handle wind and water and those velocities and at that water height."

WALSH: Yes. I mean, it's really been no secret. I mean, the city is so vulnerable to the hurricanes that swirl out in the Gulf of Mexico every year. It's a pretty dire few months for people who live there. And the city has been waiting for years for the worst-case scenario to happen. The trick and the difficulty has been impressing upon Washington the eventuality of what could happen. And now, of course, we're seeing it. And it's probably early to begin pointing fingers, because the rescue is still going on. But I don't think anyone in Washington can say now that they didn't see this coming.

Tishia Walters, (outside the Convention Center, 2 p.m.): *"I'm watching all the National Guard and all the police presence out here. I mean it's amazing. They've come in full force, . . . and we just needed the help. The crowd erupted. The clapping, crying, people shouting and waving. There's like 7,000 people out here in dying conditions. We have people starving in there. They're bringing food and water and there are bringing a lot of hope. They're coming. They are already starting taking some of the people and they're taking them away. We needed them to come and they're here. They got to get everybody out."*

National television and newspapers run with the ball, reprinting the reports, talking to professionals, demanding answers from officials who should have known the facts. It comes out that Washington has been working with state and local officials for almost 40 years on flood relief efforts, but some now say that federal funds to fix and improve the levee system in New Orleans have been cut back since 9/11. Congress allocated $70 million for work in 2001, but this year, just more than $42 million was granted. Officials rush to untangle the facts from the figures, but the facts remain: New Orleans is vulnerable to flooding. Much of the city lies below sea level. The levees were in disrepair. A hundred thousand people were at risk that would have no way of getting out of the city.

Excerpt from Wolf Blitzer Interview with Tom Foreman

BLITZER: Did officials in New Orleans have enough money to get the job done?

FOREMAN: No. I mean, that's the simple answer. No, they did not. Corps of Engineers, people down there have been saying for years, look, the levees are in pretty good shape, but they're not high enough. And here's one of the interesting things, when water goes over a top of a levee, which is exactly what happened here—and we're talking about a town that's surrounded by levees, I want you to look here, as we always do—when water goes over the top, levees fail. That's what happens if it happens long.

Once again, this is the big lake on the north. This is the river running right through the middle of town here, if we can get to it. There's the river running right through town. And all of these areas are surrounded in some way by levees all through here, all up in here, all down in here, the canals in town have levees aside them.

BLITZER: That's Lake Pontchartrain and the Mississippi River at the bottom.

FOREMAN: Mississippi River right here. Particularly—look down in this area here, see all this marshland? This is a tremendous amount of water pushing all into this area. This is Lake Borgne over here, which you don't hear as much talk about.

But all this area down here is some of the first areas that flooded. When we talked about New Orleans east, remember the day all of the pictures of the people on top of the houses then? That's what we're talking about, the areas down here.

St. Bernard Parish huge problems there. Plaquemine Parish further down, Chalmette, Arabi, these areas really got hammered by this. The money that was needed to keep this from happening has been cut back. Now, we don't know exactly why. We're going to figure out exactly why. Some people say it's because that money has been diverted to the war, some people say other things. But the bottom line is, it takes money to keep levees built up. There are people there who know how to build levees better than anyone in the country, they just haven't had the funds to do it.

BLITZER: And there was one study a few years ago, 2001, that said $14 billion was needed to redo the whole system to withstand a Category 5 hurricane, the highest level category. At the time $14 billion sounded like a great deal of money. And now, compared to how much everyone has got to spend, that seems relatively modest.

FOREMAN: Yeah. A drop in the bucket, to use a bad phrase.

BLITZER: A bad phrase right now.

A SWAT team drives past flood victims waiting at the Convention Center in New Orleans.

AP Photo/Eric Gay

Jack Cafferty: *"The* Boston Globe *reporting today that National Guard units across the country have about half their usual equipment—everything from helicopters, Humvees, trucks, weapons—available to them because all the rest of the stuff has been sent off to fight the wars in Iraq and Afghanistan. There are 78,000 National Guard troops who are now deployed in those overseas war zones. Even the hardest hit states, Louisiana, Mississippi, have 40 percent of their National Guard troops in Iraq right now."*

In Houston, the Reliant Astrodome is packed with people wandering around among strangers. Here again, because of the long, confusing days, and the sporadic bus pickups, family members have gone missing. This enormous facility, predicted to be heaven on earth in comparison to the Superdome, has become a big, broad hell of missing persons. Evacuees are at their breaking point and now that basic needs have been met—food and water and a dry place to stay—they've moved on to subtler concerns: depression, anxiety, and post-traumatic stress.

For those who are separated by buses and helicopters, it may be many days, even weeks, before they find each other again. Throughout the hurricane's arrival and after its departure, families have been suffering the worst that can happen to a family: Split up—abruptly—mothers from children, husbands from wives. They often have no idea whether the missing members are alive or dead. Some last saw each other standing on a roof as waters lapped at the eaves. Horror stories to rival any war abound: mothers offering up their babies to strangers on buses, just to get them out of the flooding. Without a register of any kind, people seize upon every possible means of finding each other. They grab reporters and ask if they can announce their whereabouts, give out the names of mothers, brothers, sisters, grandmothers . . . In response, the media opens every possible channel for family members to contact each other. Newspapers begin to run online registries, and the networks offer numbers people can call to tap into a national registry.

Toward evening, the air is heavy, hot, and filled with the odors of the rotting city. President Bush makes his last stop of the day at the stifling, mobbed Louis Armstrong New Orleans International Airport, where more misery is on full display. The injured are being transported on luggage carts, while the weary crowd the baggage carousels and lie on the floor on opened cardboard boxes.

President Bush encourages people to donate cash to the American Red Cross and the Salvation Army. Flanked by Gov. Blanco and FEMA Director Mike Brown he closes the day with, "May God bless the people of this part of the world, and may God continue to bless our country."

Evacuees of Hurricane Katrina sit on cots in the Astrodome in Houston, Texas.
Some hold signs with their relatives' names in hope of finding them.

Excerpt from Brian Todd Interview with Sheriff Steve Simpson

Sheriff Steve Simpson from Loudon County, Va., received an urgent request from the Jefferson Parish, La. sheriff.

SIMPSON: Well, we were put in touch with them by the National Sheriffs' Association. When we contacted them, I guess it was actually about eight o'clock Wednesday evening. The tone of their voice of almost panic, asking for help, how soon can you get here, what can you bring? We're losing control down here, we're in dire straits. Please get here as quickly as you can. We put everything—we worked on it overnight—put everybody together. We were ready to move, actually, one o'clock that following day. And trying to work through about 10 hours of phone calls, trying to get the approval that we needed to make it official. We went back and forth and back and forth. Finally ended up with me talking to someone in the Louisiana State Police late Thursday night who basically told us, "We're telling everybody not to come."

TODD: Did he give any reason?

SIMPSON: No reason. First it was, well, we don't have a place to put you up. Well, we were self-sufficient. We had tents, we had things to sleep in, we had food, we had water. We had already made these arrangements with Jefferson Parish. We were good to go. That was really the only explanation ever given, is that we're telling people not to come down. There's no place to put you.

TODD: We did speak to the Louisiana State Police just moments ago, Lt. Lawrence McCleary. He said that the Louisiana State Police didn't necessarily need to sign off on it. Once the governor of Louisiana lifted certain provisions in the law to supersede chains of command, then the Jefferson County Parish could have just received your team directly with no interference from anyone else. This official with the Louisiana State Police said he's not sure how that word didn't get to you. And the governor did lift those provisions either yesterday evening or late last night. What's your response to that? You never heard from anybody?

SIMPSON: No. I don't know whether that was an after the fact thing that—after about 11 o'clock last night. If it was done earlier and nobody in Jefferson Parish knew anything about it. They didn't tell us. The gentleman I spoke with at the command center in Baton Rouge did not—with the state police—did not tell me anything about that either, otherwise we were already on the road. We were three hours down the road. We would have continued. We would have been there by now.

TODD: All right. This is just an example of some of the logistical—the command nightmare that is going on with law enforcement all around the country. . . .

Excerpt from Aaron Brown Interview with Michael Parker, former head of Army Corps of Engineers

Mr. Parker had resigned over budget priorities.

BROWN: There was a plan to shore up the levee system that protects the city. At one point, money was set on the table. And then, money was lost. If the money had been spent, if the levee project had been completed, I don't think you believe, do you, that the city would be dry?

PARKER: It would not be dry. No, no. In fact, the president of the United States, when he first came into office, and we'd given him $100 million. It would not have made much difference as far as this incident.

BROWN: Why would it not have made much difference? I thought the idea was to sort of raise the level of its strength from—to withstand a Category 5 hurricane?

PARKER: But you have to understand, these projects are huge in nature. And they take a long time to build. I think we need to put it in perspective. Infrastructure is not something that we build for ourselves. We build it for our children and our grandchildren. Just like the infrastructure we have in place, we own that—we own it simply because it was given to us by our parents and our grandparents. If you look in New Orleans, in 1965 when Hurricane Betsy came through, the Congress of the United States passed legislation. And in that legislation, it was supposed to be protecting the city of New Orleans. And it was the Lake Pontchartrain New Orleans Levee and Hurricane Protection Plan. The fact of the matter is, is that Congress wanted to have that paid for—completed by, in a 10-year period of time—by 1975. We are now at 2005. Forty years after the inception, 30 years after it was supposed to be completed. And it is only 80 to 85 percent complete.

BROWN: And that is because why?

PARKER: Well, there are a variety of reasons. And a lot of them, the American people don't quite understand because there's a—it's a little secret in Washington how information gets to people. The fact of the matter is that infrastructure has a direct bearing on the standard of living of the citizens of this nation. And too many times, we have placed emphasis on things that are—that individuals, politicians look at it as self gratification, instant gratification. They turn around and say, let's take care of this now, so we can look at an election because these projects are going to be too long term in nature.

Anderson Cooper: Reporter's Notebook

Here in Waveland, Miss., you can see the destruction behind me. The reason it is so bad in this area is just in front of me: the water, the coast just there about 100 or so yards in front of me. The water is calm, beautiful tonight, deadly just a few days ago.

The days here seem to blend together. At times it's easy to forget what country you're in, what year it is, which way is up, which way is down. You drive past highways that look like parking lots. There's no gas to be had. When there is, the lines stretch for miles.

On the radio, there's no music, just people desperate to trade information.

In Waveland, you can pick any street near the water and this is what you'll see.

It's hard not to be overwhelmed by the scope of it all. I mean everywhere you turn in this town of Waveland there's just destruction. There's—look at the clothing and bedding hanging in trees. Turn left, turn right, it doesn't really matter. It all ends up the same.

Oh, look, here's a Marine jacket. . . . The rest of the world just seems so far away. I mean, you know, throughout the week we've heard politicians say, well, you know, they understand the frustration of people down here. The truth is people aren't frustrated here. People are dying here. They've died here in Waveland. They're dying still in New Orleans. So it's not just frustration. It goes much deeper than that.

Walking through the rubble it feels like Sri Lanka, Sarajevo, somewhere else, not here, not home, not America. I've covered a lot of disasters, natural and manmade, and each one is different, each one the same.

At a certain point it feels like all the words have already been spoken: devastation, destruction, disaster, sadness, and pain. Again and again it's always the same, the heat, the humidity, the sweat, the tears. This time does feel different. This time it's our home.

And it's been a privilege to be in Waveland the last two nights here, the people just remarkable, some looting here, yes, but people have just been helping one another, neighbor helping neighbor. The federal government is here. FEMA, these Virginia urban search-and-rescue personnel, have just been doing extraordinary work and continue to.

As the sun goes down, they'll continue to work. As the sun comes up, they'll be working again.

Armed SWAT policemen patrol in downtown New Orleans

Rick Wilking/REUTERS/Landov

New Orleans is the ninth poorest city in the U.S. New Orleans is 70 percent African-American. Louisiana has the fourth highest poverty rate in the country.

Christine Romans: *"Katrina couldn't have taken aim on a more vulnerable population. Crushing poverty, once invisible to the world. Now, for the poor here, their misery is on full display. Utter desperation laid bare by Hurricane Katrina."*

Eighty percent of New Orleans remains under water, and an estimated 50,000 remain left behind. It is perhaps the final irony when dictator Fidel Castro offers to send 1,100 Cuban doctors and 26 tons of medicine to help out. His offer is not accepted. Growing outrage from the public accompanies knowledge of such swift foreign aid—offers from countries as poor as hard-hit Sri Lanka and war-wracked Afghanistan—when our own government is so slow to move. Nearly 7,000 National Guard troops will sleep in New Orleans tonight.

Aaron Brown: *"Local government—which hasn't exactly dazzled anyone here—state government, federal government in the post 9/11 era, when we're supposed to be able to turn on a dime and evacuate entire communities because someone just dropped a dirty bomb in the neighborhood . . . hasn't been very reassuring."*

As darkness falls, the floor of the cavernous Houston Astrodome is a solid sea, end-to-end and hip-to-hip, of exhausted people. The Reliant Arena has as many as 15,000 harbored there, with the adjacent Reliant Center holding an additional 11,000 cots. It is full, and pleas are going out to families nationwide to open their homes to the thousands more who have not yet arrived.

While it appears to be relatively peaceful at the Astrodome, in a city safe and hundreds of miles away from the tragedy, the Convention Center in New Orleans is another story entirely. There were cheers, clapping, and tears of joy, as well as some boos and catcalls, when troops finally delivered water and food there earlier today, and President Bush himself announced that the Convention Center is now secure.

But reporters on the street refute that claim, and conditions there seem as horrific as before—senior New Orleans police officials express their great concern about possible unrest there as night falls. The thousands who have been living there amid mountains of trash, and those who have overflowed outside, where the streets have turned into an open sewer, are absolutely desperate. Bodies covered with blankets are shoved aside, no one able to give them the respect they deserve. Fires still burn and explosions still shatter the air. Help is at hand, but for many, too little too late. They have seen too much, been overwhelmed for too long, heard far too many promises.

"I am seeing moments of utter heartbreak and desperation here. There is no other word for it than unbelievable."

—Barbara Starr in New Orleans

"Pallets of food and water that have just been dropped at selected landing zones in the downtown area of New Orleans. It's an outrage because all of those elements existed before people died for lack of them: There was water, there was food, and there were choppers to drop both. Why no one was able to combine them in an air drop is a cruel and criminal mystery of this dark chapter in our recent history. The words 'failure of imagination' come to mind. The concept of an air drop of supplies was one we apparently introduced to the director of FEMA during a live interview on *Nightly News* on Thursday evening."

—Brian Williams, NBC News Anchor

"We cannot allow it to be said by history that the tdifference between those who lived and those who died in this great storm and flood of 2005 was nothing more than poverty, age, or skin color."

—Rep. Elijah Cummings [D-Md.]

"Where we've utterly failed in our preparedness thinking, actually, is in dealing with catastrophic problems. We're not prepared for a pandemic flu, this avian flu that people have been talking about. We're not prepared for major bioterrorism. And we're certainly, as we've just seen, not prepared for a major natural disaster. And it's in a way, the cover's been ripped back. And we're seeing what's underneath it. And there's not much there."

—Dr. Irwin Redlener, National Center for Disaster Preparedness

DEVOLUTION... THE UNCHALLENGED THEORY

"What inevitably happens is that the post-disaster environment is a window into the inequalities of the power structures in place before the disaster hit."

—Lawrence Vale, MIT Dept. of Urban Studies and Planning

"The fast and safe evacuation was white, leaving behind poor black people, as if time had stood still between the racial unrest of the sixties and today."

—Germany's Die Tageszeitung

"I am absolutely disgusted. After the tsunami, our people, even the ones who lost everything, wanted to help the others who were suffering. Not a single tourist caught in the tsunami was mugged. Now with all this happening in the U.S., we can easily see where the civilized part of the world's population is."

—Sajeewa Chinthaka, 36, Colombo, Sri Lanka

"It is hot. In most neighborhoods, people haven't seen anyone of any authority. People are angry. They are wandering, in many cases aimlessly. That's what strikes me about this hurricane. While there are some people who are optimistic, there are many more people than I've ever seen before who are getting more hopeless. They don't see any light at the end of the tunnel. Their kids don't have schools. They don't have jobs or houses. They have to restart their lives. I think many people just realize how big this could be. The only silver lining I see is that people in any hurricane now will know they have to get out of town."

—Gary Tuchman in Biloxi, Miss.

DAY 7

Saturday, September 3, 2005

It's 8 a.m. at Louis Armstrong New Orleans International Airport, where the normally bustling airport has been transformed into an enormous field hospital. The sound overhead is deafening, a constant, thunderous clattering as helicopters land and take off about every 15 minutes, ferrying hundreds of evacuees out of the city, and then on to Houston, Dallas, San Antonio, who knows, who cares. As long as they get out of the lost city of New Orleans.

Within a few hours, the helicopters will multiply to eight, nine, ten on the tarmac, a couple more in the air. Approximately 4,000 people huddle on luggage carousels or lie on the floor, with more arriving all the time. The most critically injured are destined for immediate care and triage on the second floor. Others, simply exhausted or less injured, are camped out in the hallways, in many cases with their small children, as they wait to figure out what their next step will be. Some clutch a dog or a pet that they've managed to hang onto throughout the past week. Many have waited for days to get here, and have nothing to go back to. But they are lucky to get out.

One day after the National Guard finally arrives in force to begin mass evacuations, the city is still full of thousands of stranded people, many still awaiting rescue in

Jarmar Johnson holds his daughter, Derrial Thomas, after arriving at San Diego's Lindbergh International Airport from a shelter in Baton Rouge, La.

their homes, on roofs, in churches, and in shelters. New Orleans is far from out of the woods, but now there's a feeling in the city that the troops and supplies won't vanish by morning, that someone, somewhere, has finally heard the cries for help. Gov. Blanco expresses her relief about the federal support, but declines President Bush's offer of a federal takeover for Louisiana's National Guard. She hires James Lee Witt, who served as head of FEMA under President Clinton, to help direct relief efforts.

Gerardo Mora/EPA/Landov

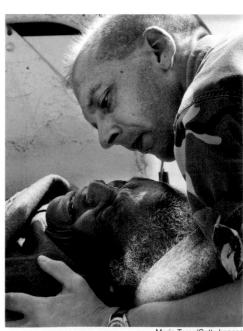

Mario Tama/Getty Images

Close Encounter of the Human Kind
Abraham Verghese, M.D.

With the first busloads of Katrina refugees about to arrive in San Antonio, the call went out for physician volunteers, and I signed up for the 2 a.m. to 8 a.m. shift. On the way, riding down dark, deserted streets, I thought of driving in for night shifts in the I.C.U. as an intern many years ago, and how I would try to steel myself, as if putting on armor.

Within a massive structure at Kelly U.S.A. (formerly Kelly Air Force Base), a brightly lighted processing area led to office cubicles, where after registering, new arrivals with medical needs came to see us. My first patient sat before me, haggard, pointing to what ailed her, as if speech no longer served her. I peeled her shoes from swollen feet, trying not to remove skin in the process. Cuts from submerged objects and immersion in standing water had caused the swelling, as well as infection of both feet. An antibiotic, a pair of slip-ons from the roomful of donated clothing, and a night with her feet elevated—that would help.

The ailments common among the refugees included diarrhea, bronchitis, sore throat, and voices hoarse or lost. And stress beyond belief. People didn't have their medications, and blood sugars and blood pressures were out of control.

I prayed, as I wrote prescriptions, that their memories of particular pills were accurate. For a man on methadone maintenance who was now cramping and sweating, I prescribed codeine to hold him. Another man, clutching a gym bag as if I might snatch it from him, admitted when I gently probed that he was hearing voices again. We sat together looking through the *Physicians' Desk Reference.* "That's it," he said, recognizing the pill he hadn't taken since the storm hit.

Hesitantly, I asked each patient, "Where did you spend the last five days?" I wanted to reconcile the person in front of me with the terrible locales on television. But as the night wore on, I understood that they needed me to ask; to not ask was to not honor their ordeal. Hard men wiped at their eyes and became animated in the telling. The first woman, the one who seemed mute from stress, began a recitation in a courtroom voice, as if preparing for future testimony.

It reminded me of my previous work in field clinics in India and Ethiopia, where, with so few medical re-sources at hand, the careful listening, the thorough exam, the laying of hands was the therapy. And I felt the same helplessness, knowing that the illness here was inextricably linked to the bigger problem of homelessness, disenfranchisement, and despair.

Near the end of my shift, a new group of patients arrived. A man in his 70's with gray hair and beard came in looking fit and vigorous. One eye was milky white and sightless, but the glint in his good eye was enough for two. His worldly belongings were in a garbage bag, but his manner was dignified.

He was out of medicine, and his blood sugar and blood pressure were high. He couldn't pay for his medication, so his doctor always gave him samples: "Whatever he have. Whatever he have." He had kept his shoes on for five days, he said, removing the battered, pickled but elegant pair, a cross between bowling shoes and dancing shoes. His toes were carved ebony, the tendons on the back like cables, the joints gnarled but sturdy. All night I had seen many feet; in his bare feet I read resilience.

He told me that for two nights after the floods, he had perched on a ledge so narrow that his legs dangled in the water. At one point, he said, he saw Air Force One fly over, and his hopes soared. "I waited, I waited," he said, but no help came. Finally a boat got him to a packed bridge. There, again, he waited. He shook his head in disbelief, smiling though. "Doc, they treat refugees in other countries better than they treated us."

"I'm so sorry," I said. "So sorry."

He looked at me long and hard, cocking his head as if weighing my words, which sounded so weak, so inadequate. He rose, holding out his hand, his posture firm as he shouldered his garbage bag. "Thank you, Doc. I needed to hear that. All they got to say is sorry. All they got to say is sorry."

I was still troubled by him when I left, even though he seemed the hardiest of all. This encounter between two Americans, between doctor and patient, had been carried to all the fullness that was permitted, and yet it was incomplete, as if he had, as a result of this experience, set in place some new barriers that neither I nor anyone else would ever cross.

Driving home, I remembered my own metaphor of strapping on armor for the night shift. The years have shown that there is no armor. There never was. The willingness to be wounded may be all we have to offer.

—*New York Times Magazine,* "Lives"

Far left–A Hurricane Katrina victim is taken onboard a helicopter, being evacuated to Texas from New Orleans International Airport.

Left–U.S. Air Force Maj. Francis Schlosser treats a victim of Hurricane Katrina on the tarmac before she is airlifted by the U.S. military out of New Orleans International Airport.

Estimates of between 2,000 and 5,000 people remain at the Superdome this morning—buses have stopped rolling once more, and no one can explain why. Despite airlifts of the neediest, the Convention Center still holds 25,000 and is indistinguishable from a Third World refugee camp—a building that has been the bedroom, bathroom, living room, and kitchen for far too many people for far too long. However, food is plentiful, and they can have as much of it, and water, as they want. They can move around safely. Many are camped along the streets. Although Tulane University Hospitals have been emptied, Charity Hospital remains unevacuated, its 200 or more patients and doctors without power, food, or water.

Miles O'Brien: *"It is an overwhelming scene . . . a city holding on by a thread. People hungry and thirsty. And a president vowing to make it right. All this amid growing criticism of the federal response to the disaster and a new dimension to that criticism—a blatant charge of racism."*

During a telethon on Friday evening to raise money for victims of Hurricane Katrina, rapper Kanye West had this to say about what was going on in New Orleans: "We already realize a lot of the people that could help are at war right now fighting another way. And they've given them permission to go down and shoot us. George Bush doesn't care about black people. I hate the way they portray us in the media. You see a black family, it says they're looting. You see a white family, it says they're looking for food." The unscripted rant had network officials scrambling to distance themselves from his remarks. The West Coast feed of the show omitted West's remarks while the East Coast carried them. The question of whether race played a part in the federal response to the crisis in New Orleans continues to be equally as divided.

Soledad O'Brien: *"This is a picture we'll show you right here of the Associated Press. And this shows a black man. And the caption underneath it says this: 'A young man walks through chest deep floodwater after looting a grocery store in New Orleans on Tuesday.'"*

"And then you have this picture. This was from the AFP media organization. And it says this—shows two white people. 'Two residents wade through chest-deep water after finding bread and soda from a local grocery store after Hurricane Katrina came through the area in New Orleans.'"

Jonathan Alter: *Newsweek* columnist (Between the Lines) *"Some wealthier refugees are saying privately that they've all but given up on the place. The pictures of looting seemed to burst a psychic dam inside them. Invest in this? Pay more taxes for them? That's a recipe for white flight—overnight. On the other side are blacks—well over half the city's population—who are fed up with a power structure that could not keep them alive, much less house and educate them. Whites and blacks in New Orleans were swimming in a fetid swamp of racial tensions long before Katrina showed up. . . ."*

—from "How to Save New Orleans"

Dr. Sanjay Gupta at Charity Hospital, one of the largest hospitals for the poor in New Orleans

GUPTA: Any hospital would have a difficult time in a disaster like this one, even one with the name Charity. At New Orleans' largest public hospital, the goal of the staff today—that nobody dies.

DR. BEN DEBOISBLANC, CHARITY HOSPITAL: We are their only hope and we are trying as hard as we can to get them some help.

GUPTA: What's going to happen to some of these patients if you don't get out them out of here?

DEBOISBLANC: Two of them have already died here on this ramp waiting to get out, in this very spot.

GUPTA (voice-over): There's no electricity, no water, no food, but more than 200 patients. And it's been this way for days.

So this is what Charity Hospital looks like in the middle of a natural disaster. We are in downtown New Orleans. This is actually an auditorium that we're standing in now. At one time, it held up to 40 patients all around this place. Several patients still remain here, as well.

DR. KIERSTA KURTZ-BURKE: We are at the point where it's developing-nation medicine, probably without the power, without light.

UNIDENTIFIED MALE: It's like a Third World country. We know the risks and we're just doing the best we can.

GUPTA (voice-over): But this is the United States. Tuesday, the governor said this place would be evacuated. Three days later, we watch as medical personnel of Tulane, right across the street, were picked up by helicopters, while Charity's patients, some on ventilators being worked by hand pumps, waited in this parking garage. Last night, this hospital had a good night because nobody died. Fortunate because the morgue, which is in the basement, is flooded. The dead have to wait in the stairwell.

GUPTA: At the hospital named Charity, it takes good doctors, quick thinking, and a lot of faith.

More than 153,000 Katrina victims have reached Texas, where officials continue to find room for the endless stream of dazed evacuees. The Astrodome and the surrounding evacuation buildings, now filled, have been given their own zip code to enable residents to get

Evacuees of Hurricane Katrina, Isaac Williams, 16 months old, and his sister, Ikea Williams, two weeks old, sleep on the floor and seats of the Astrodome.

David Portnoy/Getty Images

mail, which may be delivered as soon as tomorrow. Authorities have yet to figure out how to get evacuees' mail from New Orleans to Houston, but are now filing change-of-address forms.

In New Orleans, the Army Corps of Engineers have brought in pumps and generators from all around the nation to begin pumping out the city, as well as generators to run the city's drainage pumps. The latest estimate on how long it will take to drain the city dry is 80 days. Fires continue to burn in New Orleans, in particular a very large warehouse on the waterfront just northeast of downtown, in the same vicinity as the chemical warehouse fire that continues to smolder today. Hydrants are dry, stressed to capacity.

In Biloxi, 300 Air Force servicemen are heading home from Iraq to help families clean up, as well as an additional hundred from Keesler Air Force Base. Mississippi's worst problems is a fuel shortage—no diesel to run generators, and still no power throughout the area—which has been hindering the cleanup and recovery. Removal of the dead has turned out to take longer than residents would like. Casinos the size of ocean liners lay belly up, a half-mile inland, graphically representing the loss of the state's "economic engine." In Alabama, federal emergency officials have agreed to open up closed dormitories at Fort McClellan for evacuees. Secretary of State Condoleezza Rice says she'll visit her home state tomorrow to get a first-hand look at all of the damage.

Chris Huntington: *"We spoke to some folks just up the street here who, frankly, showed us a deceased neighbor who was wedged under a porch. And they had been told that only a local coroner could actually remove the body, even though emergency officials had identified the location and had marked it as such. The removal of that body is up to the local coroner, and, as you can imagine, the coroner here in Biloxi is overwhelmed. They described at one point finding 25 bodies washed up in an area not far from here."*

Pat D'Amuro, CNN security analyst: *"I think the response was way too slow. National Guard and the*

Reserve should have been in there moments after the storm subsided to start helping people that needed assistance evacuating, to try to restore power, to bring in food and water supplies for the people that couldn't get out, and to make sure that we didn't see the type of situation with the looting and the crimes taking place. You can't do all those other things if you don't have the security and law enforcement pieces in place to make sure you can evacuate people and offer all those other services."

As the White House continues to project the image of an aggressive, unified federal response following blistering criticism that its relief efforts have been too little, too uncoordinated, and too late, President Bush delivers a live radio address from the Rose Garden. At the end of his speech, the president ignores a reporter who asks, "Mr. President, why did you take so long. . . ?" Sen. Mary Landrieu's Web site takes the president to task for the removal of much-needed construction equipment from the site of Bush's photo op, the morning after he'd toured the broken levee by helicopter.

Hugh Hewett (nationally syndicated radio talk show host): *"There are many failures to be investigated in the aftermath of Katrina, including why the evacuation left as many as 100,000 in the city, why the prepositioning of law enforcement and National Guard in the Dome and Convention Center was inadequate, why relief supplies from the Red Cross and Salvation Army were blocked, and why FEMA seemed so slow to take control from the locals obviously overwhelmed by the size of the storm and its devastation."*

"Yesterday, I was hoping President Bush would come away from his tour of the regional devastation triggered by Hurricane Katrina with a new understanding for the magnitude of the suffering and for the abject failures of the current Federal Emergency Management Agency. Twenty-four hours later, the president has yet to answer my call for a Cabinet-level official to lead our efforts. Meanwhile, FEMA, now a shell of what it once was, continues to be overwhelmed by the task at hand.

"I understand that the U.S. Forest Service had water-tanker aircraft available to help douse the fires raging on our riverfront, but FEMA has yet to accept the aid. When Amtrak offered trains to evacuate significant numbers of victims—far more efficiently than buses—FEMA again dragged its feet. Offers of medicine, communications equipment, and other desperately needed items continue to flow in, only to be ignored by the agency.

"But perhaps the greatest disappointment stands at the breached 17th Street levee. Touring this critical site yesterday with the president, I saw what I believed to be a real and significant effort to get a handle on a major cause of this catastrophe. Flying over this critical spot again this morning, less than 24 hours later, it became apparent that yesterday we witnessed a hastily prepared stage set for a presidential photo opportunity, and the desperately needed resources we saw were this morning reduced to a single, lonely piece of equipment. The good and decent people of southeast Louisiana and the Gulf Coast—black and white, rich and poor, young and old—deserve far better from their national government. Mr. President, I'm imploring you once again to get a Cabinet-level official stood up as soon as possible to get this entire operation moving forward regionwide with all the resources—military and otherwise—necessary to relieve the unmitigated suffering and economic damage that is unfolding."

Highlights from President Bush's speech:

One of our great cities is submerged. The human costs are incalculable.

Right now, there are more than 21,000 National Guard troops operating in Louisiana and Mississippi, and more are on the way. More than 13,000 of these troops are in Louisiana.

In addition to these National Guard forces, the Department of Defense has deployed more than 4,000 active-duty forces to assist in search and recovery and provide logistical and medical support.

Hour by hour, the situation on the ground is improving, yet the enormity of the task requires more resources and more troops. Today, I ordered the Department of Defense to deploy additional active-duty forces to the region.

Over the next 24 to 72 hours, more than 7,000 additional troops from the 82nd Airborne, from the 1st Cavalry, the 1st Marine Expeditionary Force, and the 2nd Marine Expeditionary Force will arrive in the affected areas.

Our priorities are clear: We will complete the evacuation as quickly and safely as possible. We will not let criminals prey on the vulnerable. And we will not allow bureaucracy to get in the way of saving lives.

Where our response is not working, we'll make it right. Where our response is working, we will duplicate it.

The emergency along the Gulf Coast is ongoing. There's still a lot of difficult work ahead. All Americans can be

certain our nation has the character, the resources, and the resolve to overcome this disaster.

We will comfort and care for the victims. We will restore the towns and neighborhoods that have been lost in Louisiana, Mississippi, and Alabama. We'll rebuild the great city of New Orleans.

Not long after the president's speech is broadcast, the dramatic story of Charity Hospital is finally ending: Five long days after Katrina hit, all patients are finally evacuated. And at the Louisiana State Hospital, 29 newborn babies have been rescued, most of them motherless, some born prematurely. All are thriving thanks to the heroism of the doctors and nurses who cared for them under the worst of conditions—proof of the spirit of these tiniest of Katrina survivors.

Thousands of e-mails begin filtering in to news desks from coast to coast as survivors post photos of missing loved ones, hoping to be reconnected. Blogs, the new power of the Internet, chronicle the "Every Man's" experience during the hurricane. Message boards spring up every few minutes. Every Internet site has a "Missing Persons" and an "I'm Okay" listing.

CNN airs photos of victims and gives out names, locations, and numbers to call to help people find each other. They also have a Web site for hurricane victims where people can register and let their loved ones know they're alive, and where they are. By 5 p.m., more than 15,000 e-mails are logged to their Victims and Relief Desk. In Biloxi, the *Sun Herald* launches a blog, EyesOnKatrina.blogspot.com, where survivors can post up-to-the-minute news of their whereabouts and safety.

People who have been stranded at New Orleans Convention Center for days line up to be transported by helicopter to the airport and on to shelters or refuge elsewhere.

Panoramic Composite by Travis Fox/washingtonpost.com

INTERVIEW

Miles O'Brien

John Breaux,
Former Louisiana
Senator (D)

O'BRIEN: The whole thing just breaks your heart, doesn't it?

BREAUX: Yes, it's really sickening. I mean, I think it's not getting worse. It's now getting better and that's the good news. There's still so much to be done. I noted that just yesterday the USS *Comfort* you know, the hospital ship just left Baltimore yesterday.

O'BRIEN: Why? Why just yesterday?

BREAUX: They're supposed to get to New Orleans on Thursday. There's not going to be anybody left in New Orleans on Thursday. Everybody who will be sick hopefully will be evacuated to Baton Rouge, Lafayette, Houston, or other parts of the country.

O'BRIEN: I don't understand why it takes so long.

BREAUX: Well, I mean, that's the $64,000 question. I think it's going to have to be a lot of soul searching. There's going to have to be a lot of calm review about what went right and what went wrong. I mean, this is five days after the hurricane before food and supplies were being brought to the city. That's not good. That's not good for the United States of America.

O'BRIEN: Let me ask you this, Senator, just walk with me down this road here. In theory, federal troops can only be brought in if the governor asks for them because federal troops have a very specific role in the way our democracy is formed. But federal troops also have a responsibility for national security. And this is a storm that has all kinds of national security implications. Shouldn't it be almost automatic that in a case like this Northern Command should just take charge?

BREAUX: The short answer is yes. The hurricane hit. New Orleans was not hit as hard by the hurricane winds as perhaps the Mississippi coast, but as soon as those levees broke, anyone could have predicted that this was going to be a national catastrophe. This is not a surprise. We have studied this for years. Academics have written papers and volumes about what would happen when a hurricane of this magnitude hits New Orleans. It was going to be under 25 feet of water. I mean that was obvious on Tuesday.

O'BRIEN: You know, here's the thing, though. This is what bothers people. It's the bureaucracy of it all. You have a governor in Louisiana who didn't even ask for the federal troops until Wednesday and you have the military saying we would have dropped food right away but FEMA didn't ask us. There's got to be a way to cut through that red tape.

BREAUX: Somebody has to say look, we're sending food. We're sending troops. We're sending boats. We're sending helicopters because we can see that it's a big disaster. I had an example of an ambulance, American Ambulance Association said, look, we have 300 ambulances three days ago they wanted to send down there from a Florida area. They said, well, we were told we had to have GSA's permission. GSA said they had to have FEMA ask for it. As a result they weren't sent.

O'BRIEN: Let me ask you this, though. Let's flip this around for a moment. This is kind of turning in, I'm seeing shreds of this on the Web and on the blogs, of this being the allegation is that Democrats are using this as a political issue. What do you say to that?

BREAUX: I've heard the racial implications. I would categorically reject that. Our good Mayor Ray Nagin is African-American and almost all the city council is African-American. The sheriff is African-American. The areas south of New Orleans, Plaquemine, and St. Bernard Parishes, are predominantly white and the rescue efforts down there were certainly no faster. If anything, they were slower down there.

O'BRIEN: I'm talking also, though, about Democrats using this to make political hay with elections upcoming. In their own way, that's reprehensible too, isn't it?

BREAUX: That is totally reprehensible. There will be time to find out what went right and what went wrong. But I think it's not the time to start talking about political implications. I'm a Democrat. I would heartily reject that. People are trying as hard as they can to get it done. Should it have been done sooner? Absolutely, no question about it. But there will be a lot of time for soul searching later on.

O'BRIEN: Let's get real here for a moment because the people I've talked to who are evacuees, I haven't met a single one who says they're going back to New Orleans. They're moving on. Can New Orleans truly come back?

BREAUX: Absolutely. The spirit of New Orleans is more than buildings and you know and highways. The spirit of New Orleans is the people, the culture, the history. People will come back for that. I can understand them saying there's nothing to come back to now but New Orleans will rise again because as a culture and a spirit which will demand it and it will happen.

Don Hammack, *Biloxi Sun Herald* **staff writer, talking about the Web site EyesOnKatrina.blogspot.com:** *"A lot of the stories we're getting are from outsiders who are, you know, past residents who have family down here, are really worried, and really some incredibly moving pieces, you know, worried about their husbands, or sons, or daughters, or in-laws. And just people kind of dumping their guts out for everybody to see, because they don't have anything else they can do. It's just a way to kind of, you know, cope with what's going on, because it's bad for a lot of people here. It's bad for a lot of people all over the place who don't know, you know, what's going on down here. The communications are just a disaster. And nobody knows, you know, who is where. And we just got to kind of gut it out until we get past it."*

His agency under fire for causing much of the delayed reactions to New Orleans' distress, Homeland Security Secretary Michael Chertoff assures the public that his attitude is anything but bureaucratic. He promises that "the United States, as the president has said, is going to move heaven and earth to rescue, feed, shelter, and restore the life and health of the people who are currently suffering." As FEMA scrambles to restate their priorities, Chertoff assures the public that efforts now are going to "break the mold" of anything done before. Defense Secretary Donald Rumsfeld announces a tour of Mississippi and Louisiana for Sunday, and President Bush plans a return trip Monday. Chertoff holds a two-hour meeting with members of the Congressional Black Caucus to discuss the roles of race and poverty in the federal government's hurricane relief efforts.

**Excerpts from press conference, 1: 30 p.m.
Michael Chertoff, secretary homeland security**

"I want to just say that words cannot describe what one witnesses with one's own eyes when you actually see the devastation caused by Mother Nature, a Mother Nature that has been anything but maternal. I can tell you that not an hour goes by that we don't spend a lot of time thinking about the people who are actively suffering in all of these parts of the Gulf. There are people on rooftops. There are still people emerging as the water begins to recede, looking for help, looking for rescue. There are people who have been sweltering in shelters, waiting for food and water.

"The United States, as the president has said, is going to move heaven and earth to rescue, feed, shelter, and restore the life and health of the people who are currently suffering. We are throwing all of the capabilities and assets of the United States into this effort. This is a daunting challenge. I guess I would say this is probably the worst catastrophe or set of catastrophes certainly that I'm aware of in the history of the country, a devastating hurricane followed by a second devastating flood.

"In this case, I will tell that you the way these catastrophes unfolded is unprecedented in anybody's experience. We had two catastrophes: We had a Category 4 hurricane that was followed the next day by really the collapse of a levee, not merely a breach, although we had a number of breaches, but really the demolition of 300 feet of the levee, which essentially turned New Orleans into a lake the day after the hurricane. I can't think of another incident, even the tsunami, which presented this combination of events. It's as if the tsunami, we had to do the rescue while the water was still there in the tsunami.

"There has been a lot of planning for catastrophes. I will tell you that there has been over the last few years some specific planning for the possibility of a significant hurricane in New Orleans with a lot of rainfall, with water rising in the levees and water overflowing the levees. And that is a very catastrophic scenario. . . . But there were two problems here. . . . And I will tell you that really that perfect storm of combination of catastrophes exceeded the foresight of the planners and maybe anybody's foresight.

"In this case, I think we were well-prepared for one catastrophe. I think the second catastrophe, frankly, was a—it added a level of challenge that no one had seen before. But I would have to say, I think that with that, everybody has performed magnificently in stepping up to this increased challenge, reaching out for more assets, improvising additional measures that allows us to deal with what nature has dealt to us.

"Whenever you do a planning process, you have to deal with what is reasonably foreseeable. . . . I think that this major breach, not merely an overflow, but this major breach of the levee, while something itself that might have been anticipated, coming together I think, was outside of the scope of what people I think reasonably foresaw.

"To make matters worse, the storm itself was unusual in its course. It began as a comparatively low-power storm. It crossed Florida. It wasn't until comparatively late, shortly before—a day, maybe a day-and-a-half before landfall that it became clear that this was going to be a Category 4 or 5 hurricane headed for the New Orleans area. In advance of that, recognizing the danger, the president leaned forward and declared states of emergency, which is a very unusual thing, in those states in the Gulf. We began to preposition and move assets as early as possible when we realized that that hurricane was coming in."

Brad Huffines, CNN meteorologist: *"Let me show you what the National Hurricane Center forecasts were. As early as Friday at 5 p.m., the National Hurricane Center Katrina timeline shows that at 5 p.m. Friday, Katrina began being forecast to make landfall as a Category 4 hurricane. And also, the 5 o'clock advisory on Friday, again, that's three days before the hurricane struck, actually about two-and-a-half days, New Orleans was also included in the area of highest strike probability. And so, Tony, that was about two-and-a-half days out. And that's when the hurricane center really began focusing on New Orleans as the landfall, the New Orleans area and a Category 4 hurricane as the strength of this storm.*

And one of the things that they even say themselves, whenever you're looking at storm strength and intensity, that is one of the most hard forecasts, but this one, they said that they had a good idea as to where this one was going fairly early on and had a high confidence two-and-a-half days out."

A flood victim is seen among thousands of people gathered at the New Orleans Convention Center waiting for help.

As more and more eyewitness accounts of conditions in the Convention Center and Superdome surface, it becomes plain that most if not all of those who survived unspeakable days and nights under inhuman conditions were black. Survivors are often bitter and outspoken about their ordeals. Many claim that they were abandoned because they were black and poor, though leaders try to downplay this aspect of New Orleans' post-Katrina experience.

Excerpt from Ed Lavandera Interview with New Orleans survivor Phillip Holt

LAVANDERA: Phillip, what have the last five days been like for you?

HOLT: It's been hell. We have had no power. Water was shut off a few days ago. And then last night, they turned the gas off. Honestly, as I had a friend of mine tell me, the first few days was a natural disaster, the last few days have been manmade disaster. We live in what we call the Sixth Ward. Luckily . . .

LAVANDERA: That's close to the Quarter.

HOLT: Close to the Quarter. And the looting has been horrendous. Every store in our neighborhood has been looted. Last night there was a military helicopter come through. Evidently there was a shooting of some kind, because I heard almost 50 rounds of automatic gunfire go off. But they finally came in today with helicopters and pulled us out. They gave us a choice. They said, "Either you can bring your dogs with you, or you can bring your luggage. And we have—my partner and I have, well, four chihuahuas. We lost one. They let us bring three on the helicopter. They pulled us out by cable. And I just appreciate being here.

LAVANDERA: What happens next?

HOLT: I don't know. I don't know. We're trying to get in touch with family in Tennessee. We have to let them know that we're alive, and we don't know where we'll go from here, because we moved down here a year ago, because we love this city. And my partner's terminally ill. So we came down a year ago because he knew this is the place where he was going to be happy.

Tony Harris Interview with Reverend Joseph Lowery, co-founder of the Southern Christian Leadership Conference

HARRIS: I need your perspective on this. We don't want to shy away from the question of race here at CNN, but we want context and perspective. A lot of folks are asking if the face of this tragedy had been more white than black, might the response have been different? Take it in whatever direction you'd like to.

LOWERY: Well, it's not a simple issue and there's another demon other than race. I don't think anybody can deny that race was a factor, but class was also a factor. Look at the difference between how we rushed to the towers, our symbol of wealth and power, and to the levee, a symbol of poverty and hard-working people. So that in this country, we've got to deal with the demons of race and class. It's interesting that the Commerce Department issues this report on poverty in this country at the same time Katrina came, and poverty is increasing in the country, and we are not as concerned about it. Look at our difference in our response to Rwanda and Iraq. One has oil, the other has no oil so that we have to deal with the issue of class and race, and we must address the issue of poverty in this country, or we're going to see a lot more disasters akin to what's happening in Louisiana, Mississippi.

HARRIS: Is this—can this simply be—and I'm not trying to give a pass to anyone connected with this relief effort, I'm just trying to offer balance here. Can this simply be a situation where this was an overwhelming natural disaster and it just simply took the federal government, the state, the local officials, time to assess the gravity, to catch up, to get up to speed?

LOWERY: Oh, I think that's a factor, it's not—it's too complex an issue to say one thing, it was . . .

HARRIS: To say race. To say . . .

LOWERY: To say just race, or just incompetence. What bothers me a little bit is that—well, not a little bit. Is it FEMA?

HARRIS: Yes.

LOWERY: Our Homeland Security that been rehearsing how to deal with a storm of this severity for two years. What did they learn? Why weren't they ready? All the predictions, it seems to me, pointed to the fact that that levee was in trouble. And Louisiana has been begging for help for the levee for eight to 10 years, so either a lot

of heads ought to roll for incompetence or we have to accept the fact that we have come a long way, but we still have a long, long way to go on the issue of race and the issue of class.

HARRIS: You know, when we get to the core of you, as a man, you are a man of God, Reverend Lowery. When you see these pictures of human suffering, what can you tell us? What has your experience as a pillar of the civil rights movement in this country, what can you tell us to help us through this enormous period of suffering?

LOWERY: Well, I think God never closes one window that he doesn't open another one. And I think while tragic as it is, it does provide an opportunity for us to seize the moment, to recognize that, yes, we were unprepared, because we ignored certain factors that should have been obvious. Yes, we perhaps would have responded differently if it had been the faces of other people. But here's an opportunity to prepare for the future. We're messing with God's creation, and we've got to deal with those factors, those environmental factors that may help precipitate a Katrina, so we've got to live in reverence. We've got to stop being irreverent where creation is concerned and we've got to address the issue of poverty. We cannot—we cannot stick our heads in the sand. And poverty, if you don't—you either pay me now, or you pay me later. And the price later goes up, inflation.

The Great Mississippi River Flood of 1927 left a disastrous impact upon the entire [ten states] 1.25 million mile river drainage . . . The flooding began at Memphis in the fall of 1926 and it was late August of 1927 before the last of the floodwaters flowed into the Gulf below New Orleans. The levee system was decimated with over 120 crevasses and 165 million acres were inundated. There were 246 fatalities and over 600 thousand people were made homeless. The total damage was estimated at $230 million. A major portion of the 600 thousand people made homeless were black tenant farmers which made up the labor force of the agriculture-based Delta. Those refugees were not allowed to leave and were forced to work and live on the levees that year to provide damage control.

—Paul S. Trotter, G. Alan Johnson, Robert Ricks, David R. Smith, National Weather Service Forecasting Office

New Orleans evacuees, who recently arrived by bus, wait in line to be processed for shelter inside the Astrodome.

Along with questions about whether race was a factor in the five-day wait for an effective show of force and aid, now there is curiosity about just exactly what happened in the New Orleans police force, rumored to have lost, in some cases, up to 30 percent of its capacity during the peak violence in the city.

Jamie McIntyre: *"Well, a lot of the police force left. Again, there were about 1,500, about 400 left. Some of them had their homes wiped out. Some of them simply couldn't get to work. But many of them apparently felt like there was such a breakdown in their capability to do their job that they simply left.*

"There's a lot of controversy about this in New Orleans, about why the police didn't stay on the job. But whether it was justifiable or understandable, it nevertheless complicated the military mission, according to the Pentagon. They say that was one of the factors that produced a delay in getting troops in there. They said they had to go in, when they did go in, in substantial numbers, so that they would not face any sort of problem from armed gangs or anything. They feel if they went in in small numbers immediately, there could have been a potential problem to put their own troops at risk."

New Orleans Deputy Police Commander W. S. Riley: *"We expected a lot more support from the federal government. We expected the government to respond within 24 hours. The first three days we had no assistance. We have been fired on with automatic weapons. We still have some thugs around. My biggest disappointment is with the federal government and the National Guard. The guard arrived 48 hours after the hurricane with 40 trucks. They drove their trucks in and went to sleep. For 72 hours this police department and the fire department and a handful of citizens were alone rescuing people. We have people who died while the National Guard sat and played cards. I understand why we are not winning the war in Iraq if this is what we have."*

In many respects, the failure of the federal government to react quickly has brought New Orleans underlying problems to the surface, igniting a bonfire of concerns about poverty, race, and vulnerability of the city's infrastructure. But it has also suggested that the country, despite years of color-coded alerts and reassurances that the war on terror is being fought on foreign soil so that it will not be fought here, is in no way prepared for a terrorist attack.

Help pours in from everyone, everywhere. Foreign aid. Corporate aid. Private citizens, sports stars, celebrities, and state after state, all join in to offer, send, or pledge money and aid. Alabama plans to offer up as many as 20,000 beds within the week. Gov. Phil Bredson signs an executive order to speed up the medical coverage for more than 12,000 Katrina evacuees in Tennessee. California universities offer to take those who can't finish school. Walt Disney donates 10,000 backpacks. Benefit concerts spring up, all the proceeds donated to Katrina victims. The National Next of Kin registry is taking 1,500 names per hour. Feed the Children, Second Harvest, Habitat for Humanity, Mercy Corps—the list is endless of organizations donating food and help to the tri-state areas. Beds, rooms, tools to rebuild, chainsaws, shoes— in a tremendous wave of goodwill and compassion, neighbors are pulling out the stops to help neighbors.

As former President Clinton says tonight, "It's been overwhelming to me that, you know, the American people are never a problem. They're always there when you need them. They're always there and the rich are, the poor are, the middle class are. We're coming forward."

Jonathan Reckford, pastoral leader and CEO of Habitat for Humanity: *"Habitat for Humanity is undertaking a three-tiered approach to helping recover from Hurricane Katrina. While we're not a first-order relief organization, we hope to be instrumental in helping families after the initial recovery is started get back into homes. And we're calling it Operation Home Delivery. The first part is to help local affiliates get back on their feet. As you can imagine many homes have been*

Volunteer Linda Ledford from Fletcher, Okla., sorts clothing at Falls Creek Baptist Camp outside of Davis, Okla. Volunteers are preparing for an influx of Hurricane Katrina refugees who will be arriving at the camp.

AP Photo/*The Oklahoman*/Paul Hellstern

Top–Members of a search-and-rescue team prepare to search for victims and survivors in Biloxi, Miss.
Bottom–A convoy of Wal-Mart trucks with supplies is guarded by police as they wait to enter the battered city of New Orleans near Raceland, some 30 miles west of New Orleans.

damaged or destroyed and our affiliates have lost their offices, construction facilities, tools, and vehicles. And their staff have suffered personal losses as well.

"So our first order is to get them going so that they're in a position to serve all of the families and partners down there. At the same time we want to be a catalyst, pulling together corporate partners, churches, other not-for-profits, and local governments to build a coalition around low-income housing and recovery on a scale that we could never do all by ourselves. And finally the centerpiece of Habitat's effort is something we're calling, 'A Home in a Box Project.' And this is the boldest part of our plan and what we want to do is assemble materials and pre-build homes in communities all around the country. And then we're going to disassemble these homes, put them on containers and as soon as the infrastructure is in place ship them down to the Gulf areas that have been most affected. And this way we can build many more houses

far more quickly and most importantly get families in those homes as quickly as possible.

"So what we're asking people to do is first donate money to help because we're committed to repair and build as many homes—hopefully in the thousands—as we can fund. And then at the same time people can go to www. habitat.org and find ways first to donate. And then second we hope to get personally involved, to lift a hammer and become part of the process."

The Story of Three Duke University Students Who Just Did It

AARON BROWN: I don't know how many stories there are like the one we're about to tell. This is the story of three young men, college students at Duke University who, while watching us late last week, decided to get in a car, drive to New Orleans, and save a life or two, ending up loading relief supplies at a TV station. And in doing so, they were generous and ingenious and energetic and a little larcenous. They left behind good deeds and brought back some wisdom. We talked with Sonny Byrd, Hans Buder, and David Hankla late today. [left to right in photo]

Millions—literally millions of people, tens of millions of people— were sitting around the other day watching all of this play out. What is it about you or the three of you that made you think, you know what, let's go there and do something?

KATRINA'S HEROES   NEWSNIGHT

HANS BUDER: You know, I've always criticized myself for dreaming big, but not having the initiative to go through with it. And just this one time I decided I'm not going to be an armchair humanitarian. So I just talked to Sonny and Hankla and we went down.

BROWN: And, Sonny, when he turned to you and said, let's go there, did you think for a second, that's crazy?

SONNY BYRD: That did cross my mind, but the first thing that left my mouth was I'll be there in five minutes.

BROWN: David, you're on the road now, you're heading toward the great unknown, and I suppose to some extent, a great adventure. Did it feel like you were off on a great adventure?

DAVID HANKLA: It wasn't so much a great adventure as a great opportunity. Everything that we can do and everything that's available for us to do to really help people, we need to do that.

BROWN: Did you have any idea, not so much what you'd find, because you'd seen pictures of it, so you had some idea what you'd find. Did you have any idea of what you'd do?

HANKLA: We'd hoped to do basically what—exactly what we did.

BUDER: What we did. That was our plan. We got to the Convention Center.

HANKLA: Exactly. Our goal was to get to the Convention Center, where no one else seemed to be going, and find a way to get people out. Just get our way into the heart of the city and find people who need help and find a way to help them.

BROWN: Hans, let's talk a little bit about getting to the Convention Center itself. Actually, driving there wasn't the hard part. I guess getting past the security along the way was. Whose idea it was to steal the press passes?

BUDER: This was Sonny Byrd. We actually took a business card, an AP pass and also a television shirt with the embroidery from the station. And we scanned in the business card and the press passes and changed the names to our names. And we went past the military blockade, just waved, and didn't even roll down the windows, and they let us through.

> **"Our goal was to get to the Convention Center, where no one else seems to be going, and find a way to get people out."**

HANKLA: It was unbelievable. Literally, like, we're sitting there, working at the station, and we were just like, I really wish there was some way to get past. And Sonny was like, yes. Seems like a lot of press people seem to be going. I was like, I wish we had a pass. And Sonny just kind of paused, walked out of the room, came back a couple of minutes later and said now we do. What can we do with these?

BROWN: All right. You get to the Convention Center and, in truth, things are better than they had been the day before. But they're hardly pleasant. Sonny, what did you see? What do you remember? How did it feel?

BYRD: The first thing, we were extremely surprised when we came upon the building, because we really didn't think we would be able to drive right up to it, but we were able to do that. And there were military helicopters flying through the sky, there were National

Guardsmen and women all over the place with guns and military supplies. And just the entire Convention Center was trashed. It was just a disaster. And we walked up to it, and we walked right inside. And there was just the impression that we got, the smell was overwhelming, there was feces and urine everywhere, and it was just an absolute nightmare.

BUDER: We saw a kid on the corner who had a sign that said "NEED FOOD AND WATER." One gentleman had been stranded in a tree when the flood waters came up, he didn't know how to swim, so he was trapped in the tree, and fire ants devastated his face, welts on his face, all over his body. Took him out and three women the first trip and then we came back the next morning at first light.

BYRD: When we were leaving New Orleans, the ladies in the backseat were jubilant when they saw street lights. And we passed a dumpy little strip mall and they were just like, "Oh my God, look at this, look where we are." They were crying. They said at last we're free, God almighty we're free. And we were just leaving the city, you know?

BROWN: Where did you take them when you took them?

BUDER: We took them to Baton Rouge to reunite with family, and eventually to get them on buses to Texas.

HANKLA: If we'd had another day to run people in and out, we probably could have gotten appreciably more people. I mean—

BUDER: A hundred.

HANKLA: Yes. We could have just gone in and out, in and out all day. I mean, we found places to get gas. It really was not that big of a—it wasn't that hard once we actually got in there and had a plan in action.

BROWN: Are you shocked that it was—I don't want to say it was easy, you guys went to a fair amount to do it—but it wasn't swimming across the ocean either. But it was no harder to do what you did. There were so many people who needed to be moved that weren't moved.

BUDER: Yes, shocked.

HANKLA: Extremely, extremely shocked.

BUDER: The overarching question that we had was, how did we get in there, we've never been to New Orleans before, how did we get in there where these people have been stranded for four, five days with no food and water, living in a lawless anarchy environment, how do we get in there in 20 minutes in a Hyundai Elantra? And why did they not get out four days before that?

HANKLA: Why couldn't anyone else allegedly get in when we could, with such relative facility. I mean, once we were past the National Guard, it literally, it was a direct drive.

BUDER: We saw 150 empty buses driving the other way on I-10 as we were going into the city.

HANKLA: As we were driving in, bus after bus after bus that was completely empty, no people they were evacuating, driving away from the city or parked roadside.

> **"A lot of people, including the people at the Convention Center, they weren't trapped by hurricane damage, they were trapped by red tape. And if we could drive right in there in 20 minutes, there's no reason why help couldn't have gotten to them sooner."**

BYRD: A lot of people, including the people at the Convention Center, they weren't trapped by hurricane damage, they were trapped by red tape. And if we could drive right in there in 20 minutes, there's no reason why help couldn't have gotten to them sooner.

BROWN: Well, we're lucky to talk to you and we're pleased at what you did. Don't be so hard on yourself. You went out and did a great thing. Good for you.

BYRD: Thank you, Mr. Brown. Thanks very much.

BROWN: Nicely done, guys.

BROWN: So imagine getting a call from your kid saying, I want to go to New Orleans and help. Hope you'd say yes. Hope I'd say yes.

Note: Actual interview took place on Tuesday, Sept. 6th

DAY 8

Sunday, September 4, 2005

> "The spirit of death has been over this city for seven days, and it's got to go. Okay?"
>
> —*New Orleans Mayor Ray Nagin*

Although gospel songs and voices raised to the heavens accompanied the final evacuation of the Convention Center yesterday, on this Sunday morning the city is quiet. After six days of chaos, an eerie silence overtakes the city. Half of it lies beneath lakes of deceptively tranquil water. Labor Day weekend, usually a time of celebration and bustling tourist activity, passes unacknowledged. New Orleans is a ghost town. But it is far from empty.

The National Guard's presence has streamlined evacuations, clearing 30,000 out of the Superdome and another 20,000 from the Convention Center, but there are still an estimated 40,000–50,000 people remaining in the city. Stragglers, hundreds of them, continue to show up at the Superdome, hoping to get a ride out of town on the next buses. About 200,000 evacuees have arrived in Texas, where the governor says his state's hands are just about full. The thousands at the New Orleans airport have disappeared as well, and only a few dozen remain.

But the rescues continue, and police, soldiers, game wardens, and other volunteers meet with resistance— even gunfire—as they discover that many still hidden away in the flooded houses have no intention of leaving. The Coast Guard, boating into the St. Bernard and Plaquemines parishes, finds people in attics and on second floors who are utterly exhausted, having endured without food and water for days. Despite their ordeals, and isolated by stinking, mosquito-infested waters, these holdouts are unwilling to be taken to unknown destinations, unwilling to leave their money, belongings, and pets behind.

Despite much-touted "boots on the ground," the take-charge personality of Lt. Gen. Russel Honore, and countless official promises of food, water, blankets, cots, meals, aid, and more aid, everything is still moving in slow motion to thousands of desperately tired, frightened, and ill people. But they're not too tired, too frightened, or too ill to take it lying down that they waited six days for help. People on the streets—some wandering aimlessly, some emerging from their hideouts to finally give themselves up—voice their disgust with sluggish federal help.

Monroe Hodgkins, survivor: "*To be the richest country in the world, this is a disgrace. How can you take care of other countries when you cannot take care of home? Is this racist? Is this a racist statement that you're making? Come on, take care of us. We need you. Our people have fought, have died, have built this country.*"

Napoleon Avenue remains flooded in the historic New Orleans Garden District.

A rescuer from Houma, La., uses his boat to tow another boat loaded with three dead bodies down Read Blvd.

Biohazard is what authorities are calling the indescribably filthy Superdome and Convention Center, where the stench of rotting garbage, waste, and dead bodies can be smelled for blocks. The same fetid bouquet rises up from the city streets; the floodwater, which is black and smells like bad fish, is still in some places from eight to 10 feet deep. A rough estimate has come in for the cleanup of the city: about $100 billion.

Chirs Granger/*Times-Picayune*/NNS /Landov

Peter Berkowitz, stranded tourist: "*It's a disgrace. It was a disgrace to treat people the way they were treated. They were treated like animals. You'd walk down the street with nothing, each day being told there's buses coming and nothing happening, no food, no anything. It was a disgrace to see 20,000–30,000 people lined up there, waiting for buses, waiting for food, waiting for anything, with nothing and everybody here is calling them looters and calling them this and calling them that when they were trying to survive like everybody else, like we were. Yes, I am furious. It's an absolute disgrace.*"

Refrigerated trucks are rolling in, soon to begin the horrific job of what is politely termed "processing" the dead. Bodies are everywhere: floating in canals, slumped in wheelchairs, abandoned on highways and medians, and hidden in attics. For days, they have been bloating in the sun, hidden in closed-up houses, trapped beneath debris, decomposing, even preyed on by rats and starving animals. Records—dental, hospital, DNA, all forms of identification—may possibly be destroyed.

Panoramic composite by Travis Fox/washingtonpost.com

Search-and-rescue teams use boats and helicopters during operations in the aftermath of Hurricane Katrina in New Orleans.
REUTERS/David J. Phillip/Pool /Landov

BUISSON: Well, actually, I grew up here and that was part of the reason for us deciding to come back. The fellas from Lake Charles, a bunch of Cajun boys with flat bottom boats who like to hunt and fish, just rallied and decided to come over. . . . In fact, three of our guys went out with the SWAT team on Wednesday night because the SWAT guys had lost one of their fellas. They took the boats out, helped them to recover them, but we are out of supplies. We took off about two in the morning, got home about six. We regrouped and came back yesterday.

O'BRIEN: I think even just some military walking around and kind of giving a sense that control is back in the city as we hoped. But, still, you're from here. How strange is it to see?

BUISSON: Oh, it's very surreal. We were in areas of town that used to be the nice uptown areas of New Orleans yesterday. Carrollton Avenue, in six feet of water, and it's disheartening to me. I love this city. I grew up here and haven't lived here in quite some time, but we always come back. But I'm telling you, it's encouraging. I wish you could see the volunteers and the folks from all over the country who have driven in here, slept in their cars.

Excerpt from Soledad O'Brien Interview with Andy Buisson, civilian and volunteer rescuer . . . "A Cajun Boy From Lake Charles With a Flat Bottom Boat"

O'BRIEN: How many people do you have?

BUISSON: We got 17 boats and 36 volunteers, all come from a construction company in Lake Charles, La. . . . I think we probably pulled out about 1,000 people from the eastern area of New Orleans [on Wednesday]. We're going back today because we left some and told them we'd come back.

O'BRIEN: What was it like to see someone who is clearly begging for help and saying, 'Don't just take my friend, take me, too?'

BUISSON: We didn't have to make those decisions. Unfortunately, the last few, there were some who had just had surgery, and we were intent on getting them proper care. We didn't want to hurt them getting them out, because we were [going to be] bringing them down into a dark stairwell with about four feet of water and then putting them into the boat. We actually brought the boat up into their dining room—what used to be their dining room—and we just didn't think we could safely do it. We're not trained EMTs or ambulance guys. So we wanted to get them proper medical removal, and we're hoping we can do that today.

O'BRIEN: You're a local person. What was it like to know that you had to step in when the police could not do the job because the violence in the city had gotten so bad?

As they have been for days, Army engineers are laboring to plug the breaches in the levees, saying it will take anywhere from 36 to 80 days from the time they start the pumps until the water will be gone from city streets. Black Hawk helicopters roar overhead, picking up 3,000 lb. sandbags and dropping them into the 500-foot breach in the 17th Street Canal levee. The Corps has built a rock road to the gap, then piled rock aggregate into the breach. Workers maneuver a backhoe to the site by hauling it on a floating bridge by pulling on cables. By 6 p.m., all that will remain to be sealed is a 20-foot gap.

In eastern New Orleans, 24 pumps are draining 700 cubic feet of water per second. In St. Bernard Parish, water is being drained through breaches in the levee. In Plaquemines Parish, the Corps is "notching" levees with gaps up to 100-feet wide so that water can flow back into the Gulf. The notches will be plugged with rocks after the area is drained.

VERA'S STORY

At the edge of the Garden District, on the corner of Jackson Avenue and Magazine Street, a woman's body remains lying in the same place it has been since at least Wednesday. Pointing to it is a spray-painted arrow, along with the numbers "29." After five days, the corpse is unrecognizable. Someone has covered it with blankets.

But today, neighbors bury the body on the sidewalk. A short wall of bricks surrounds the grave, holding down a plastic tarpaulin. A simple cross lies on top. In black letters, the inscription reads, "Here Lies Vera. God Help Us." The letters are big enough for everyone in America to see.

The photographs of Vera's makeshift grave quickly become a poignant symbol of the dignity residents have had to seize from circumstances beyond their control.

A passing bicyclist stops to look at the grave. "That's Miss Vera," she says.

Everyone knew Vera Smith, who had gone out the evening following the hurricane and never returned. Vera had survived the hurricane only to become the victim of a hit and run the following night. She left the house to go out to get something from the store, and her husband, Max Keene, got worried when she didn't return. He found her on the corner, covered with a piece of cardboard. Police were clearing the streets, and he says when he asked them to remove Vera's body they told him to go home. After repeated pleas to collect the body went unanswered, friends of "Miss Vera" took shovels and buried her as well as they could.

Neighbors told of how Smith, aged 65, loved shopping and wigs and casinos and her two small dogs. Keene and Smith had been together for 25 years. He said she liked books and was originally from Mexico. When they met, she was married and Keene had a girlfriend, but both relationships ended. "It was the right time. We just got together," he said, with tears in his eyes. "We used to lie in bed. I'd drink bourbon, she'd read books."

In Mississippi, an area that will take untold billions to repair, residents are angry that after losing so much, they have been shuffled to the side. Every man-made structure, every human-made element for a 50-mile stretch of coastline, has been destroyed—the only thing left standing are the magnificent oak trees. Major industries—casinos, shrimping—are completely out of commission. The water supply is so dangerous that a shelter in Biloxi shut down, after 20 people contract dysentery. But attention continues to focus on New Orleans, leaving Mississippi to wait as they run out of fuel.

Gulfport Mayor Brent Warr improvises imaginative, and not entirely legal, ways to cope with shortages, in one instance stealing a stove to feed his 500 first responders. He also makes off with a portable kitchen belonging to a local restaurant, using it to serve meals—with its owner's permission.

Residents of an apartment complex have placed a sign outside their homes in Biloxi, Miss.

"When you send your law enforcement out to steal things, that's when you know you're in a different situation" —*Gulfport Mayor Brent Warr [R]*

Excerpt from "By Hook or by Crook," by Sally Jenkins, *Washington Post*

Gulfport was still without help three days after the storm, and Warr's control over the situation was slipping. Looting broke out downtown. When Warr drove a utility vehicle down U.S. 90, he watched as his longtime family business, Warr's Men's Clothing, was ransacked. Worst of all, the city was running out of fuel. Generators were about to fail, rescue vehicles were running out of gas. One local hospital radioed that it was on backup power and had no water, and that looters were circling. Warr turned to his chief of police, Stephen T. Barnes. There was a private fuel transport vehicle—Warr doesn't remember whose—parked in a lot behind a chain-link fence. Warr had the lock cut.

"Can we hot-wire it?" he asked.

Barnes said, "I wasn't cut out to be a crook; that's why I went into law enforcement."

"Well, can we get someone from the jail to do it?" Warr asked. Thirty minutes later, the truck was sitting in the City Hall parking lot. That was just one episode in Warr's life of petty crime over the past three weeks.

Mississippi first lady Marsha Barbour hauls supplies into hard-hit areas in her pickup. Sen. Trent Lott uses his own office to run a supply line, commandeering two 18-wheelers filled with baby supplies, disinfectant, and medical goods. "If anyone from FEMA tries to confiscate anything," he tells a sheriff worried about FEMA diverting supplies, "arrest them."

Though roads to the area are impassable and dotted with military checkpoints, a Sunday service this morning took place at the oldest Episcopal church in Mississippi, built in 1846. Parishioners bring in folding chairs and two altar rails and set them up on the floor, all that remains of St. Mark's Episcopal Church outside Gulfport. About 30 people show up for the service.

Excerpt from Soledad O'Brien Interview with Rev. Roberts of Saint Mark's Episcopal Church and Rev. Gray, the Bishop of Mississippi

O'BRIEN: We want to take you east now, to Mississippi, where the devastation is just as complete and in fact, there is a remarkable story. The story of a church that has decided to go ahead with services even though there's nothing left. It's a church with a lot of history. I want to introduce you to the Reverend Bo Roberts of Saint Mark's Episcopal Church and the Reverend Duncan M. Gray, he is the bishop of Mississippi. Reverend Roberts . . . You're trying to hold services now in an hour. But it's completely damaged. How are you going to do that?

ROBERTS: Well, there's still a slab here and there's still a lot of hope and a lot of future here. So, we asked people to bring a chair and we'll set up and just get about God's work.

O'BRIEN: How have you been getting the word out with the damage so complete as it is?

ROBERTS: That's been a tough one, because even though those with cellphones are having difficulty with communication. We put us up a little makeshift sign on the property and as members came by to check on things, they've seen the sign. And of course we've done it by word of mouth, and door to door as best we could. We had it in yesterday's newspaper that many people receive and it has been on the Web sites and also on the local television station.

O'BRIEN: Bishop Gray, if I may ask you a question, what is the scope of the loss that we can see in front of us outside of just the physical structure? What's been lost here?

GRAY: Well, the loss beginning with the physical structures, is six churches along the coast looking like this. But . . . this is the second time this has happened to their churches, to their homes and within 35, 36 years. And that's a pretty heavy blow emotionally, psychologically. But one of the great joys, as I've been traveling down here in the last two or three days, is to have people say we're building back. There's a T-shirt being minted even as we speak that says, "The church is still standing," and that's going to be distributed throughout at least the Episcopal community here on the coast. Some of them are halls that are standing, some of them, like Bo's church here at Saint Mark's, are not standing physically, but certainly spiritually. The church continues to stand and will continue to do the work that God has called us to do.

FRANK POLICH/Reuters /Landov

facilities that spread throughout cities like Austin, San Antonio, Dallas, and Corpus Christi. Partnered with the National Center for Missing and Exploited Children, CPS adds the missing children to the national database, as well as the names of parents searching for their children. So far efforts have been successful, and some 50 children have already been reunited with their parents.

Everyone is looking for someone. The media offers up airtime to desperate survivors who have lost mothers, sisters, grandparents, and children. CNN devotes airtime throughout the day and evening to trying to reconnect family members, then follows up with the news when they're found. Here are some of the callers:

"Hi. This is Kaneisha Moore. I'm looking for my grandmother, Corinne; my mom, Arlene; my uncle, Elmo; my niece, my cousins. And I hope you're all right. I'm all right. It's hard out here. We're striving; we're surviving."

Now that the families and residents of the Gulf Coast are mostly in shelters and safe places, it is becoming alarmingly clear that hundreds and hundreds of children are lost, adrift, and alone, separated from their parents, their families, in Katrina's aftermath. At the Astrodome in Texas, Child Protective Services has set up one of 17 lost children

Above–Rev. Harold Roberts (center) delivers his sermon to parishioners during a church service at Redeemer Episcopal Church in Biloxi, Miss., September 4, 2005.

Right–Thomas Walker, the sexton of the Episcopal Church of the Redeemer carries a bronze plaque from the church which was destroyed by Hurricane Katrina.

Win McNamee/Getty

"My name is Dennis Washington. I'm concerned about my mother, Wilhelmina Robinson, to find out if she's all right in New Orleans. And I want her to know that I'm safe here in Houston and the people are treating us very, very kindly. And we're at the Convention Center. So Mother, if you get my message, try to call and let me know that you're all right."

"I'm trying to get ahold of my fiancé who's here in Houston, Charlene Williams, staying with William Genetta. I'm at the Convention Center. Please come and get me. I've been waitng. I'm safe."

"What did you say your name was?"

"Nathan. Nathan Chaquis."

"Keith Darbonne is looking for 'Mr. Eddie,' his grandfather, Eddie Gabriel, who played at Pat O'Brien's for 70 years. 'He's like Mr. New Orleans to a lot of people. He just turned 95.'"

Meanwhile, the New Orleans police force, staggering under the guilt over losing control of the city, is cause for concern: Two officers have committed suicide, and Mayor Ray Nagin is urging that they need help—psychiatric counseling, after what they've gone through.

Mayor Ray Nagin: *"I've got some firefighters and some police officers that have been pretty much traumatized, and we've already had a couple of suicides, so I am cycling them out as we speak. They need—they need physical and psychological evaluations.*

"They've been holding the city together for three or four days, almost by themselves, doing everything imaginable. And the toll is—it's just too much for them. But we have a problem. . . . [We're] running into a little bureaucracy about what FEMA can pay and I said, 'Screw it, I don't care what they pay. I'll pay it and then we'll figure this out later. But I have to get these men out.'"

At about 4 p.m., the *Times-Picayune* reports that police opened fire on eight people crossing the Danzinger Bridge. The report is swiftly picked up by network TV, but the details change from moment to moment: The contractors were killed, then, none were injured. Five or six people were killed, not eight. It was eight people who were shooting at the contractors. Finally, a corrected report emerges. But it is still troubling. Amid concerns that police have deserted their districts and even turned to looting, Superintendent Eddie Compass comes forward to defend the reputation of his officers.

About two dozen people gather this afternoon in the French Quarter for the Southern Decadence Parade, an annual gay Labor Day celebration that normally draws thousands. Matt Menold, 23, a street musician wearing a sombrero and a guitar slung over his back, says: "It's New Orleans, man. We're going to celebrate." Wearing beads, hula skirts, and wigs, the small contingent dances down Bourbon Street.

Scott Threlkeld/*Times-Picayune*/NNS /Landov

Excerpt from Soledad O'Brien Interview with Eddie Compass, New Orleans police superintendent

O'BRIEN: Yesterday we were hearing that 60 percent of the officers walked off the job. Is that true or not true?

COMPASS: That is totally ridiculous. You know, we had about 1,300 officers we could account for. We're a 1,700-person police department. We're off radio communications. We had 150 officers trapped in a hospital with 12 feet of water. You know, my job was to protect the citizens of this city, to keep my officers safe. And I didn't have time to deal with the press, to quell all rumors.

Now that the situation is under control, I'm going to set the record straight. The men and women of this New Orleans Police Department fought bravely. We did something no police department in the history of the world was ever asked to do. The only thing I can make this analogous with is the Spartans at the Battle of Thermopylae—except we won.

This police department was so tactically proficient. We did not have radio communications. The commanders that we had on this police department kept this police department intact. We worked with other agencies throughout the parishes, throughout the federal system. It went off without a hitch with almost no radio communications.

O'BRIEN: How tough is it to know that there are people to rescue and they can't get to them because either someone's shooting at you, or someone's sniping, or you have to sort of help regain control of the city. And so people who need your help, who are flooded out, couldn't get your help?

COMPASS: It's extremely difficult and frustrating. Just imagine doing it under the conditions where we're sleeping in the street, had no restroom facilities, had no food, had no water. We were running out of ammunition. No radio communications.

And we did not lose one police officer, despite the many firefights that we've had during this entire ordeal. And that's a tribute to men and women in this police department, the federal aid, the sheriff's departments throughout the state.

O'BRIEN: You were quoted as saying, "I don't see anything yet on the ground." This was back when I was in New York. I think it was either on Thursday—maybe it was Thursday. You said, "I don't see anything yet on the ground." And this is when a lot of federal aid had been promised and the troops were coming in. How frustrating was it to know that you had sort of battled on a lot of fronts and you didn't have any backup with 1,700 officers under the best circumstances?

COMPASS: You know, it makes you do one of two things. It brings out all your strengths. It displays all your weaknesses. We couldn't sit down and complain without the strength of this enormous police department. We adapted. We withheld the resistance. We still saved people's lives. We protected people.

News comes to light of an altercation in Jefferson Parish between a sheriff and about 200 people from New Orleans who tried to cross the bridge into West Bank to reach higher ground. Mayor Nagin criticizes the parish for closing the doors to the exhausted group who trudged over the Crescent City bridge. He's especially angry that the group was told that Jefferson Parish did not want "another Superdome" in their community. "When we allowed people to cross the Crescent City Connection because people were dying in the Convention Center, that was a decision based upon people," Nagin tells reporters. "Now, if they made a decision based upon assets, to protect assets over people, and to have attack dogs and armed people with machine guns, then they're going to have to live with that."

FEMA charters three Carnival Cruise Line ships to help house up to 7,000 evacuees for the next six months. The *Ecstasy, Sensation*, and *Holiday* were pulled from regular use and are now heading to Alabama and Texas. This will end up costing about $1275 per week per person—a $236 million contract—a deal that comes under harsh criticism when it's revealed that a seven-day western Caribbean cruise out of Galveston can be had for $599 a person. Many evacuees don't want to live on the ships anyway, saying they have seen enough water for a while.

Aaron Broussard, the Democratic president of Jefferson Parish, appears on NBC's *Meet the Press.* In the course of an emotional interview with host Tim Russert, he is critical of the federal disaster-response effort, and during an account of the death by drowning of his emergency services manager's mother, he breaks down.

Excerpt from NBC's *Meet the Press* Interview with Aaron Broussard:

TIM RUSSERT: Hold on. Hold on, sir. Shouldn't the mayor of New Orleans and the governor of Louisiana bear some responsibility? Couldn't they have been much more forceful, much more effective and much more organized in evacuating the area?

MR. BROUSSARD: Sir, they were told, like me, every single day, "The cavalry's coming," on a federal level, "The cavalry's coming, the cavalry's coming, the cavalry's coming." I have just begun to hear the hoofs of the cavalry. The cavalry's still not here yet, but I've begun to hear the hooves, and we're almost a week out. . . . Nobody's coming to get us. Nobody's coming to get us. The secretary has promised. Everybody's promised. They've had press conferences. I'm sick of the press conferences. For God sakes, shut up and send us somebody.

As if to back up Broussard's claims, the *Chicago Tribune* reports that the USS *Bataan*, which has been in the region since the worst of the storm subsided, has offered its extensive hospital facility and supplies to the relief effort, but that so far federal authorities haven't made use of most of the ship's resources, which include doctors, six operating rooms, 600 hospital beds, food and water supplies, and the ability to produce 100,000 gallons of clean, fresh water each day.

> **"I'm sick of the press conferences. For God sakes, shut up and send us somebody."**
> —Aaron Broussard

Mayor Nagin's focus now is on draining the city, a job he optimistically states could be finished within "a week or two weeks." He hopes that a system of using dredging pipes to pull water out over the levees may speed up the process. But he's not nearly as hopeful about what the receding waters will uncover.

Nic Robertson: *"How many bodies are there . . . thousands?"*

Mayor Ray Nagin: *"I think so, thousands. If you do the math, there's 500,000 people in the city. We probably evacuated 80 percent after the mandatory evacuation. First time we've ever done a mandatory evacuation. We probably have moved about 50,000 people out as it relates to 50 or 60 of these shelters of last resort, so you probably have another 50,000 to 60,000 out there. You do you the math, man. What do you think: five percent, is that unreasonable? Ten percent, 20 percent? It's going to be a big number."*

Richard Johnson sits stunned on the steps that are all that remain of a house in Biloxi, Miss., that was destroyed by Hurricane Katrina.

BLOGS

Posted: 4:10 p.m. ET Ted Rowlands in Biloxi

They continue to find more and more bodies. The coroner in Harrison County here is completely overwhelmed. They're using mortuary employees to help out with duties to collect the bodies.

The residents are telling people where the bodies are. A CNN crew was shown a body here in Biloxi by neighbors. The body was under a porch and the neighbors said they talked to law enforcement but were told not to touch the body, but it's still there.

It is a very, very difficult process. There's no electricity here. They're taking the bodies and putting them in white vans, semi or cooler trucks, and that is where they are sitting now. The identification process is going on simultaneously but as every day goes on, that process gets more and more difficult.

It is going to be a long rest of the weekend into next week collecting bodies, and they're technically looking for signs of life. We haven't heard reports of anybody being rescued but they're still looking actively for signs of life.

When FEMA, under fire for its inefficient response to the plight of the entire Gulf Coast, tries to lay blame on everyone from the local government to the National Weather Service, responses range from icily corrective to outright anger.

On behalf of the people of New Orleans, the *Times-Picayune* sums up their reactions in their "Open Letter to the President."

Dear Mr. President:

We heard you loud and clear Friday when you visited our devastated city and the Gulf Coast and said, "What is not working, we're going to make it right."

Please forgive us if we wait to see proof of your promise before believing you. But we have good reason for our skepticism.

Bienville built New Orleans where he built it for one main reason: It's accessible. The city between the Mississippi River and Lake Pontchartrain was easy to reach in 1718.

How much easier it is to access in 2005 now that there are interstates and bridges, airports and helipads,

Charlene Veillon hugs her grandson, Thearon Ellis, after they learned that her daughter, Joanna Ellis, was killed during Hurricane Katrina in Waveland, Miss.

Joe Raedle/Getty Images

cruise ships, barges, buses, and diesel-powered trucks. Despite the city's multiple points of entry, our nation's bureaucrats spent days after last week's hurricane wringing their hands, lamenting the fact that they could neither rescue the city's stranded victims nor bring them food, water, and medical supplies.

Meanwhile there were journalists, including some who work for the *Times-Picayune*, going in and out of the city via the Crescent City Connection. On Thursday morning, that crew saw a caravan of 13 Wal-Mart tractor trailers headed into town to bring food, water and supplies to a dying city.

Television reporters were doing live reports from downtown New Orleans streets. Harry Connick, Jr., brought in some aid Thursday, and his efforts were the focus of a *Today* show story Friday morning.

Yet, the people trained to protect our nation, the people whose job it is to quickly bring in aid, were absent. Those who should have been deploying troops were singing a sad song about how our city was impossible to reach.

We're angry, Mr. President, and we'll be angry long after our beloved city and surrounding parishes have been pumped dry. Our people deserved rescuing. Many who could have been were not. That's to the government's shame.

Mayor Ray Nagin did the right thing Sunday when he allowed those with no other alternative to seek shelter from the storm inside the Louisiana Superdome. We still don't know what the death toll is, but one thing is certain: Had the Superdome not been opened, the city's death toll would have been higher. The toll may even have been exponentially higher.

It was clear to us by late morning Monday that many people inside the Superdome would not be returning home. It should have been clear to our government, Mr. President. So why weren't they evacuated out of the city immediately? We learned seven years ago, when Hurricane Georges threatened, that the Dome isn't suitable as a long-term shelter. So what did state and national officials think would happen to tens of thousands of people trapped inside with no air conditioning, overflowing toilets and dwindling amounts of food, water, and other essentials?

State Rep. Karen Carter was right Friday when she said the city didn't have but two urgent needs: "Buses! And gas!" Every official at the Federal Emergency Management Agency should be fired, Director Michael Brown especially.

In a nationally televised interview Thursday night, he said his agency hadn't known until that day that thousands of storm victims were stranded at the Ernest N. Morial Convention Center. He gave another nationally televised interview the next morning and said, "We've provided food to the people at the Convention Center so that they've gotten at least one, if not two meals, every single day."

Lies don't get more bald-faced than that, Mr. President.

Yet, when you met with Mr. Brown Friday morning, you told him, "You're doing a heck of a job."

That's unbelievable.

There were thousands of people at the Convention Center because the riverfront is high ground. The fact that so many people had reached there on foot is proof that rescue vehicles could have gotten there, too.

We, who are from New Orleans, are no less American than those who live on the Great Plains or along the Atlantic Seaboard. We're no less important than those from the Pacific Northwest or Appalachia. Our people deserved to be rescued.

No expense should have been spared. No excuses should have been voiced. Especially not one as preposterous as the claim that New Orleans couldn't be reached.

Mr. President, we sincerely hope you fulfill your promise to make our beloved communities work right once again.

When you do, we will be the first to applaud.

Times-Picayune, Mark Schleifstein

Dr. Max Mayfield, director of the National Hurricane Center, said Sunday that officials with the Federal Emergency Management Agency and the Department of Homeland Security, including FEMA Director Mike Brown and Homeland Security Secretary Michael Chertoff, listened in on electronic briefings given by his staff in advance of Hurricane Katrina slamming Louisiana and Mississippi and were advised of the storm's potential deadly effects.

Mayfield said the strength of the storm and the potential disaster it could bring were made clear during both the briefings and in formal advisories, which warned of a storm surge capable of overtopping levees in New Orleans and winds strong enough to blow out windows of high-rise buildings. He said the briefings included information on expected wind speed, storm surge, rainfall, and the potential for tornadoes to accompany the storm as it came ashore.

"We were briefing them way before landfall," Mayfield said. "It's not like this was a surprise. We had in the advisories that the levee could be topped. I keep looking back to see if there was anything else we could have done, and I just don't know what it would be," he said.

Chertoff told reporters Saturday that government officials had not expected the damaging combination of a powerful hurricane levee breaches that flooded New Orleans. Brown, Mayfield said, is a dedicated public servant. "The question is why he couldn't shake loose the resources that were needed," he said. Brown and Chertoff could not be reached for comment on Sunday afternoon.

In the days before Katrina hit, Mayfield said, his staff also briefed FEMA, which is under the Department of Homeland Security, at FEMA's headquarters in Washington, D.C., its Region 6 office in Dallas and the Region 4 office in Atlanta about the potential effects of the storm. He said all of those briefings were logged in the hurricane center's records.

As the sun goes down in the Big Easy tonight, surreal scenes at twilight, reported by the *Times-Picayune*: "On the corner of Chartres and Dumaine Streets in the French Quarter, two cross-dressing bicyclists carrying a music box swerve down the street until one of them crashes, opening a nasty gash in his right elbow. And as the sun disappears and the sky turns pink, four horses led by a white stallion burst from the flood waters on Claiborne Avenue and started grazing on the neutral ground on Elysian Fields Avenue. Their backdrop? Heavily armed drug enforcement agency teams roving through the neighborhood in pickup trucks and an SUV."

New Orleans jazz musician, Wynton Marsalis speaking with Larry King: "*I want to say to the American people, it's important to understand that this is a very profound moment in our history, and it's important for us to realize that our political leadership is not reflecting the will and the feelings of the American people. As a musician I've been around the country, around the Untied States of America for 25 years touring and representing the city of New Orleans and our country, also, around the world. I've been at the tables of Americans all over our country, Iowa, Minnesota, Alaska, I don't care what state you want to name, we have been there swinging, teaching people's kids, and doing other things. And I have to tell you that I know as people around our country of all hues look at these images and hear these people talk, they will understand that these are beautiful people.*

"*And there's nothing to fear. So the whole history and legacy we had for polarization, using race and other issues, pointing fingers at each other, this was at the root of slavery, it was argued when the Constitution, Bill of Rights, Declaration of Independence was being established, the Civil War, it was at the center of that, the Civil Rights movement. We've had a whole legacy of these things. It's time for us to dig down into our souls . . . And realize that this is the time for us to redefine American greatness.*"

He ends this testament of hope by playing the great mournful song, *The Saint James Infirmary Blues.*

"If your're poor, your're powerless. Not just in America, but everywhere"
— Bill O'Reilly, Fox News

"The real disaster of Katrina was that society broke down. An entire community could not cope. Liberalism, the idea that good intentions and government programs can build a Great Society, was exposed as fraud. After trillions of tax dollars for welfare, food stamps, public housing, job training, and education have poured out since 1965, poverty remains pandemic. But today, when the police vanish, the community disappears and men take to the streets to prey on women and the weak."

—Pat Buchanan

"It makes me think of what my friend Rev. Goat just told me: 'Let me say this before it goes any further; New Orleans didn't die of natural causes; she was murdered.'"

—Bluesman Dr. John

"We have been abandoned by our own country. Hurricane Katrina will go down in history as one of the worst storms ever to hit an American coast, but the aftermath of Hurricane Katrina will go down as one of the worst abandonments of Americans on American soil ever in U.S. history. . . . It's not just Katrina that caused all these deaths in New Orleans here. Bureaucracy has committed murder here in the greater New Orleans area, and bureaucracy has to stand trial before Congress now."

—Jefferson Parish President Aaron Broussard

"The temperature of the tropic oceans is warmer than it's been in 150 years."

—Kerry Emanuel, author of Divine Wind

"But I just think as an American, forget Republican, Democrat. As an American, you can't look at these pictures and see a great American city in this kind of a mess, and think that things were working."

—Former House Speaker Newt Gingrich

"What we saw in New Orleans was, in some part, the poor demonstrating the very behavior that made them poor in the first place, and the behavior that keeps them poor. We saw a complete and utter lack of self sufficiency and sense of responsibility. It was as if they had no sense of responsibility for their own safety. Did they deserve help? Of course! That's the role of government, and it's clear that the mayor of New Orleans did next to nothing to make sure that the poorest citizens had a way out. But somewhere along the line someone has to recognize that the so-called poor do have some responsibility for their own lives and their own safety."

—Neal Boortz, WSB-AM radio talk show host

"It's not just a lack of preparedness. I think the easy answer is to say that these are poor people and black people and so the government doesn't give a damn. That's OK, and there might be some truth to that. But I think we've got to see this as a serious problem of the long-term neglect of an environmental system on which our nation depends. All the grain that's grown in Iowa and Illinois, and the huge industrial output of the Midwest has to come down the Mississippi River, and there has to be a port to handle it, to keep a functioning economy in the United States of America."

—Former U.N. Ambassador Andrew Young

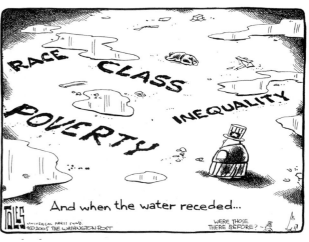
And when the water receded...

DAY 9

"It is a very, very—it's a dark time here in New Orleans." — *Anderson Cooper*

Labor Day, 2005 . . . a national holiday and day of rest for Americans to escape the daily grind of the workplace, greatly anticipated for its three-or four-day weekend status. But for thousands on the Gulf Coast, this September 5th is a day when many wish they still had a job. Or a house to go when the work day ends. Or a city to work in. For most, as far as the eye can see, it's either miles of water or miles of debris. It's been exactly one week since Hurricane Katrina turned back the clock on the Gulf Coast.

"When this thing happened, you got people shooting each other, stealing from each other. The only thing I trusted was my dog. I'm not going to leave her. You guys are going to have to shoot me to get me to leave."
—Unidentified man, New Orleans

The most significant change in New Orleans is that levees have been repaired and the pumps are now working. The city is not expected to be drained, though, for months, and the water grows increasingly filthy. Mosquitoes breed and bacteria multiplies in the heat and humidity. The threat of forced evacuation looms for those who still won't leave—it's estimated there are about 10,000 remaining. The elderly, injured, homeless, mentally challenged—thousands are still out there in wheelchairs, or walking down the streets, their worldly possessions stacked into a shopping cart. Some are too afraid to come out, convinced that if they do, they'll never find their way back. Other determined citizens who have clung to their property in hopes of waking up to a drier tomorrow begin to emerge from their hiding places. Exhausted, hungry and numb. Ready to get out.

Christiane Amanpour: *"Streets that are now rivers, houses that are still flooded, bloated bodies that still bob in the putrid water. And into this festering filth wades a man desperate to be rescued. Forty-two-year-old Tommy Thomas has survived on M&M's and chocolate bars for days now. Stunned, exhausted, he's hauled to safety and given food and fresh water."*

Tommy Thomas, hurricane survivor: *"Water was so deep, you know, I had to come out, you know. Running out of food. That's why I came out. I was running out of food."*

At last count, a quarter of a million Katrina victims were sprawled over 20 states, living in close to 800 shelters. Dozens of evacuees arrive in Los Angeles this morning; four planeloads of survivors have landed in Phoenix, Ariz. Some will take up a new life in those places. They have lost everything that means anything to them.

"When all is said and done, this will be the largest displacement of Americans since the Civil War."
—*Aaron Brown*

This morning, some that did make it out are already trying to return. A line of cars formed Sunday night in New Orleans, after an announcement that residents of

Homes destroyed by Hurricane Katrina line the main road in Port Sulphur, La.

Chris Graythen/Getty Images

The trip may not do much, though, to alleviate some of the resentment brewing among people living in small towns devastated by the storm who feel they are forgotten and neglected: Prichard, Ala.; Hattiesburg and Port Gibson, Miss. These small cities have not yet received any assistance and are in dire need of generators, water, food, supplies. Their water systems are shut down. They have no power, no phone lines. But where FEMA falls short, Americans come to the rescue. Volunteer physicians pour in. National Guard. Someone from a small town in New York raises money to fly a plane load of people from Alabama to safety. Mayors from around the country manage to get through with firemen and supplies.

Vanessa Williams, the executive director of the National Conference of Black Mayors: *"The problem that we're finding in a lot of our small cities is the fact that there was just no help. Many of our mayors reached out to a lot of the larger organizations, as well as FEMA. And, unfortunately, have not yet received any assistance. Therefore that is why we are now on the ground assisting them . . .*

We actually formed the National Conference of Black Mayors' Disaster Relief Fund in which we now have mayors on the ground that are members of our organization that have taken truckloads of supplies to these communities, that are helping mayors evacuate these communities and just have been just a blessing and a resource."

Mario Tama/Getty Images

The dead body of a female victim of Hurricane Katrina floats in the water surrounding the Superdome.

Jefferson Parish could return, provided they had photo ID and proof of residence. The line is three miles long at 6 a.m. When they get to the checkpoints that are part of the security there, they find police. Further into the city, National Guard. No one can stay. They can look, examine, search through the rubble, find the ring or the yearbook or the wedding picture. That's it.

President Bush tours the Gulf Coast again today, with stops in Baton Rouge and Poplarville. He is bringing the First Lady, who will tour some schools and shelters. The President's parents, George H. W. Bush and Barbara, at home in Texas, will tour the Astrodome today.

Due to either a mix-up or some ruffled feathers—perhaps some lingering tension over Gov. Blanco's refusal to accept the President's offer of martial law, or her nose-thumbing choice of James Witt as her personal advisor for disaster relief—the governor initially plans to leave town, but by noon, changes her schedule in order to meet the President. They will tour some of the affected areas together. The outcome of their meeting will be, on the surface, agreeable.

AP Photo/Anja Niedringhaus

Weary search and rescue workers catch a ride in a pickup truck after ending their efforts in St. Bernard, La. Workers continue to search for victims of Hurricane Katrina in this hard-hit area south of New Orleans.

Bill Broadway searches for his daughter's car in the debris in Pass Christian, Miss. The Broadway family returned to their home to find it completely destroyed by Hurricane Katrina. They will rebuild.

No longer in the shadow of the horrors that have dominated headlines from New Orleans, Mississippi's calls for help are finally heard, but not necessarily answered. Reeling from the worst storm to ravage the region in a generation, places like Gulfport, Waveland, Pass Christian, Pascagoula, and Bay St. Louis—where the eye of the hurricane hit directly—desperately need attention. Water. Food. Someone to help them pull out and bury their dead. To help them cope with the fact that their communities are all but destroyed. But help to these isolated areas is slow. Today, they are only starting to get the supplies they need to survive.

Their history was swept away with their homes, businesses, and churches. A week ago, Bay St. Louis boasted antebellum mansions. Now, nearly all of the historical buildings, including the 100-year-old Our Lady of the Gulf Catholic Church—rubble. Mississippi newspapers report that Beauvoir, the last home and presidential library of Confederate President Jefferson Davis, is totally destroyed.

The communities have no infrastructure to speak of. In Gulfport, Katrina destroyed police headquarters, and the storm waters swamped emergency vehicles. Most of Biloxi remains without water or power. Trucks loaded with food, water, and ice are arriving but distribution has been slow and unreliable. "Camp Restore" is finally up and running, with 500 Marines and up to 4,000 Navy personnel available for deployment. Their job description includes everything from repairing the sewer systems to feeding the survivors. They sleep on the beach in tents, ferried in and out by transport ships.

Katrina leveled nearly every building in the beach town of Waveland, population 7,000. The roads to the beaches are mostly inaccessible because of the sheer density of the debris. The parking lots of the malls have become impromptu refugee camps. The newly homeless have pitched tents in the parking lot of the Kmart. What's left of their houses form massive, indistinguishable heaps of wood that clog the streets. An ominous odor emanates from the piles. K-9 squads, led by their corpse-sniffing dogs, travel from lane to lane on foot, searching for bodies. During search-and-rescue efforts, workers break residential windows to find bodies floating in flooded houses. When they move piles of tree limbs, wood planks and rocks, there are more bodies underneath.

Pass Christian took the full force of Hurricane Katrina, slammed by an 23 foot tidal surge that leveled nearly all 2,500 homes in this once-quaint community. Officials say 8,200 of the town's 8,500 residents are now homeless. About 15 houses survived. "Bodies are still being pulled out of trees, out of houses," say residents. "You drag somebody out of the rubble you grew up with, it's pretty tough." In Long Beach, a local insurance agent goes downtown to survey the damage. "Everything south of Second Street is gone. The harbor is gone."

"Thank God you are alive, everything else can be fixed," reads a sign in Biloxi, but help is slow to come and fixing may take a long time. As Gov. Barbour points out, rebuilding will be a slow process. About 22 percent of Mississippi residents live below the poverty line, the highest percentage in the nation. The state ranked next to last in household income in 2004.

Meanwhile, in New Orleans, three DMORT teams move through the city, 31 medical examiners and morticians on each team, securing bodies found floating in the streets to fence posts. Officials spray paint codes on the houses to indicate bodies or lack of. Bodies are everywhere but the grisly task of collecting them hasn't begun yet. They will need to retrieve the bodies, remove them to dry land, load them in refrigerated trucks, and move them to a central mortuary. But that job will come later.

Anderson Cooper: *"We set up our live shot and suddenly noticed that there is a body in the water not too far from where we are standing. It is, frankly, the kind of thing that we are seeing an awful lot of here, every day. We just saw some other bodies today. . . . They can't even, at this point, collect the bodies. I mean, they're not at that stage of rescue operations. They simply kind of look, they know generally where some of the bodies are, where the most obvious ones are, but there are so many bodies they haven't even found yet. They don't even mark down houses at this point in some neighborhoods. They're trying to find the living. They're going to deal with the dead, and, of course, deal with the disease and all the germs and bacteria. I mean, this city's going to have to be cleaned and evacuated. And that is what people here are gradually realizing. It is a very, very— it's a dark time here in New Orleans. And it's going to be dark days ahead as well."*

Faraway in Houston, away from the stink and the memories of chaos, families housed in the Astrodome and adjacent buildings find their only way of reuniting with each other after days of separation is through the media. Phones don't work and family members are frantic. With the help of TV and, to some extent, Internet Web sites,

Marianne Todd/Getty Images

Rosa Carrillo (left) tends an outside kitchen with a relative. This is the first food the family has had for days in Biloxi, Miss. Carrillo said until they were able to get chicken and corn from a distribution truck, the family lived off water for three days following Katrina's strike.

A woman writes a message looking for a relative on a makeshift bulletin board for Hurricane Katrina victims at the Astrodome in Houston, Texas. Between 10,000 and 11,000 New Orleans victims of Hurricane Katrina, have found shelter in the Astrodome before it was closed to new arrivals late September 1.

people come together to end days of agonizing doubt. Using forums and message boards, survivors can find out news, look for friends and family, even find out whether houses are still standing. TV cameramen are also on hand to record those countless, unheralded acts of courage by people who would otherwise go unthanked. Many an impromptu interview with bystanders turns into a story of surprising ingenuity and touching bravery.

Excerpt from Larry King Interview with three heroes of St. Bernard Parish

KING: We have some heroes joining us now from the Houston Astrodome. These are evacuees, heroes because they helped scores of people in St. Bernard Parish, just east of New Orleans. They're Brian Anthony Kaufman, Errol Brown, and Corey Williams. And for several days after Katrina struck, they brought people out of their housing project and ferried them to relative safety, first using an air mattress, later using a boat they had to physically pull through the water, because it had no motor. Brian's parents told him to take them out after he helped everyone else. Finally, after three days, the National Guard showed up. Corey, how did you get the idea to use an air mattress?

COREY WILLIAMS: Well, I was bringing dressers up in my house, emptying all the clothes out, and I was nailing some dressers together, and we threw it in the water, and it sank. So I said, "Something else has got to work."

So we were sleeping on the air mattress on the porch, so I said, "Hey, let's throw that in, see if it works." So we did. And we used some brooms for paddles, and it worked good.

KING: Errol, where did you get the boat that you used later?

ERROL BROWN: Well, me and Brian here, we was on the air mattress after Corey told us to use the air mattress. After we evacuated at least about 100 people, we found the boat under the bridge that was just abandoned. So somebody must have left it there after they evacuated the scene. And we just took the boat. Brian said, "Well, let's grab the boat." And we grabbed the boat, and we left on out with the boat.

KING: Brian, you ought to be very proud of yourself.

BRIAN KAUFMAN: Well, actually, I am, but the idea was like this. When we woke up on Monday, right after the hurricane hit, it was—the power went out immediately. The water started rising, so we didn't hit the panic mode, but we were sort of speaking like, "We have to do something," because we seen helicopters flying over. We don't see nobody coming to the area trying to get people out. The water started rising. The rain hadn't stopped after the hurricane, but we wondered where the water started rising from. So like you said, we went to (INAUDIBLE) boats to a raft that we had, actually a raft, which was made out of four pieces of plywood. That didn't work, like he said. So when we did use the air mattress, we tried with two adults. So we figured me and him, that's at least 370 pounds. You're looking at two adults. That's another 180 pounds to 200 pounds. So once we passed that first test, we wanted to get adults on first, so we can at least have an idea of what type of weight we was able to maneuver well on a mattress.

KING: Wow.

KAUFMAN: That's when we took four infants on the next trip. And once we made it with those four little babies, everybody else knew it would be a successful thing.

KING: You deserve the salute of all of us, Brian Anthony Kaufman, Errol Brown, and Corey Williams. What a job they did. There are lots of heroic stories like this. We're happy to bring them to you.

Donna Brazile, CNN political contributor, a New Orleans native who had family there: "There are so many angels in Texas right now and all over the country that are helping the people of Louisiana. They are taking care of them. They are treating them like their own family and bringing them food, bringing them water. And I want to say to you, Wolf—and I've talked to President Clinton and others—my father, like many other seniors and elderly people, lives paycheck to paycheck. So when they get their check at the beginning of the month, they buy their medicine and food for the month.

"And many of these people need medicine. They need their insulin. They need their heart pills, whatever. And we're urging people to make sure that they have medicines. They don't have ATM cards. They don't have the wherewithal to purchase anything. And so people need to be understanding and help the people of Louisiana rebuild and restart their lives. . . . I'm begging friends to help adopt families so that we help these people. They can't afford to start rebuilding their lives.

"Tell FEMA to get rid of all these regulations. I tried to get Section 8 housing for a family member today, and they wanted to know if my sister qualified. I said, 'Hello? They have nothing.' So Wolf, I'm coping because I have a lot of friends and I have a lot of faith."

As the rest of the world watches the Gulf Coast struggle to recover its balance from a week of devastation and, as some believe, federal neglect, reactions range from disbelief to shock to sympathy. Foreign aid pours in, unconditional and generous. At home, though, Americans are just as giving—the Bush-Clinton-Katrina fund has raised between $40 and $50 million so far. The finger pointing is mounting as well. With the revelation that FEMA Director Michael Brown's prior "emergency management" experience was managing an Arabian horse show circuit, calls come for him to step down. There are those who think all blame should be set aside to save lives. And there are those who think lives should be saved faster, or who think lives were lost and someone needs to take responsibility. Rumors now surface that Brown's résumé was padded.

"In far less time than it took to rescue the people in New Orleans, the price of gas at pumps surged. Capitalism is apparently far more efficient than government."—Aaron Brown

Christiane Amanpour: "You know, in the parts of the world we go to, you know, we do see these things. But this is America. And that is what has shocked so many people from abroad. And what continues to shock many people who are left here, fending for themselves, still not getting the kind of information they think they need to know what to do next and really sort of feeling that they are on their own, despite the fact that so many of these agencies are starting to trickle in, and volunteers as well. But it's still very much kind of a piecemeal effort. You don't see a very, very—you don't see the results of a massive organized campaign."

> **Excerpt from Wolf Blitzer Interview with Clark Kent Ervin, former inspector general of the Department of Homeland Security**
>
> **BLITZER:** Your department is under enormous fire right now. Was it a blunder to make FEMA part of the Department of Homeland Security?
>
> **ERVIN:** I'm not convinced, Wolf, that that really is the issue here. The FEMA director reports directly to the secretary of Homeland Security, who reports directly to the president.
>
> **BLITZER:** So, why did FEMA apparently miss the boat here?
>
> **ERVIN:** It's inexcusable. There's absolutely no excuse for it. This is the kind of thing that ought to have been planned for. Whether it was a terrorist attack or a natural disaster, the consequences would be the same. There would be survivors who would need to be tended to so there should have been prepositioned supplies of food and medicine and water. Not only was this foreseeable but it was actually foreseen by people within FEMA and outside FEMA.
>
> **BLITZER:** Some are suggesting incompetence at the very top, a political appointee Michael Brown, the FEMA director, with limited experience coming in. What do you say?
>
> **ERVIN:** I know Michael Brown and I think he's a wonderful fellow. He's actually been praised for the response to the hurricanes in Florida last year. So, I must say that I'm rather surprised by the response at this point. This was, as I say, not just foreseeable but it was actually foreseen, so it's inexcusable. . . . I don't think it's a structural issue. I think it's an issue of leadership.

Michael Brown FEMA Director : "[I] Started out as general counsel of FEMA, ran operations at headquarters through 9/11, and since then 164 presidential disaster declarations, including the California wildfires, the historic outbreak of tornadoes in the Midwest a couple of years ago, and last year's historic four hurricanes that struck Florida. So yeah, I've been through a few disasters in my life."

William Cohen, former U.S. Secretary of Defense: "Well, first, let me say what an incredible job the men and women who are serving us today are doing today, as well as the first responders, the police, the firemen, all those who are trying to help in this massive disaster.

"In terms of what could have been done, should have been done, this was not an unforeseeable event. There had been report after report predicting what would happen with a Category 4 or 5 type of hurricane. So it's not something that was unforeseen. It may have not been foreseeable by the local officials, but it was not unforeseeable in terms of all the people who have studied this issue.

"This was Mother Nature's weapon of mass destruction—wind and water. The consequences are the same. Whether this was a one-kiloton bomb, nuclear bomb going off in that area, or Mother Nature wreaking this kind of devastation, the response has to be the same.

"Number one, you need evacuation. Number two, you need to have medical supplies. You need to have transportation, communication, which they still don't have.

"All of these preparations would be needed whether it's a natural disaster or a terrorist action. So it's clear that we were ill prepared for this type of incident."

The U.S. Border Patrol moves in as it gets dark. They stop and search all the rescue boats. Everyone is armed these days. Despite a military presence and early curfew, as evening descends, the New Orleans Police Department lock themselves in for the night. Out of the 1,700-man police force, between 400 are unaccounted for. Some fled to look for family members or because their houses were flooded. Some couldn't cope with the triple role of rescuer, law enforcer, and victim. Now the ones who stayed aren't sure they want those who left to come back. Ever.

Excerpt from Drew Griffin Interview with Lawrence Dupree, member of the New Orleans Police Department

DUPREE: People who left, I feel abandoned by them, you know? I feel abandoned. And with that being the case, if they were to come back on the department, it would be hard for me to work next to that type of person.

GRIFFIN: Detective Lawrence Dupree is sick about what happened. He and his buddies all stayed. They fought off the looters. They helped rescue people who were so poor, they were afraid a helicopter ride off their roof would cost too much.

DUPREE: That they'd have to purchase a ticket. I'm like, No.

GRIFFIN: To get on a helicopter?

DUPREE: To get on a helicopter out. They thought that they had to purchase a ticket and were afraid that they couldn't afford it. You know, so it's—that kind of hits you.

Tough, even heartbreaking, decisions have become commonplace during this disaster. Thousands of evacuees were forced to leave something very important behind—perhaps, for some, the most valuable thing in their lives. With the majority of New Orleans' human population in safekeeping, rescuers have more time, and sympathy, for the thousands of abandoned pets at large, roaming and hungry. Some are still tied to porches, trapped on roofs, even trees. They don't understand why there is water everywhere. Why their masters can't be found. They are scared, starving, and in many cases, isolated from rescue boats by water too deep and too wide for the animals to cross.

Luckily, hundreds of people pitch in to help. Trained animal rescuers have begun to show up, to carry these lost pets to shelters. Animal welfare groups from around the country pool their resources, and various animal rescue groups are take reports of missing or abandoned pets including the ASPCA branches in Louisiana or Houston; the Humane Society of the United States; and groups like petfinder.com.

Anderson Cooper: *"When you're going around in the neighborhoods, it's hard to tell where you can go. First of all, the street signs are gone, but you also don't know how deep the water is. You don't want your boat to get stuck so you have to constantly test to see how deep it is. Right now, we're in about two feet of water. So, it's pretty shallow. We're here on an off-ramp off of I-10, which is, if you can look over my shoulder, completely flooded. . . .*

"Even now, seven days after the storm, rescuers are still finding people trapped in their homes in flooded areas. They're trying to pluck somebody out right now from their home. It's amazing to think that this person has lasted this long living in this condition. They're right over there. I don't know if you can see that, they're right there, look over there, look there on the porch. A boat of rescuers from a nearby town try to radio the chopper they can help, but they don't have direct communication. There they go! What's frustrating for a lot of rescuers, though, is the lack of coordination. There's people here— there's a crew here from Destin on boats that could have gone in, had they known these people were here. They tried to signal to the chopper, that they could do it. He's going down again, the rescuer's going down, we believe there may be at least two more people in the house. He re-enters the water and . . . wraps some protective bindings around the people and then hoists them up. It is remarkable to see.

"On the next block, we find the Humphrey family, Deirdre and her son, Manuel. They've rescued several dogs and don't want to leave them. If forced to leave, they say they plan to hide the dogs in their bags."

Deirdre Humphrey: *"Just be quiet. We taking him, yeah, we don't want him to die, too."*

Andy Nelson/The Christian Science Monitor via Getty Images

Michael DeMocker/Newhouse News Service/Landov

Top—Police officer Rebecca Ruspoli helps three dogs stranded on a damaged roof. The dogs quickly ran home.

Bottom left—Donnie Panarello, Sr. (right), and Donnie Pan-arello Jr. (left), pull dogs Chance and Buddy down a flooded street, as they evacuate the hard-hit Chalmette community of Saint Bernard's Parish.

Bottom right—Sgt. Jason Smith of New Orleans walks through floodwaters in the 2800 block of Calhoun Street with a cat he rescued while patrolling the area.

Mario Tama/Getty Images

Donald Civelo (left) and wife Joan greet rescuers from their flooded house in the Gentilly neighborhood of New Orleans. The couple said they wanted to stay at home.

If only it were as easy to coax the last thousands of humans from their lairs. By now they are just as scared and exhausted as the gaunt, helpless animals awaiting some compassionate person's outstretched hand. The water is receding slowly, inch by inch, going back to where it came from, but it won't vanish in time for the stubborn contingent of New Orleanians who, having held out for so long and at such a cost, just don't want to go. They don't want to end up in California or Arizona, with everything they love and feel safe around gone, possibly forever. They don't want to wake up in Oklahoma, surrounded by nothing. When the authorities threaten to cut off food and drinking water, they close their minds to the news, to the warnings. "This water is going to kill you," rescuers tell people. "Don't swim in it, don't get in it. Come out now." Still, there are as yet no forced evacuations. Rescuers try to be gentle. People are so angry.

"The goverment picking you up, telling you, Come on, let's go, let's go, let's go, let's go. After that, they'll drop the ball again. You're just out there somewhere. Might as well be in space."
—*Johnny Jones, New Orleans*

The water in the streets and houses is black, a toxic mix of gas and mud, oil and excreta, garbage and human remains. It's best not to think about what's really in it. One thing's for sure: It's different than what it was when it surged over the levees and plunged through the breaches—but there's no time to clean it up, just pump it back over and out. Back where it came from.

For now, the most wonderful sight in the world is simply a pump, doing its job on Labor Day.

Water pours out of pipes connected to pumping stations sucking water out of flooded neighborhoods in New Orleans. The water is flowing back into Lake Pontchartrain, causing concern because of possible toxins.

Excerpt from Aaron Brown Interview with Michael Rogers, Army Corps of Engineers

BROWN: How dirty is the water that's going back in the lake, by the way?

ROGERS: Sir, the water that you would see on the ground where we are is just like the lake water.

BROWN: So it's no different? It's not that it's contaminated with chemicals? It's not any worse for the lake than what came out of the lake a week ago?

ROGERS: Sir, we have coordinated our efforts of putting that water into Lake Pontchartrain with the Environmental Protection Agency, and they'll be glad to answer any questions along those lines.

BROWN: Are you telling me you're not sure if there is risk in that water, or not risk in that water?

ROGERS: Sir, we have not—we do not know anything more about the water than most folks.

BROWN: OK. Well, here's one thing we all know is that there's no option. It's not like it could go somewhere else. It has to go back in the lake, fair enough?

ROGERS: Yes, sir. And I think that's a fair thing to say. We are at the point where we have to make a decision. The city of New Orleans is flooded in many places in eight feet of water. We must remove that water to get to a lot of people that are still trapped in the city. Our number one goal is to get that water out of the city and help protect lives within the city.

BROWN: So it may not be as clean as a mountain stream, but there's just no option to it. We see this picture of this pipe and all the water flowing out of the pipe back into the lake. Is this a significant amount of water, or are we looking basically at a straw in the ocean?

ROGERS: Sir, that's an important stream of water. It may not be a significant amount, but that water is (INAUDIBLE) we are using, removing, to help us de-water the power plant, the pumping plant you see just behind that. And that pumping plant is key to us being able to de-water the city of New Orleans.

BROWN: In any case, it sounds like they're trying to clear the water out of the large pumping station, or at least the water that surrounds the large pumping station. And it's not necessarily the cleanest water on the planet, but if you've got a better idea what to do with all of that water, I'm sure they'll be glad to hear from you. I know I will.

A Chinook helicopter drops sandbags to plug a levee break on the east side of the London Avenue Canal in the Gentilly neighborhood of New Orleans.

DAY 10

"Take whatever idiot they have at the top of whatever agency and give me a better idiot. Give me a caring idiot. Give me a sensitive idiot. Just don't give me the same idiot." —*Aaron Broussard, president, Jefferson Parish*

For members of Congress returning from a five-week recess this morning, the day begins—not in the darkened morning of New Orleans, not on the sweltering beaches of Mississippi and not in the desolate streets of Waveland—but in a large, comfortably air-conditioned room in Washington, D.C. There, Congress grills top emergency officials about what happened and why after Hurricane Katrina. There, suited officials and Cabinet members argue the facts. When they are done speaking, the room erupts. Lawmakers can't find enough ways to express their outrage at the planning and response to the disaster.

Meanwhile, Aaron Broussard, president of Jefferson Parish, goes on CBS's *Early Show*, pleading for Congress to investigate the delays and malfunctions, and to find someone to head FIMA, presumably, more effective than FEMA Director Michael Brown. "Bureaucracy has murdered people in the greater New Orleans area,"

he says. "And bureaucracy needs to stand trial before Congress today. So I'm asking Congress, please investigate this now. Take whatever idiot they have at the top of whatever agency and give me a better idiot. Give me a caring idiot. Give me a sensitive idiot. Just don't give me the same idiot."

And so the day that begins with accountability, nowadays known as "the blame game," in full swing. Every politician, every talking head, everyone with an opinion gives one. The consensus is that yes, the government failed the people of New Orleans. The problem is how to remedy that fact?

Democrats want an independent commission to investigate the federal delay. Republicans want to focus on relief and rescue efforts. Give more money to the victims, say the Republicans. Get rid of the incompetents, say the Democrats. One thing they're agreed on: the price tag,

Rescue workers approach a destroyed home in Gulfport, Miss., during a search for victims still trapped in houses.

Nicholas Kamm/AFP/Getty Images

and it's growing. Congress asks for another $50 billion for relief efforts. Senate Democrats said the government's share of relief and recovery may top $150 billion. By the way, say several senators, restore FEMA to Cabinet-level status. And oh, yeah: Replace Michael Brown. President Bush and Congress pledge separate investigations. Moving to get ahead of a storm of criticism, the president declares that he personally will head up a probe of the government response to the disaster: however, he is the head of the federal bureaucracy, and Democrats aren't crazy about his idea.

President George W. Bush: *"What I intend to do is lead an investigation to find out what went right and what went wrong. I'll tell you why. It's a—very important for us to understand the relationship between the federal government, the state government, and the local government when it comes to major catastrophe. And the reason it's important is that we still live in an unsettled world. We want to make sure that we can respond properly if there's a WMD attack or another major storm. So I'm going to find out over time what went right and what went wrong."*

He plans to send Vice President Dick Cheney to the area to investigate how things are going. "Bureaucracy is not going to stand in the way of getting the job done for the people," the President says.

The Senate Homeland Security and Governmental Affairs Committee announces its own investigation into the response to the disaster. Republican Sen. Susan Collins of Maine and ranking Democrat Sen. Joseph Lieberman of Connecticut will lead the charge.

Sen. Susan Collins [R-Me.]: *"Well, it is disturbing that almost four years to the day after the attacks on our country, we see some of the same lack of preparedness, despite the billions of dollars that have been spent to shore up our homeland defense and emergency preparedness. And certainly that is a key question that the committee will be focusing on in the weeks and months ahead."*

Sen. Joseph Lieberman [D-Conn.]: *"What we saw in the last week was not only a humanitarian tragedy, it was a national embarrassment. . . . The fact that New Orleans is effectively a bowl, and that if the levees gave way, that New Orleans would drown, is not a surprise. The experts have been telling us that for years. . . . The shocking and unsettling question is, why didn't we all do something about it?"*

After the meeting, Rep. Tom DeLay (R-Tex.) blames local government. Mississippi Sen. Trent Lott, who has been coming to his state's rescue since the storm hit and is in line for more federal funds, is practical "My mama don't raise no idiot. I ain't going to bite the hand that's trying to save me," he said.

Jerome Crenshaw, a Miami, Fla., firefighter, takes a break from the recovery efforts in the aftermath of Hurricane Katrina in Gulfport, Miss.

Ross Taylor/Getty Images

Tom DeLay [R-Tex.] *"The emergency response system was set up to work from the bottom up. And it's the local officials trying to handle the problem. When they can't handle the problem, they go to the state, and the state does what they can do. And if they need assistance from FEMA and the federal government, they ask for it and it's delivered."*

Just as it seems that FEMA's liability couldn't get worse, a memo surfaces that Director Michael Brown wrote to Secretary of Homeland Security Michael Chertoff after the storm hit. In it, Brown asks for "at least" 1,000 volunteers, and gives them two days to arrive, one of which will consist of a day of training; he asks for 2,000 more within a week. Although he uses the term "near catastrophic event," the memo is polite, refers to the deployment of volunteers as "a field assignment," and includes a list of "personal supplies" The memo was written five hours before Katrina's landfall. Director Brown, whose résumé is under close scrutiny today, is keeping a low profile.

Adding to the debate about whether race played a part in the disaster, many now question whether, in fact, it was class that dictated the tardy government response, and the fact that the people of New Orleans are poor. But there are still those who think accountability lies with the general populace, who should have known to get out when they were told to evacuate. It is hard for many people to conceive of the sort of poverty that might prevent this. There are still those who think that any charges of racism are an attempt to exploit the tragedy.

Excerpt from Carol Costello Interview with Bob Parks, a former Republican congressional candidate

COSTELLO: So, Bob, it's your turn now. You wrote a column on americandaily.com. And you're very upset at the images of blacks looting. You write, and I quote: "Black people in New Orleans should be made to understand that the whole world is watching. Any racism people may have is being justified every time they turn on their televisions." Some might say that statement is racist. Aren't you using a broad brush?

PARKS: Well, when the perception is given on worldwide television that the only people who are doing the looting are black, first of all, I just don't understand in a situation like that is this need to loot. We have been through this before with the Rodney King riot. I mean, there's just times when you need to get everybody together. There are boneheads in the world that will do things. And, you know, the looting, the lawlessness in New Orleans set back any progress that could have been made to get initial relief in. Right now, there obviously is a concerted effort to make this look like—it was planned as a racist thing in the first place, like the Bush administration just decided they were going to try to exterminate black people on worldwide television. I think that whole notion is absurd. And I think the real story, which a lot of people are being very careful to navigate around, is to find out what was the lack of response from the local and from the state.

COSTELLO: Well, Bob, why is the sentiment out there that many in the black community feel that this was the reason that the response was so slow, because these people were poor and black?

PARKS: Well, because that is the story that a lot of pundits are putting out right now. I think there's a lot of damage control going on as far as the people who were really on the ground there who could have made the decisions. They did not. And it is an attempt to—and anytime the people who make money on race, whether they be civil rights activists, these people are always looking for a reason to play the race card and say that Republicans and conservatives really just want to kill all black people. And here was a perfect opportunity.

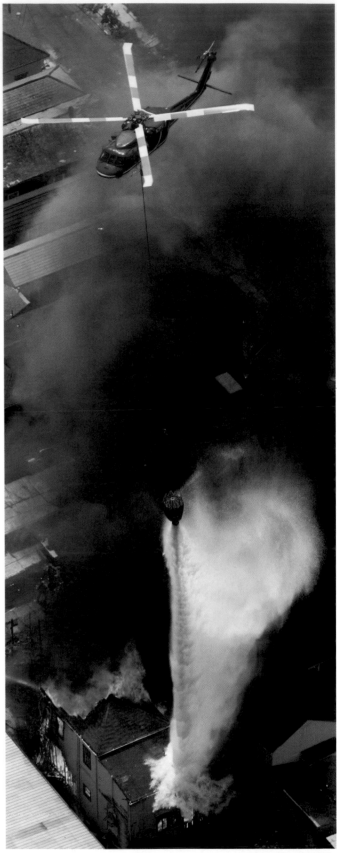

AP Photo/David J. Phillip

A helicopter drops water on a fire in New Orleans. In many cases this was the only method to fight fires as the streets were impassable and there was no water pressure, making street hydrants unusable

Callie Crossley, a media critic and social commentator: *"I think the journalists really have been struggling with really how to describe using a language for poverty, because this is not an arena we cover. These are people who are mostly invisible to us. They do the service work, and they disappear. I think it's really hard for people to understand folks without means, folks without ability to get themselves from one place to the next, because they don't have the financial wherewithal. I think some of the journalism that's been reported recently has been brilliant and really detailing, I mean detailing. For example, describing from one man, he said, I make $340 a month. I mean, how could I get myself out, you know?"*

And so the shoving match continues, while the real work on the ground gets done by first responders, volunteers, and people who are so determined to let nothing get in the way of helping Katrina survivors—they are the real heroes of this tragedy

Habitat for Humanity, former President Jimmy Carter's relief organization of choice, plans to build thousands of homes for Gulf Coast residents. Carter says it's the group's most important mission yet in the United States. The Georgia-based organization plans to launch "Operation Home Delivery" later this month and will assemble housing frames and put them on trucks bound for Alabama, Louisiana, and Mississippi. Habitat officials said they've had an overwhelming response, with more than $450,000 from just on line donations pouring in during the four days after Katrina made landfall.

Donations to the Red Cross top $400 million, but problems arise with the organization getting into New Orleans. A statement on the group's Web site states that Louisiana Homeland Security Department has requested "the American Red Cross not come back into New Orleans following the hurricane." Their presence would, LHSD says,

keep people from evacuating and encourage others to come into the city. "Red Cross access to New Orleans is controlled by the National Guard and local authorities and while we are in constant contact with them, we simply cannot enter New Orleans against their orders," the statement also notes.

The numbers sound good, as always: 41,000 National Guardsmen and 17,000 active duty troops on the ground along the Gulf Coast, nine million meals have been handed out; hundreds of helicopters, aircraft, and naval ships assisting in rescue operations. Yet it is the Coast Guard, in much smaller numbers of 2,400, that has saved more than 22,000 people using boats and helicopters throughout the crisis following Katrina's landfall.

On the beaches of Biloxi, Miss., the wreckage of casinos shares the sand with 5,000 sailors and 500 marines. "Camp Restore" has landed, a platoon of soldiers geared to repair everything from sewers to cooking meals. The recovery effort moves forward unevenly, and a sense of optimism and relief a couple of days ago in the area has given way to a depressing reality check—it's going to be a long time before life returns to normal. Tens of thousands of people remain homeless, and the state is struggling to provide shelter for them. Sen. Trent Lott (R-Miss.) continues to negotiate the release of 20,000 trailers sitting idle in Atlanta, Ga. mired in red tape. Somewhere, an enterprising someone realizes that a government warehouse full of seized contraband—knockoff "designer" clothing, accessories, shoes, even dog food—is sitting idle while Katrina victims go without. The fake Tommy Hilfiger shirts and faux Ralph Lauren jeans are distributed to evacuees at the Houston Astrodome.

Military soldiers unload supplies as they prepare to patrol the uptown section in New Orleans.

The first responders are still out there; embattled, stressed out, and still at it. The local officials and some state officials, who have been working under deplorable conditions and continuing to do their job, even as their families are unaccounted for, their homes destroyed—keep going. They are the unsung heroes of this disaster, the heroes with a human face who survivors will remember. They are the ones who got through when everyone else said it was impossible.

Marko Georgiev/Getty Images

Excerpt from Anderson Cooper Interview with Dr. Jeffery Wiese

COOPER: We talked earlier with Dr. Jeffrey Wiese, a psychiatrist at Tulane University. It wasn't for my own personal mental health, although that I certainly could use it, but what we talked to him about is he has been working for the last several days with the first responders, with the New Orleans Police Department officers, who he says really haven't had anyone, any medical personnel working on their behalf. He's quite upset about what he has seen over the last several days, about some of the things that happened here, and that failed to happen here in his opinion. I talked to him a short time ago.

COOPER: What has frustrated you most? What has angered you most that you have seen here?

WIESE: Everything. The fact that people have died when they didn't need to. The fact that the cops didn't get the credit they deserve for holding down the fort in the beginning. And the fact that there wasn't food, water, and medical care made immediately available, forward deployed. We knew this was coming. We could see it. You can predict these things to an extent, see where they're coming. There are models that show what parts of the city would have flooded under these circumstances. That's what climatologists do.

Chris Graythen/Getty Images

COOPER: Right, in 1995, a study was done showing what a Category 4 or a Category 5 hurricane would do on this city.

WIESE: Absolutely. This was not a failure of pre-planning from the scientific standpoint. This is a failure of planning from the response standpoint. This is the only chance we get for a test run if something even more horrible happens or something as horrible happens with a nuclear device in this country. And we botched this one. We won't get a chance to botch it again.

COOPER: If this is a model for how we respond to a nuclear disaster, it is not a good sign at all?

WIESE: Not really. There's medical care needed, still, by every one of these rescue workers, by every one of these law enforcement officers.

Win McNamee/Getty Images

AP Photo/Eric Gay

Clockwise from top left–SWAT police officers Cris Mandry (front) and Todd Morrell (back) comfort a person who was too weak to say his name during the search-and-rescue operation in the Lower Ninth Ward.

New Orleans firefighter Mike Seaman takes a break from battling a fire in the lower Garden District.

New Orleans police officer Alfred Celestain drops to a knee after police lost radio contact with a fellow officer who was trapped up to his neck in rising water in New Orleans. Police later found out the officer freed himself from the rising water by breaking through to the roof of his house.

Joseph Baumgarten, a member of a search-and-rescue team, searches for victims and survivors in Biloxi, Miss.

Rescue crews search for survivors New Orleans.

COOPER: These first responders. They're not wearing masks, they're not wearing, in many cases, protective gloves. Do you worry about their health?

WIESE: Absolutely. Who knows what's in the water? And who knows what happens when all that stuff gets mixed together? Who knows what happens when you breathe it? There are lots of unknowns.

COOPER: Basically all the New Orleans Police officers who need attention are coming to you, and the few people you have been working with.

WIESE: Yes. I have been working with an excellent federal agent. I've been working with the good people of the New Orleans Police Department and doing what we can. But we needed more help. And it finally got here today. Why did it get here today? You know, I know they've been medically evacuating people from over there. I know there has been some civilian stuff, but where was the help for the helpers? And if a psychiatrist has to come in on his own with a gun and a backpack to do it, that's not a failure of an individual, that's a failure of the entire system.

COOPER: And that's what you did? You came in with a gun and a backpack of medicine?

WIESE: And a backpack of supplies for myself, including medicine, bandages, you know, scalpels, I mean, just anything I could get my hands on.

COOPER: Do you carry the gun with you?

WIESE: It's right here. I was not coming back to this town without this. I was not coming back in this town checking my house without this. I have a sworn oath to help. And the last thing I want to do is hurt somebody. But I had to get here to help.

COOPER: And so, the heroes of this disaster and this continuing disaster are—I mean, you're modest, you wouldn't say it. But I mean, I would say it's you and you would say it's the other people who just ignored the bureaucracy and just decided to come down and do what you could, even though no one—there was no organization?

WIESE: Yes. The heroes of this disaster are the local officials, some of the state officials, who were here working under deplorable conditions . . . the New Orleans Police Department, the New Orleans Fire Department, the local officials, whatever state offices of emergency preparedness, good to go, excellent, doing what they could. They're the heroes.

Mario Tama/Getty Images

Anderson Cooper: *"A special unit from the military is coming to help identify bodies. It is coming. I mean, there are bodies, but no one is picking up bodies at this point. There are bodies just floating out there that we drive by in boats every day. They're lying out on top of cars. And there's no telling how many bodies are in these homes once this water goes down.*

"It is remarkable. I mean, there are so many first responders here from small towns all across Louisiana and all across the south and all from different states who want to help and start picking up these bodies. Often, it seems like the left hand doesn't know what the right hand is doing here. And there's a lot of duplication and a lack of communication.

"And we're hearing that every day from all the first-responders that I talked to privately. They don't want to say it on camera because they don't want to get in trouble. These are small-town guys who don't want to make waves. But they are incredibly frustrated.

"So, earlier, you heard Tom DeLay talking, blaming basically the very same people, from the low levels, I believe was the term he used, from the bottom up. This man who has been working on the bottom, he sees it, of course, the reverse. He sees it as the heroes are the people who work, were working and continued to work throughout this storm and in these dark, difficult days ahead.

And who, by the way, are out there in this water all day long, getting—drinking this water and getting it in their eyes, without protective—much protective gear. I mean, some of them have latex surgical gloves on. But, I mean, this water is just—it's a health hazard. And one doctor I just talked to who responds to these medical personnel all the time describes it as a crime, what is happening here. He describes it as a crime, the response to this, and the fact there are first-responders out there without the right gear, risking their lives every day still."

As for New Orleans, a week and a day after Hurricane Katrina, it's secure. Order has been restored, the military patrol the streets, no one is living in fear, the looting is under control. The critical breach in the 17th Street Canal levee has been repaired, the pumping system has been partially restored. Slowly but steadily, the floodwater is being drained from the city. With two pumping stations working, water is leaving the city

EPA/Paul Buck/Landov

A police boat returns with people rescued from high waters in New Orleans. Police and fire department rescuers are heavily armed because of reports of frustrated locals firing shots at rescuers.

at the approximate rate of 27,000 gallons per minute. It's being forced back south into the bayou below the Ninth Ward and St. Bernard Parish through a couple of breaches the Army Corps has made. It's also being pushed back up over the levees and north using pumps. This will clear water from where it covers tens of thousands of homes in Orleans and Jefferson Parishes. Estimates are that draining the city could take up to three months.

The water, by the way, is a witch's brew of garbage, human waste, toxic chemicals, and germs. The CDC tested it for bacterial levels and found it to have more than 20,000 colonies of fecal coliform per 100 milliliters. The levels in water runoff into rivers is usually 200, so that's roughly a hundred times higher than normal. It is only one of several elements of life today in New Orleans that is causing the diehards—stragglers is the undignified term used by the authorities—to relinquish their stranglehold on their beloved city.

Unfortunately, it's uninhabitable. Authorities say that the water in the city, though it has receded slightly, is deadly. Even to touch, it is dangerous. Wade through it, they say, and you could end up with anything from nausea to e-coli to tetanus to Hepatitis A. And yet, it is the same water that's being pumped back into the Gulf of Mexico.

Anderson Cooper Interview with Hugh Kaufman, Environmental Protection Agency

COOPER: Hugh Kaufman, a senior analyst for the Environmental Protection Agency's office. He's speaking as an expert who's worked on countless disasters in the last 35 years, and makes it clear that he is not speaking for the EPA and that he is not involved with Katrina cleanup. Hugh, thank you very much for joining us.

KAUFMAN: Thank you, sir.

COOPER: What is wrong with pumping the water into Lake Pontchartrain? Is it drained too quickly?

KAUFMAN: Well here's what you've got. And you put it out there. You've got a toxic soup. And, that toxic soup, we don't know how toxic it is. The testing hasn't been done. We should have told the rescue workers a week ago how toxic it was. We should have told them to take precautions. We're still not telling them. Just before your show, EPA and the federal government finally told the public that the water is contaminated, and that they should limit contact

Mario Tama/Getty Images

A police officer keeps watch as people walk through filthy water in downtown New Orleans.

and not even smoke around it. Notwithstanding us not knowing the full magnitude of the toxins, we are going ahead and pumping it to the Gulf of Mexico which will have enormous adverse environmental affects. On top of that—

COOPER: Did the EPA know that all along and they're just announcing it now? Or—when I heard that statement, I thought, OK, maybe they just did some study and just got the results, no?

KAUFMAN: No. Everybody—the old pros at EPA and FEMA, what few are left that haven't been decimated, know that this material got into the water. Anything that went into the sewers—hazardous material from industry, feces, etc., etc., is all in the sewers. And now it's all in the toxic soup. So—

COOPER: OK, Hugh. Hugh, let me just tell you what the EPA says about what you're saying. We got a statement from them. And I say, quote: "The EPA believes it's the right decision in an effort to limit public contact with flood water due to potentially elevated levels of contamination associated with raw sewage and other hazardous substances."

That's why they say it's the right thing to pump this out. No? And what are the long-term effects?

KAUFMAN: You've got very few people in contact with the water except the rescue workers and the few people are there. Now they're going to take the toxic water and spread it to a larger area where more people will have contact with it. In other words, the bungling continues by these incompetents who are running the federal government right now on this area.

AP Photo/News & Observer/Chuck Liddy

Members of the Oregon National Guard cruise through flooded streets in a light armored vehicle near the Superdome.

Ted Jackson/NNS/Landov

Firefighters try to get a small portable pump going so they can spray a meager amount of polluted water on a neighboring house to keep the fire from spreading on Columbia Street.

people—the elderly, the handicapped, a merchant marine with a shotgun—out of their homes; Lt. General Russel Honore says U.S. troops are forbidden to perform law enforcement within the country.

But even if it weren't for the fact that their world now reeks of stagnant water and sewage, more and more hold-outs just can't take it anymore. Decomposing bodies, animal and human—in houses, lying under bridges or debris, floating by in the water—by now are doing the forcing, along with the constant roar of helicopters overhead. The smell everywhere is overpowering, a mixture of garbage, human waste, toxic chemicals, and germs. Shell-shocked storm stragglers wander out from their hiding places. Wave from rooftops. We give up. Come get us.

Carey Bodenheimer, CNN assignment editor: *"People are walking around like zombies, these people who have been stuck. And they are—it's really unbelievable. They have almost no energy. They're walking around with their possessions in small, white plastic bags like you get when you buy something from the drugstore."*

The estimates of New Orleans' dead have been extreme. The mayor has repeatedly warned that he expects up to 10,000. While so far it's been substantially less—about 100 bodies recovered—there are still areas underwater, many houses unentered. More, it's assumed, will come to light as the city dries out.

Broken gas lines and people using candles and improvised methods of cooking create major fire hazards all over the city. Four fires blaze in the Garden District, where wooden homes, some more than a century old, are packed closely together. And if you have a fire on your block, it's not as if you can pick up the phone and call 911. Despite equipment as 20th century as a helicopter, it takes two hours to alert one to bring the water and drop it on the flames. Two Chinook CH-46 helicopters fly over the Mississippi, lowering giant buckets and scooping up thousands of gallons of water from the river. The choppers then drop the water onto the fires to try to keep them from spreading. Too late. For all intents and purposes, the city has returned to the dark ages, where a single candle burning by a bed can ignite an entire row of houses and burn them to the ground.

Lethal water. Fires out of control. Air full of gases released from long-dead bodies and rotting garbage. In short, an environment toxic enough that Mayor Nagin now says "It's time to go." He issues a formal order authorizing force to remove the remaining people from New Orleans, and threatens to withhold the water and food that many have only just begun to receive. But no one has the heart to carry out the threat. Even the military begs off on the prospect of having to force

Reuters/David J. Phillip/Landov

Two women are rescued by a U.S. Navy helicopter in New Orleans, after changing their mind about staying in the city.

Soon, those bodies will have a temporary home. St. Gabriel, population 6,000, average annual income $9,000, has been chosen by FEMA as the site of the first morgue for bodies collected from New Orleans. Some of the townspeople say it's the least they can do for the victims of Katrina: to give some dignity to these individuals and their families, provide some finality, the knowledge of where their relatives are.

Excerpts from Paula Zahn Interview with Dr. Louis Cataldie, Los Angeles emergency response medical director

ZAHN: This is such a grim story to talk about. How many bodies have you received so far, and how many are you expecting?

CATALDIE: Well, Paula, I don't know how many we're going to expect.

We are—you know, I think it's important for everybody to understand that it's about the individual and not about the number. You know, it's about the little lady with the big brown eyes who is in the Superdome in all that filth who looks at you and you can't do anything for. And somebody hands you a limp kid. And when you come back to her, she's dead. It's about the individual. It's about the one.

And I don't want people to lose track of that, that we handle every person as the individual and with the dignity they deserve. We're coming into probably close to 100 bodies right now, 100 individuals. Certainly, the count is going to go higher. We're not keeping score.

With each recovery, you know, there's more trauma, certainly, for our city and probably for our nation. I don't know how many individuals we will find, Paula. . . .

ZAHN: And then, Doctor, finally tonight, there are reports that the state of Louisiana is thinking about buying land to create some sort of cemetery for all these victims. Is there a possibility that there might, given all the difficulties you talk about, end up being a mass grave for these victims?

CATALDIE: Absolutely not. We will not do a mass grave. We will have individual plots for each person— each victim that we track through the morgue. We are looking at various locations right now. A task force has submitted various options to our governor. There is no way our governor's going to allow a mass burial. We're not going to treat Louisiana citizens like that.

Here in rural Lousiana is where the dead will be photographed, X-rayed and fingerprinted. DNA will be taken, dental records checked. A Disaster Management Operational Team, or DMORT, can process up to 140 bodies a day. Each team consists of 31 people, experts in the details of death—funeral directors, medical examiners, coroners, pathologists, forensic anthropologists, fingerprint specialists, x-ray technicians, and dental assistants. These same teams spent nine months identifying victims of 9/11.

Once the grisly task of processing the remains of the dead is done, the bodies will be released back to the state, where families can reclaim them, and then bury them. For bodies that are not claimed, the state is looking for a piece of land to use as a cemetery.

For those who survived Hurricane Katrina and managed to get out, the prospect of relocation was simple: anywhere but here. Now, as evacuees settle in different cities around the country, the prospect of moving yet again—even back to New Orleans—doesn't seem as likely as it did a week ago.

When the U.S. government charters three Carnival Cruise Line ships with plans to move 4,000 evacuees from the Astrodome into two of the vessels docked in Galveston, long lines are anticipated. There is much talk of what an improvement berths will be over cots. But there are no takers. It seems that people fleeing floods are reluctant to move onto the water.

"I can't live over water. I can't swim. I wouldn't want to see no more water. I saw enough already."
—*Donna Smith, 24, commenting on FEMA's plan to house 4,000 evacuees on Carnival Cruise Line ships*

Kyra Phillips: "Ecstasy *can wait, so, too, the* Sensation. *With the health and welfare of flood evacuees still mission critical in 16 states, plans were afoot in Texas to move thousands of people from the Astrodome and Reliant Arena on to cruise ships, Carnival's* Ecstasy *and* Sensation, *at the nearby port of Galveston. Few want to go. The Coast Guard acknowledges, 'Another immediate relocation is too much, too soon.'"*

Efforts are made to turn the Astrodome into Dome City. The Reliant Center is being called Center City. Officials try hard to turn the mass environment into little towns. They set up a temporary banking center. They create bus stops for kids to go to school next week. Evacuees tell officials they would rather stay put for now and focus on finding their loved ones and other places to stay. Of the 250,000 who came here, many no longer want to leave.

Estelle Lewis took advantage of an offer by Wal-Mart to find jobs for its workers displaced by the hurricane. Just four days ago she was sleeping on an overpass in New Orleans, wondering if she would live or die. Now she is starting work in the deli of a Houston Wal-Mart. She says she will never go back to New Orleans.

Mona Lisa Wright, a certified nurse assistant, wants to find a job in Houston and bring over her 13-year-old son, who is temporarily staying in Mississippi. "I like the atmosphere," she says. "I like the people. They're nice and kind. I think this is where my new life is going to start, right here in Texas."

At the end of the day, New Orleanians fall asleep in strange places all over the U.S.: Texas, Pennsylvania, Colorado, Arizona. Some have left New Orleans for the first time in their lives. Others were just being born as the hurricane hit, and may never see the city their parents called home. The most unique of all American cities. If it does rise again, as the politicians keep promising, will it survive another hurricane?

In response, some are asking if such a defenseless city should ever be rebuilt. It is so far below sea level. The levees can never be high enough. It would be a waste of money to even attempt it. And won't the same things happen again?

Others insist it must be rebuilt. But its vulnerability must be taken into account. Its poverty and helplessness eliminated. Its protective coastline restored. Only then can one of the most well-loved cities in the world rise again. And even then, a more profound question: With so many of its long-standing residents possibly never to return, has the soul of New Orleans left with them?

Excerpt from Aaron Brown Interview with Douglas Brinkley, historian

BROWN: The historian Douglas Brinkley has deep ties to New Orleans. He's a professor of history at the University of New Orleans. He evacuated to Houston early on, but he's been back to check on things, do some work, as well as the World War II museum in the city. It's always good to see Doug, and we welcome him tonight.

The whole idea of rebuilding the city is something to talk about. But to some degree, unless you're going to do the work to protect the city, it's almost pointless.

BRINKLEY: Well, that was a great piece you just had about the barrier islands. Coastal restoration's been a big issue in Louisiana. And 100 years ago, Theodore Roosevelt, who had, of course, created our national forest and national monuments, went to those barrier islands and said, We've got to keep them, not just for bird rookeries, but to prevent hurricanes that hit the city of New Orleans.

A hundred years later, nothing's been done that T.R. recommended. New Orleans is a city surrounded by water, it's been called a fishbowl lately. Many great cities in the world are—Venice, Amsterdam. We've

got to save New Orleans. We've got to start a rebuilding, but we're going to have to rebuild it with coastal wetlands restored, and with a new system of levees and dikes.

BROWN: You know, it, Doug, it's easy, I don't know if it's easy, but it's easier, to build buildings again. I mean, you take a lot of money and you can build buildings and the French Quarter can be the French Quarter and it's the math. I wonder if you think that the culture of New Orleans, this most unique of American cities, has been destroyed.

BRINKLEY: No, because culture's in the souls of people, and it means something to be from New Orleans. I can't tell you how many—you talk about jazz, it's not just going to a jazz museum or a jazz club. It's in the schools of New Orleans, the people that you see in the Astrodome, or you're seeing in Baton Rouge. They have that spirit, that free expression which jazz is the world's great gift of democracy all over, the concept of the spontaneity and expressing oneself through music.

New Orleans is one of the most-loved cities in the world. It's not really even an American city. It's an international heritage site. And that energy of those people and that soulfulness of those human beings are around, and they're going to stay in New Orleans.

And on a purely architectural note, the French Quarter's in pretty good shape. So are the historic homes up St. Charles and what's known as uptown, or Audubon Park, Tulane University, area. So some of it, tourism, which is the number one industry in town, is intact, what people come to New Orleans to see.

What's been destroyed, and what, the tragedy of New Orleans, is one of neglect. Some people call New Orleans the Big Easy. But the other term is The City Time Forgot. And one of the charms of New Orleans was its Mom and Pop stores and this kind of localism.

And I'm afraid some of that has been taken away. And I hope it doesn't get rebuilt in a strip-mall, fast-food, franchisey way, because New Orleans has always kept an individual identity as an international port city. And I hope and pray that it'll continue to remain as such.

BROWN: You know, one needs to take conversations this proximate to a tragedy with a grain of salt. But we talked to a number of people, some of whom were able to get out because they had the means and the resources to get out, and others who had to be evacuated who talked about they just never want to go back.

The soul is something, as you talked about, that exists in people, it doesn't exist in buildings. And if these people don't come home, then New Orleans really isn't New Orleans.

Anderson Cooper: Reporter's Notebook

So many words have already been spoken about what's happening here. So many words; what more can be said?

You drive down streets and don't recognize a thing. The water, the waste, New Orleans is buried. You clear trees and debris and feel on your own. It's a flooded frontier; the edge of the world.

Police at the station in the French Quarter put up a sign that says Fort Apache. That's pretty appropriate. It feels like it's the Wild West here. One officer just told me it's a war zone and every night they take fire; snipers shooting into the police station. They've now posted snipers on the buildings to shoot back. .

Every day we put on waders and motor through back streets in shallow bottom boats. Every street you go down, every corner you turn, another story, another shock of surprise. Desperate dogs, abandoned by owners dead or alive, scared, hungry. In a place of priorities, they're low on the list.

There are so many dogs which are just starving. And you try to feed them as much as you can, but there's too many of them roaming around. It's a health hazard.

We've all found ourselves in positions we're not used to—searching for survivors, taking chances every day. We were videotaping a helicopter rescue, two people plucked from their home by this massive machine. The helicopter's rotor churned up filthy water, spraying it on our cameras, getting it into our mouths.

Charlie, my producer, had to hang on to a stop sign to keep our boat from getting swamped. Chris, our photojournalist, cut off his shirt to keep Kevin's camera lens dry.

You do what you can. You try to stay clean and you try to stay safe. But it's not always possible in conditions like these.

When you're out in these flooded neighborhoods, the water is so contaminated. I mean, it's got human remains in it. It's got human waste. There are bodies floating in it. There are dogs defecating. You know, there's gas leaks. There is oil in the water. There are all sorts of just toxic chemicals. And you know, when these helicopters come down, they spray the water in your face you really have to try to keep your mouth shut, keep your eyes shut. But you know, we do what we can to try to clean up immediately afterwards.

There's no telling how long the cleanup of New Orleans will take. No telling how many days, how many bodies, how much money it's going to cost. For some, I suppose, the story has already gotten routine—same pictures, same rescues day after day.

If you ask me, that only adds to the horror of it all. I realized today that all week I'm referring to the dead I have seen, as bodies and corpses. I should be ashamed of myself. These are human beings, Americans, our neighbors. They had families. They had friends. And now they have nothing—no life, no future, not even dignity in death.

Radhika Chalasan/CNN/Getty

DAYS 11–14

Wednesday–Saturday, September 7–10, 2005

"Talk to these survivors, hear their stories and what they have been through. Look into their eyes. You will never think of America the same way."
—*Hemant Vankawala, a doctor with one of the medical teams set up at the New Orleans airport*

If everything that came before was Act One, then this is Act Two of Hurricane Katrina. The curtain goes up, and all sorts of things are revealed that couldn't be seen before. The players in this scene are the holdouts in their hideouts; the disease, bacteria, and waste beneath the water; the as-yet-undiscovered bodies, still trapped in flooded buildings and houses. Even the mistakes, the delays, and the bungling are players here. In the days to come, receding water and forced evacuations will slowly uncover a second tier of life—and death—in the City of New Orleans and beyond.

Mayor Ray Nagin has said repeatedly that there could be thousands of dead out there, under the water. The sniffer dogs are out. The mortuary teams are riding in their trucks. The National Guard is marking the houses. It isn't long before the news breaks of a gruesome discovery in Chalmette, in heavily damaged St. Bernard Parish—30 bodies at a single nursing home. Within a day, shrimpers on a search-and-rescue mission will make another horrific find: 15 bodies in the New Orleans Methodist Hospital. On Sunday, the bodies of 45 people are uncovered at Memorial Hospital.

Carol Costello: *"Our top story this morning is a devastating discovery near New Orleans. More than 30 bodies have been found at a single nursing home in Chalmette, La. Chalmette is in St. Bernard Parish. A state representative from the parish says residents of St. Rita's Nursing Home were left behind when the staff evacuated* [there were later conflicting reports about when this occured] *and a rescue that was supposed to take place never materialized. The New York Times is reporting that some residents tried to barricade the doors and the windows from the inside in an effort to keep the rising floodwaters from getting in. They were using their wheelchairs to do that.*

"It's just such a sad story. They tried to pound nails in the door. As many as 40 people from the home did manage to escape, but then again those 30 people could not."

AP Photo/Anja Niedringhaus

The wheelchair with a slipper still on the footrest sits in the mud left behind by Hurricane Katrina at St. Rita's Nursing Home in St. Bernard, La. Over 30 people died while waiting to be rescued from the floodwaters.

Now that the furor has died down—the Convention Center, the Superdome, the looting, the violence, the terror—a new landscape appears. It's made up of all the lesser-hit towns that, as it now turns out, barely survived like St. Bernard and Plaquemine. Each day, another dot on the map suddenly comes into view, with someone to tell the story of how Katrina took away everything that made life as they knew it normal, and how long they have waited for someone to come and help them pick up the pieces. Yesterday it was Bay St. Louis, Waveland, or Pass Christian. Today it's Pascagoula, where 80 percent of the town was flooded and the survivors comb the wreckage looking for something salvageable. But nothing is.

Beth Nissen in Pascagoula, Miss.

NISSEN: This is Pascagoula, Miss., home to 28,000 souls. All but a handful survived the hurricane winds, the 22-foot surge of sea water. But the city was half erased. The white shoe part of town, where Republican Senator Trent Lott had his home. The blue collar part of town, where the shipyard and refinery workers lived.

UNIDENTIFIED MALE: The south part of Pascagoula was totally devastated by this hurricane. I would guestimate that probably 80 percent of the houses in Pascagoula had floodwaters in them.

NISSEN: Now, the 58 police officers in Pascagoula, all of them still on the job and working 12-hour shifts, are dealing with a flood of a different kind—an overwhelming amount of relief supplies.

UNIDENTIFIED MALE: They're sending generators, chainsaws, clothing, diapers, food. You name it, it's coming in here.

NISSEN: Pascagoula has no one staging area right now for donated supplies. A local Baptist church is serving as one distribution point. But police here say officials don't have the manpower to offload incoming trucks, the ability to sort and label supplies, the means to distribute the contents, or any real idea of who needs what, except that thousands need just about everything.

UNIDENTIFIED MALE: The hardest part is going down and seeing people's lives all over the street, seeing people's lives piled up in front of their houses. And they're pulling everything out of their houses onto the streets—carpets, rugs, furniture, everything—because nothing is salvageable, absolutely nothing.

WARREN LUSH, HURRICANE SURVIVOR: It was a pretty place.

NISSEN: Still, on Belair Street, Warren Lush, age 84 and a World War II veteran, was on a mission to salvage something, helped by his daughter who had driven down from Pennsylvania. The water had marked its growth on his wall, giving everything he and his wife owned a putrid veneer of mud and sewage, turned family photos into inky blurs, ruined his old Bible. But he had his American flag up, was trying to keep his spirits up. Over on 12th Street, Douglas Francis had his flag showing, too, or what was left of his flag on what was left of his home.

DOUGLAS FRANCIS, HURRICANE SURVIVOR: Everything we own is up under there.

NISSEN: He, too, was trying to keep his spirits, his strength up.

FRANCIS: Oh, that was a brighter day. That was a brighter day.

A family walks around a destroyed house in Pascagoula, Miss.

NISSEN: FEMA is here. They had a dispatch, a fleet of 18-wheelers with emergency relief—food, water—which is being distributed at the county fair grounds. But there's been virtually no communication, coordination between local authorities and the FEMA team.

UNIDENTIFIED MALE: One of them will stop by the station to download some information from the Internet or use e-mail or something. So I know they're here. Now, what their organizational plan is, I'm not sure yet. I've been told they're going to set up at a local high school.

NISSEN: And people in Pascagoula, he says, are desperate for more than just emergency aid—for housing, tents, trailers. So are people in the next town and the next.

UNIDENTIFIED MALE: The further west you go, the worse the devastation is. We got the edge of the hurricane here. And you can see what the edge has caused.

NISSEN: But that gives Pascagoula the edge, he says, in recovering.

UNIDENTIFIED MALE: We're going to rebuild. Eventually we're going to rebuild. It's going to take time. This is a beautiful area, and it was a beautiful area before the storm. It's going to be a beautiful area again. It's just going to take time.

Fishing boats pushed ashore by Hurricane Katrina are shown where they came to rest on Highway 23 in Empire, La.

Below–(left to right) Sgt. 1st Class Uranga Pete, Staff Sgt. Paul Miera, and Specialist Anthony Bustillos from the New Mexico National Guard wade through water and debris as they check for bodies in homes destroyed after Hurricane Katrina in Port Sulphur, La.

GARY TUCHMAN: Route 23, the main road in Plaquemines Parish, La., a road that is now being used by the vessels of the sea. Southeast of New Orleans, sticking out into the bayou, most of Plaquemines now looks like the lost continent of Atlantis, the houses, the businesses, the parks, the memories of life under water. Three bodies have been recovered here, but dozens of people who are not believed to have evacuated are still missing. The search for them is taking place with local police and the military. Many people have been rescued, including crusty John Woodward, who realizes he's lucky.

JOHN WOODWARD: Well, the more you think about it, if you keep thinking about it, you'll go clean insane. Thirty-foot waves are not fun.

TUCHMAN: This parish is 67 miles long, from the outskirts of New Orleans in the north, to the mouth of the Mississippi in the south. It's the bottom two-thirds of the parish, the part behind me, that became submerged after Hurricane Katrina arrived.

What you see here is surreal and depressing. Shirts still hanging in the closet of a house that is destroyed, caskets that have washed up from cemeteries and floated away, confused cattle hunting for the last pieces of dry land, and a truck, somehow perfectly balanced on an air-conditioning vent.

Russell Gainy owns an excavating company and volunteers for the sheriff's department. His home and business are gone. He uses his bulldozer, which was spared, to do his small part in the huge cleanup effort.

RUSSELL GAINY: It's just—everything is just leveled. It's like a bomb went off.

TUCHMAN: The water levels are receding and will continue to do so. But the damage is immense.

TUCHMAN: Mississippi River barges are on land. And towns like Home Place are now places in the sea. Life has given all here a detour.

"Open up, police!" could be the most frequent phrase heard over the next few days in New Orleans. Mayor Nagin, whose mandatory evacuation order seems to have had little effect, now authorizes his policemen and National Guard to use force. Many bodies, loosely covered, still lie in the open, threatening to spread disease like wildfire through this watery graveyard. Nagin wants everyone out. Everyone meaning the same 10,000 that were here yesterday. And the day before. And will probably be here tomorrow.

The stragglers and holdouts remain in New Orleans; in fact, some estimates say there are up to 15,000 still out there. Sleeping on porches, guarded by their dogs in houses with no ceilings or windows, foraging for canned goods at burned-out convenience stores. They seem oblivious to the water, the odors, and the health hazards these present. In fact, some of them seem right at home. The threat of force, however, causes many who stockpiled guns during the violent days following the hurricane to

A holdout talks to a search and rescue officer. Efforts to evacuate the remainder of New Orleans' weary population are met with some resistance.

Shannon Stapleton/Reuters/Landov

turn those same guns on whoever comes to pull them out. It's also a civil rights issue that raises eyebrows around the country.

Eddie Compass, New Orleans police superintendent: *"Well, right now people cannot believe this, but we're still in the process of evacuating individuals who are voluntarily wanting to leave. We still have thousands of people that are in the city under water, so I'm not going to use my efforts for forced evacuation until we take care of all the people who want to voluntarily leave. "*

The battlefield has shifted: from saving the people of New Orleans to fighting them. But no one has the heart to take from these survivors the only thing they have left: the dignity of remaining in their homes, however meager. Their defiance and doggedness puzzle newscasters, who have smelled the garbage, waded through the filthy swamp that still covers the city, and have boated by the dead bodies. And yet, every interview and encounter sheds more light on what gives New Orleans its particular flavor: The locals know that if they leave, something will disappear with the leaving, and it will never come back.

Most police and National Guard, in the end, are the ones who offer little resistance, advising the exhausted, hungry citizens where to find water or rations. It's rare that the authorities use force. It's not just the sight of a shotgun in someone's lap, or a frail woman in her eighties struggling at her threshold. Something about it won't work with these folks.

Joe Raedle/Getty Images

AARON BROWN: In talking to people in New Orleans, today, I've had no sense that they're on any timetable or, in truth, have much desire to forcibly remove anybody. Do you?

ANDERSON COOPER: Yeah, you know, it's weird, it depends on who you talk to, I mean, some people I met were removed and they said soldiers came to their home, banged on their door, and said, "Look, you got five minutes, you're packing out, you're getting out." Then I've seen other people told, "OK, it'll be a couple days, you can, you know, work on your house, get yourself together." So, often, you know, here the left hand doesn't know what the right hand is doing and so there's conflicting reports. And this thing Jeff mentioned about pets is a huge deal. Some people are being told you can bring your pets . . . I've seen pets being loaded on to helicopters; others are being told, "No you can't" and they're staying.

BROWN: The evacuation story, when it happens, will be interesting. It's one thing to be told you have five minutes to leave, and then another thing, if you say "No, I'm not going" then they don't really know what to do, and nobody wants to be pulling people out of these houses, regardless.

Rose Adams, rescued from St. Bernard Parish: *"They're not supposed to force you out of your house. And I told my son that. I'm sure I could have stayed there. Nobody could have forced me out. I want to die in my own house, if I have to die. I'm old. And I'm ready to go, I'm not afraid of death. And if I could stay there and die in the same house where my husband died, which we bought together and lived together for a number of years, I want—I would be happy."*

Soledad O'Brien: *"People here carry weapons, and people are stockpiling weapons in their homes because they're not going to leave their homes. Wait until you start seeing pictures of the actual way the removals are forced. I mean, I'm curious to know, will they put handcuffs on a little old lady and haul her out? Will they draw weapons? Will a SWAT team go in and remove an 87-year-old who doesn't want to leave her home?"*

Soledad O'Brien Interview with Delia Labarre, New Orleans Resident

S. O'BRIEN: We want to tell you the story of the folks who have decided that they are going to stay in spite of the mandatory evacuation order. You'll recall on Thursday, you met Delia Labarre. She told us that she has no interest in leaving and invited us, in fact, to come and see her home after the show, which is exactly what we did.

Delia Labarre has water and candles, a hurricane lantern, a gas stove, and a hardy constitution.

LABARRE: The gas. It's very nice to have gas.

S. O'BRIEN: She's refusing to leave her house in New Orleans Warehouse District.

LABARRE: We were high and dry. It never came up at all. We never saw water on this street.

S. O'BRIEN: And she's angry—no, make that furious about the mayor's plan to forcibly evacuate all of the residents of New Orleans.

LABARRE: There was no real plan to evacuate. So I don't think—it's difficult to trust that there is any plan to revitalize the city.

S. O'BRIEN: She spends her days cleaning up after Hurricane Katrina. The sandbags in her courtyard lie useless. The water never got that high. Delia says local citizens have the right to have a say in the future of their city, and local leaders, like Mayor Ray Nagin, have had the wrong priorities.

LABARRE: If they had been as obsessed with an evacuation plan in protecting the people as they were with the Saints and whether or not we were going to keep a professional football team, this would not have happened.

S. O'BRIEN: Delia is even convinced she's got legal grounds to fight her evacuation.

LABARRE: Just thinking about it, you know? I know, and I feel for them, and I understand completely, because there are worse things than death. And people do have a choice. I think, you know, even at this point, because they have failed miserably.

S. O'BRIEN: When you go to Delia's house, you see how she is living, which is fairly comfortably, with running water. Granted she doesn't have electricity, but she's got batteries for a little TV and batteries for a radio and communications. You do sort of wonder if she is the kind of person who should be moved into a shelter if all of the folks whose homes were not devastated, who did not have to wade through water to get out of their front doors, actually are living pretty well.

MILES O'BRIEN: Well, and I'm sure, Soledad, a lot of people watching that and say, what's the matter with her staying there? What is the city line on this? Why does she have to go? She is high and dry and self-sufficient.

S. O'BRIEN: The city line has been that every single person has to leave the city. That there is an evacuation order, and it applies to everyone is what she's been told.

M. O'BRIEN: But the truth is, you know, if she is truly self-sufficient, which she appears to be, by leaving she becomes a burden to somebody. And so, in a sense, you would think they'd want to allow people like that to stay on if they could.

Travis Fox/washingtonpost.com

Carol Costello: *"There's an interesting article in the Wall Street Journal. And it's talking about how some of the very wealthy people of New Orleans have managed to stay. There's a part of New Orleans called Audubon Park. And they're talking about—I'm just going to read a bit of the article: 'The green expanse of Audubon Park and the city's uptown area has doubled in recent days as a heliport for the city's rich and a terminus for the small armies of private security guards who have been dispatched to keep the homes there safe and habitable.' In fact, they talk of one wealthy man who hired Israeli security guards. He helicoptered them in to guard the homes in that area from looters. You know, you just wonder, these people are still in their homes and there's no water around them.*

"Will they also face that mandatory evacuation like the others who are trapped in their homes and don't want to go? I'm just reading more of this article and it's just—I guess it just highlights the huge gulf between the rich and the poor in New Orleans."

Johnny White's Bar on Bourbon Street, "the bar that never closes," lived up to its reputation and stayed open while Katrina struck the city. The bar never closed and the locals never stopped drinking. It's a place short on space but long on character and atmosphere. It became a bastion for the holdouts.

The curtain rises, too, on the missing—those countless hundreds who were separated from their families—those who climbed onto buses and helicopters, those left behind in hospitals and on rooftops. Where are they and how will they ever be found? Efforts are in motion to compile a national registry, but there are obvious obstacles: Too many of them are children, too young to tell their rescuers who they are. Too many are elderly, who are so stunned by events that they can't recall where they came from or who they belong to. It begins to look as if some will be lost forever, accidental citizens of wherever they end up.

Hundreds of agencies open their doors to help hurricane victims find each other. Everyday exposure through the media gives those separated by the disaster ample air-time to try to reconnect: Faces and names of the children are broadcast each day, with toll-free numbers to call. The National Center for Missing and Exploited Children launches a Web site to help reunite children and their parents using photographs taken of children and parents at shelters in Alabama, Mississippi, Louisiana, and Texas.

Excerpt from Soledad O'Brien Interview with Ernie Allen, CEO of the National Center for Missing and Exploited Children

O'BRIEN: How many children are we talking about? How many are missing from their parents who are looking for them?

ALLEN: As of yesterday, we've reached 1,500 missing child reports. And the numbers are growing.

O'BRIEN: What percentage do you think are children who are displaced? And what percentage do you think are children whose parents did not survive the flooding, do you know?

ALLEN: We have no idea. Obviously a large percentage of these children are not missing in the traditional sense, we know where they are. We just don't know where their parents are. So this is an atypical search process for the National Center for Missing and Exploited Children, but one in which we are working closely with state and local law enforcement, the FBI, social services agencies. And we're making real headway. We've already recovered 258 children and reunited them with their families.

O'BRIEN: How is that being done? I know you have a phone number, 1-800-THE-LOST which is the number that usually anybody can call to get in touch with your organization. But what happens when somebody calls? How does it work?

ALLEN: Well, Soledad, the Justice Department asked us to set up a special Katrina missing persons hotline. So we're asking people to call 888-544-5475. When those reports are received, they captured that information on missing children and adults by our volunteers here, all retired law enforcement officers. They are then validated and verified by a second team of retired law enforcement here beside me. They then go to our case managers on the second floor of this building, who are working with law enforcement. And we have our Team Adam staff on the scene on the ground in the affected areas.

O'BRIEN: I wanted to ask you, we're looking at these pictures as you were talking of your Web site. Some of these kids are really little. I mean, that must be a huge logistical challenge in the teeny tiny ones, you know, whose aren't really old enough to be helpful with the basic information like their name.

ALLEN: Absolutely, Soledad. Many of these people can't even—these children can't even tell us who they are. So we're using every resource.

In some cases, we've been able to identify the child. And then we search for the parents. In other cases, we're trying to use the power of photographs. Our Team Adam staff with digital cameras is taking pictures of these little people and trying to get them on the air. We're really grateful for all that CNN has done in helping us do that.

O'BRIEN: Well, we're more than happy to be helping out. I want to show a couple of pictures today. A little girl named Kirarra Roberts. I think she looks like she's about two years old. Outside of showing her picture and putting that information, what else are you able to do for kids like this?

ALLEN: Well, we are working with school authorities. She's preschool age, but social service agencies, we have worked very closely with the Louisiana and Texas social service agencies trying to track down the parents. One of the challenges here is we've had cases in which children have been in one shelter, parents in another shelter in another state. And there's been no ability to link the two. That's getting better. Information sharing, database access is really improving.

O'BRIEN: That's good to know. Let's show a final picture of this little girl. I know you don't have a name for her yet. And she looks about two-ish?

ALLEN: She may be two years old, and [she] is not able to tell us who she is.

O'BRIEN: Do you think she's traumatized? Or do you think she's just, you know, a lot of two-years-olds actually don't talk quite yet.

ALLEN: Absolutely. And so many of these children are traumatized. They've seen their whole worlds, everything they have known in their life to date washed away. So it's really important that we make them feel safe and secure and give them hope.

The curtain has also been pulled back on FEMA, and consequently on the wealth of red tape entangling rescue efforts and deliveries of supplies. Despite FEMA's countless promises of relief aid, the presence of the military and visits by President Bush, many of Katrina's victims are still awaiting the government's helping hand.

Embattled FEMA Director Michael Brown's assurances to the contrary are unflagging, and at a Sept. 7 press conference, he explains at length that his agency is going to rebuild the infrastructure of the New Orleans police, give Governor Blanco everything she needs, supply over 100,000 trailers to Mississippi, and basically save the Gulf Coast. Of the over 50,000 offers of private donations, and countries all over the world offering help, Brown continues to explain away FEMA's failure to utilize them: "That has to be coordinated in such a way," he says, "that it's used most effectively, that it's used where it's needed. And that's the same with the firefighters and the police officers and that's why we're going through that process."

Brown fields questions from openly hostile reporters, including one who asks if he's offered his resignation, and another challenging FEMA's choice of Pat Robertson's Operation Blessing as one of three charities they suggest Americans make donations to in support of Katrina victims. By Thursday, *Time* magazine, has pulled his résumé from the FEMA website and is taking a long hard look at it. The discrepancies that come to light include a professorship that never existed and a job as an assistant city manager that was more along the lines of assistant *to* the city manager.

His hot seat gets so hot that Nancy Pelosi, the outspoken representative from California, urges Bush to fire him.

He is not fired and seems in no hurry to resign. However, he is recalled to Washington on Friday, September 9.

"I'm going to go home, and walk my dog, and hug my wife, and maybe get a good Mexican meal and a stiff margarita and a full night's sleep and then I'm going to go right back to FEMA and continue to do all I can to help these victims."—Michael Brown, Sept. 9, 2005

He continues to direct the flatfooted agency, whose latest goof is a call from FEMA to state officials in South Carolina, announcing that a plane with as many as 180 evacuees was headed to Charleston. The health official says FEMA told them there were some on board who would require medical assistance. Health officials scrambled, lining up buses and ambulances at the airport, but the plane never arrived. Well, actually it did, but not in Charleston, South Carolina. It was sent to Charleston, West Virginia.

FEMA also runs into a wall with its latest idea, a debit card worth $2,000 offered to hurricane victims so they can get back on their feet. The program was aimed at those most in need, to be issued on a one-per-household basis, specifically to those at major evacuation centers such as the Houston Astrodome. Candidates who line up and wait for hours in anticipation of the promised cards are turned away the first day. On Thursday, lines snake around the Reliant complex before the sun comes up, but by evening, even though the Red Cross chips in to issue their own debit cards, all the money is gone. Not unexpectedly, the crowds go wild, and police lock the doors in defense. FEMA swiftly changes the plan, and offers to make direct bank deposits into evacuees accounts provided each applicant fills out a form on FEMA's Web site. Since not many will have access to a) a computer or b) a bank, this plan is soon scrapped as well.

A family of nine sits outside their demolished home in Pascagoula, Miss. With no gas to leave and their food and water running low, many families in the area face a bleak future.

FEMA Director Michael Brown: *"We're putting together a very unique program for the debit card to get it to folks that register with us, or are in the shelters right now, to get them a debit card with a minimum of $2,000 on there so they can start utilizing that money for emergency supplies they may need, clothing, if they need to, you know, do some minor repairs if they happen to be in some of the areas that weren't hit quite as hard.*

"But the concept is, is to get them some cash in hand, which allows them—empowers them to make their own decisions about what do they need to have to start rebuilding their lives. . . . This is something that FEMA has not done before. We think it's a great way to, again, empower these hurricane survivors to really start rebuilding their lives."

Rep. Nancy Pelosi [D-Ca.], Minority Leader: *"[President Bush] chose someone with absolutely no credentials. And you know what? When I said to the president that he should fire [FEMA Director] Michael Brown, he said 'Why would I do that?' I said, 'Because of all that went wrong, with all that didn't go right last week. . . .' and the President said: "What didn't go right?"*

ED HENRY: *"The Republican National Committee chairman, Ken Mehlman, just put out a tough statement saying that that is completely over the top, [Pelosi statement] a sign that even over these relief efforts, there's real partisanship digging in here."*

Brown resigns on Monday the 12th of September, but FEMA sticks around. Even a new director, Coast Guard Vice Admiral Thad Allen, can't go very far to turn the tide of the agency's tangled red tape—sometimes so stunning that even eyewitness accounts are hard to believe. Doctors prevented from helping dying people; firefighters diverted to Atlanta for FEMA training sessions on community relations and sexual harassment; trucks hauling water to staging areas stopped for

INTERVIEW

Miles O'Brien

Dr. Jeffrey Guy,
Vanderbilt Burn Center

Ken Rusnak,
Angel Flights America

O'BRIEN: Did mid-level bureaucrats interested in protecting turf make it harder for people to help those hard hit by Katrina? Our next guest answers emphatically yes.

Dr. Jeffrey Guy is with the regional burn center at Vanderbilt University in Nashville. He says doctors were thwarted in their efforts to help. And in Dallas, Ken Rusnak, executive director of Angel Flights America, which provides emergency medical flights by private pilots for those in crisis, he says his pilots ran into all kinds of road blocks. Let's begin with you, Dr. Guy. Tell us what doctors encountered as they tried to help out?

GUY: We've had reports from all over the country where doctors and nurses using assets bought by the United States government were basically diverted or detained, because they didn't have the appropriate authorization or they had been authorized perhaps by the wrong government agency.

want of "tasker numbers;" Amtrak trains turned back; volunteer morticians barred from New Orleans . . . the list goes on and on.

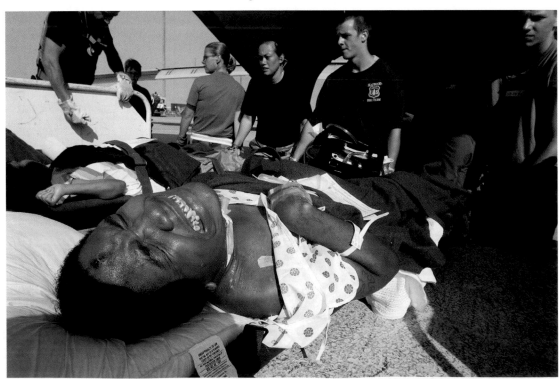

A victim of Hurricane Katrina winces in pain while waiting to be airlifted by the U.S. military out of New Orleans International Airport.

Mario Tama/Getty Images

O'BRIEN: Authorization is a good thing, though, when you're talking about medical care, right?

GUY: Absolutely. But when somebody is dying, we have clearly people in need, and the first response, whether it's a disaster like this or it's somebody who is bleeding on the highway, you need to match the resources to the needs immediately.

O'BRIEN: And the kind of response you got was what?

GUY: Well, basically more bureaucracy. And we're seeing that even until today. What you're now seeing in the public eye is the kind of mid-level fighting between various agencies in different jurisdictions that have been going on for the past week is now becoming in the public.

O'BRIEN: Talk about a disaster Ken Rusnak, I've been hearing from all kinds of pilot friends all this past week or so just trying to use airplanes to try to help out and running into just silly regulations, temporary flight restrictions, unable to carry people because they didn't have the proper forms filled out. Has any of this been rectified?

RUSNAK: As far as I know, it's running pretty smoothly now, Miles. We have not had any problems getting our pilots in and out of Baton Rouge.

Our problems occurred really sort of early on when we began to realize that there really was no command and control in place down there as far as the aid situation. We dispatched pilots last Friday trying to get 80 what we call medically challenged people out of Baton Rouge at the request of the River Center shelter, and ran into a situation where we arrived and there were no patients. And when we called the head of the shelter to find out what happened, we were told that the governor's office had denied us access to take them out of state because . . .

O'BRIEN: So let's get this straight. This is the governor of Louisiana, correct, denying you access?

RUSNAK: Well, we don't know if it was the governor, Miles. We know that it came out of the governor's office.

O'BRIEN: OK. But denying you the permission . . .

RUSNAK: Right.

O'BRIEN: . . . to get these people to some proper care on what basis?

RUSNAK: Well, we got several explanations. One was that if we took them out of state, they would lose their FEMA reimbursement.

O'BRIEN: Really? That sounds like nonsense.

RUSNAK: Well, we were unable to verify that. We sent one of our people to the governor's office, and we were unable to get really any information. So, we just created our own command and control after that, set up our own op center at the Baton Rouge airport, and our people did a really yeoman's duty.

O'BRIEN: So, you just stepped into the vacuum and kind of took over.

RUSNAK: Well, we've got a lot of ex-military on board, and they jumped in there and said, we know how to do this, and they did. And they started circulating in the shelters. They got a hold of shelter people, Red Cross people, found patients that needed help and started moving people out of there with our aircraft.

O'BRIEN: All right. Dr. Guy, back to you for a moment. On the one hand, these stories really outraged people. It compounds a disaster.

GUY: Right.

O'BRIEN: On the other hand, this is such an unprecedented disaster that a lot of confusion, which a lot of this could be attributed to confusion, would be understandable. Where do you come down on that?

GUY: Well, Ken's story is not unique. I mean, we can tell you stories of 60, 70 ambulances being dispatched to areas and not being accessed to patients, because they don't have the right hanging government I.D. Ken made a good point. There was clearly a void of leadership. And in their organization, they created leadership where there was none.

What we have to be focused on here are the people, not the processes. And there's an over-focus right now on the processes. When people are in need, they need that now. I'm sure that a person in need does not care that a bottle of water came from FEMA or the Coast Guard or the Red Cross or some Baptist relief organization.

O'BRIEN: All right. I want to get before you get away. People, not process, that's something to take away from this. Quickly, gentlemen, Dr. Guy first, do you think people lost their lives as a result of this?

GUY: Yes.

RUSNAK: Yes, I'm afraid I'd have to say, because there were a number of diabetics and dialysis patients that we were unable to move, I think. And I don't know how well they fared after we were unable to move them.

Michael DeMocker/*Times-Picayune*/NNS /Landov

Outside a rug shop on St. Charles Avenue in New Orleans, SFC Eusebio Perez of the Texas Army National Guard stands by a humorous sign after a group of soldiers stopped to take pictures of it during a patrol.

President Bush announces his third trip to the region on Sept. 11. In the preceding days, Vice President Cheney arrives to survey damage to the area. After touring New Orleans, Cheney says that tax increases will not be needed to help pay for the enormous cost of reconstruction.

Daryn Kagan: *"Another VIP visit to tell you about today. First Lady Laura Bush heads to Iowa and Mississippi. She'll visit schools in Des Moines and South Haven to put the spotlight on the plight of displaced children. The first lady will be accompanied by Education Secretary Margaret Spellings during her travels. The visits by the first lady, the vice president, and the attorney general are part of a major offensive by the White House. They have been stung by criticism that they moved too slowly. Officials are pulling out all the stops to regain lost ground."*

In an effort to provide Americans the answers he says they deserve, Senator Bill Frist (R-Tenn.) announces a joint House-Senate panel that will investigate the initial response to Hurricane Katrina. The panel will review, "at all levels of government," both the preparation and recovery from the hurricane. It will report its findings to Congress on Feb. 15, 2006. Democrats are informed about the panel by the media.

The latest $51.8 billion relief aid that President Bush requested passes, though there is some question about the percentage—roughly 90 precent—that will go to the much-criticized FEMA.

ED HENRY: *"A unique disaster that clearly begs a massive federal response, but the bulk of the new funds, $50 billion, is going directly to an agency [FEMA] under fire for alleged incompetence. Congress does give FEMA some suggestions for how to spend the money, such as $23 billion in housing assistance and direct aid to victims, $4.6 billion for FEMA operations, three billion for the Army Corps of Engineers, $1.6 billion for trailers for temporary housing. But the bill specifically gives FEMA wide latitude to shift those suggestions as it wishes."*

Jeff Greenfield, CNNs senior political correspondent: *"Four years and tens of billions of dollars later, some of what plagued the rescuers in New York were on painful display in New Orleans. Communications collapses, responders without a clear picture of the disaster, or directions to handle it. But while Sept. 11 was literally a bolt from the blue, Katrina was a disaster in plain sight for days, whose potential consequences were known, literally, for years.*

"There will be no shortage of hearings and task forces and media investigations to try to answer that question. But part of the answer does seem clear. The response to the attack of Sept. 11 was a classic bureaucratic response, aimed at a direct immediate threat. And part of that

response may have left the country less able to respond to threats less dramatic, but much more probable. Consider the central response of Washington to the terror attacks, the creation of a new Cabinet-level department, the Department of Homeland Security, with 180,000 people. That's the biggest new department since the Defense Department was created in 1947, with an annual budget of $30 billion. That department's focus, understandably, was terror.

"But that meant that when the Federal Emergency Management Agency was placed in the department, its traditional focus, natural disasters, was played down. For instance, as the Wall Street Journal reported on Tuesday, officials in Shelby County, Ala., were permitted to use department funds to buy chemical suits, but not to fund an operations center to improve communications during tornadoes. Shelby County, Ala., is not exactly a prime terrorist target, but it has experienced 20 tornadoes in the last half century."

Tim Roemer, former Democratic congressman and member of the 9/11 Commission: "We had our first post-9/11 test and we've miserably failed. We're not prepared for a disaster. We're not prepared for large-scale terrorist attack. Our government couldn't drop water to our most needy citizens. We couldn't get generators to people in hospitals. We didn't go by an evacuation plan. I think the first place to start here is not just pointing the finger, it's to get things right and be accountable."

Excerpt from Miles O'Brien Interview with David Gergen editor-at-large for *U.S. News & World Report,* **Adviser to Presidents Nixon, Ford, Reagan, and Clinton**

GERGEN: Let's give credit where it's due. This president has shown enormous compassion when he has been exposed to things. When he went to New York for the 9/11 and picked up that bullhorn and talked to the firefighters, he did show enormous compassion. As governor, he showed enormous compassion. Somehow this just didn't—his aides didn't bring him in to let him see the suffering so he didn't pick up on it . . .

M. O'BRIEN: Is he in too much of a bubble, David?

GERGEN: Well, you wonder about that because it's—in the first term, these folks seemed to be enormously sensitive to what was going on around them. They were. And they were politically adept. But this second term, you know, with the Schiavo case and then when Cindy Sheehan was out there on the driveway in Crawford, and here in the initial reactions to New Orleans, this doesn't seem like the same team on the field. And I—it's—there is an imperial quality about it, which I am sure that does not represent what the president himself wants. I do believe in his heart of hearts he really does care about suffering.

Two dogs run past a house marked with a note, "Dead Body Inside" in the Ninth Ward district of New Orleans.

Residents ride in the back of a truck through toxic floodwaters from Hurricane Katrina in St. Bernard Parish near New Orleans.

Reuters/David J. Phillip/Landov

Excerpt from Sophia Choi and Sen. Mary Landrieu (D-La.)

LANDRIEU: I know what the people are suffering. The governor knows, the president knows, the military officials know. And they're trying to do the very best they can to stabilize the situation. Sen. Vitter, our congressional delegation, all of us understand what is happening. We are doing our very, very best to get the situation under control. But I want to thank the president. He will be here tomorrow, we think. And the military is sending assets as we speak.

CHOI: But those assets were a long time coming. And when the fingerpointing began, with federal officials responding to criticism directed at them by blaming Louisiana state and local officials for the problems on the ground, Sen.Landrieu took offense.

LANDRIEU: If one person criticizes them or says one more thing, including the president of the United States, he will hear from me. One more word about it, after this show airs, and I might likely have to punch him, literally. But their infrastructure, our infrastructure, is devastated. Their lives are in shatters. The region is torn to pieces. Would the president please stop taking photo ops, and please come see what I'm trying to show him?

Bad water. Toxic mud. Lack of information and relief. It adds up to another crisis of mismanagement and failed intentions.

And in one final insult to the dignity of those trapped in the floodwaters, a persistent rumor that the levees were breached on purpose. While this so-called "urban myth" has no basis in fact, there is a historical basis. During the Great Mississippi Flood in 1927, wealthy city fathers in New Orleans persuaded the federal officials to dynamite the main Caernarvon, La., levee in order to flood the mostly poor, rural southern parishes, in order to protect their own business interests. The river rushed through St. Bernard and Plaquemines parishes at the rate of 250,000 cubic feet per second. The water did not recede until July, six months later. Although the residents of those parishes had been promised restitution for the loss of their homes, none ever materialized.

In 1965, many who had lived through the late '20s in the region were still alive. And when Hurricane Betsy came ashore, residents of the still-poor parishes were convinced that once again, the levees were purposely breached to save the rich, white neighborhoods from destruction—and sacrifice the lower Ninth Ward in the

With 23 out of 148 pumping stations working, the water drains slowly but surely from the city—the Army Corps reduces the estimate from 80 days to a month; they are pumping the equivalent of 432 Olympic-size swimming pools out of the city every hour. In St. Bernard Parish, the water has fallen five feet. What it leaves in its wake is just one more gathering storm of problems: sludge. About a million tons of it throughout the Gulf Coast, mud that's almost certain to be as dangerous as the water. And because bacteria and pathogens can live in it, once it's dry, steps need to be taken to decontaminate it. Fuel spills, too, stick around in the soil. Chemicals in the lake sediment are likely to be stirred up anytime there's another storm. Household pollutants—pesticide sprays, oil cans, gasoline containers, acetone—have seeped into the water, and ultimately, the soil. And that's not counting everything that's already been floating around in the floodwater for the past two weeks. People in isolated districts are living in houses coated with it, and still may not know to boil their water before drinking it.

process. Although no proof ever existed that this occurred, many in the Ninth Ward to this day believe that then, Mayor Victor Hugo Schiro ordered the levees to be blown up in order to protect his own Lakeview neighboohood.

Katrina's threatening winds and rains evoked memories of both 1927 and 1965, memories that were summed up in these interviews by David Remick in a recent *New Yorker* article:

At the Houston Astrodome, for instance, people made statements and asked questions that mixed the logical with the conspiratorial.

"Where were the buses?"

"Why is it, do you think, that the French Quarter and the Garden District are high and dry and the Ninth is flooded and gonna get bulldozed?"

"In Betsy I know the mayor blew up the levee to save those big homes on the lakefront. A lot of people believe that, especially the people who were on their roofs!"

"I couldn't leave. I was terrified. I didn't have any money, no car, nothing. Where was I supposed to go? They shoulda had some buses. It's me and my five kids. I live in Desire, the Ninth Ward. I think it was a setup to get black folks out of New Orleans forever. Look around. Who's here? Nobody but the black and the poor. They ain't got but ten white families in the whole Astrodome."

At the Reliant Center, in Houston, Patricia Valentine, a 54-year-old woman from Treme, a black neighborhood near the French Quarter, told me that her area was "waist high" in water and the restaurants down the street "got nothing." She was sitting in a wheelchair and said that she had no intention of returning home. "They can have New Orleans," she said. "It's a toxic-waste dump now. I was in Betsy forty years ago: September, 1965. And the levee broke. What are we, stupid? Born yesterday? It's the same people drowning today as back then. They were trying to move us out anyway. They want a bigger tourist attraction, and we black folks ain't no tourist attraction."

Fifteen days after Hurricane Katrina struck, California Task Force members rescued an elderly man, who was near death, from home where he had been trapped by floodwaters.

Bruce Chambers/*Orange County Register*

INTERVIEW

Anderson Cooper

Dr. Gregory Henderson,
Pathologist

COOPER: Let's talk about this water. I mean, how bad is it? CDC says its got high levels of e. coli. What else does it have?

HENDERSON: This water has got everything. This water is not only—I mean, we've been talking about infectious organisms. Everything that lives in your colon is out here flourishing in this heat. Everything, every bacteria that you could probably think of you could probably culture out here. I think, right when I was out there for the first time experiencing that, that's when I really appreciate just how much chemical there is in this water. We took a big splash in our face.

COOPER: You got it on your face?

HENDERSON: Yes, we had a bunch of it.

COOPER: Did you or any of those guys out there have safety gear on?

HENDERSON: No. They're all wet. They're all getting evac'ed out to the zephyr spot to get cleaned up. I mean we hit—you know, you're driving on streets with cars that are sunk. And so the boats are hitting cars.

COOPER: It's incredible. You've been working with the first responders. You don't know this at home, but this man is a hero for what he has done. You have been here when no one else was. You were working in the Convention Center. Virtually the only medical personnel there was you walking around trying to treat 15,000 people with a stethoscope.

HENDERSON: Trying, not doing a very good job, but doing the best I could.

COOPER: How frustrated, angered, whatever the word is, are you by what you have seen by the response here on the ground these last days, these last weeks?

HENDERSON: Well you know, the last few days we're coming together. So we're starting to get a response. Obviously the first few days there was no response, so my level as a physician was incredibly frustrated. My job, the way I think as a physician, the way I'm hardwired is, you see a problem, you make a diagnosis and you fix it. You do everything you can to fix it. And you're in a situation where you have got innumerable medical problems laying out right in front of you and no means to do anything about it.

COOPER: People died, in your mind, from what you have seen with your own two eyes, people died because of the lack of response?

HENDERSON: People died, yes. People died because there was no medical care here to give them. Absolutely.

COOPER: Children, babies died because there were no IVs for them.

HENDERSON: People got dehydrated. Babies, old people, more old people than babies, thank God, but some babies did die. One night we had one woman give birth and I think the baby did die that evening.

COOPER: You've also been treating New Orleans Police Department, New Orleans Fire Department, these local responders who, I mean, they don't even have these protective masks, in many cases, which I have just started to wear. When you hear politicians in Washington saying, well you know what, response to this start from the bottom up, and if they couldn't do it they should have asked for the federal government. And it's got to go from the ground up. You probably haven't heard them say that, but that's what they just said.

HENDERSON: I haven't heard what everybody's been talking about. I can tell you something right now, that all I have seen for the past nine days is ground up inaction. I have seen people, I've seen—you called me a hero, I'm not a hero. The New Orleans Police Department, individual men who didn't vacate their job and stayed 24 hours a day and did exactly what I did. Those are the heroes on the ground. The people on the ground didn't have the structure to tell them what to do. And they figured it out on the fly. We've all figured it out on the fly.

COOPER: So, what do you want to tell people in Washington who are, you know, pointing fingers and playing the blame game?

HENDERSON: Look, we are going to waste a lot of time spending time blaming everybody about everything. People can make careers out of blaming things. Let's solve the problem. I'm willing to get together with them and solve the problem.

What this entire episode has exposed for us, just like 9/11 exposed a problem, OK, this exposed a massive problem. The problem is put very simply, this, is we really do not have any immediate civilian medical response team to drop into a disaster area that can handle the population and give them what they need. I mean quickly. Not four days, five days, I mean now.

We are all used to, we are very familiar—we are the generation of M.A.S.H. as a television show, you know, military army surgical hospital. We need to start thinking about civilian mobile hospitals where we can drop in and treat these people quickly. And that's what we need. Because we can't have me running around with a stethoscope, holding hands and patting shoulders. That's not going to do any good.

Points of View

"But to my country I want to say this:
During this crisis you failed us."

—Anne Rice, author, native of New Orleans

"The CNN footage does not even begin to do it justice—the roar of the motor blades, the smell of jet -A [fuel] and the thousands of eyes looking at us for answers, for hope. . . ."

—Hemant Vankawala, a doctor with one of the medical teams set up at the New Orleans airport

"There were many decent, innocent people trapped in New Orleans when the deluge hit—but they were trapped alongside large numbers of people from two groups: criminals—and wards of the welfare state, people selected, over decades, for their lack of initiative and self-induced helplessness. The welfare wards were a mass of sheep—on whom the incompetent administration of New Orleans unleashed a pack of wolves."

—Robert Tracinski, editor of TIADaily.com and the Intellectual Activist

"We have grown accustomed to the best-case scenarios in the U.S.; we have come to assume that we will always have electricity and fresh water and an endless pipeline of goods and services. We assume that we can always control our fate, that we are exempt from chaos, and that governance is a necessary evil rather than an essential good, the ultimate civilized defense against the rudeness of nature."

—Joe Klein, Time Columnist

"In Katrina's collision with New Orleans, the essence of primitivism, howling nature, met one of mankind's most sophisticated works, a modern city. But what makes cities such marvels—the specializations and divisions of labor that sustain myriad webs of dependencies—also makes them fragile. Forgetting that is hubris, an ingredient of tragedy.

So Katrina has provided a teaching moment. This is a liberal hour in that it illustrates the indispensability and dignity of the public sector. It also is a conservative hour, dramatizing the prudence of pessimism, and the fact that the first business of goverment, on which *everything* depends, is security."

—George Will, The Last Word," Newsweek

"Everything I own now is in that truck, but the shelters are too overcrowded and uncomfortable. I was born and raised on this coast, so I'm a good little redneck. I got a bow and arrow to kill food, and that's what I'm going to be eating . . . at least in the woods I don't have to smell the dead bodies."

—John Padgett, a boat captain in Pass Christian, Miss.

"Everybody is out there saying, 'We need a Giuliani!' What was Rudy Giuliani? He was a mayor. Has anybody seen Ray Nagin? Was Ray Nagin in the Superdome? Was Kathleen Blanco in the Superdome? Yeah, we need a Rudy, fine, but Rudy was not part of federal government, folks."

—Rush Limbaugh, syndicated radio talk show host

"Your job is going to be community relations. You'll be passing out FEMA pamphlets and our phone number."

—FEMA official instructions to firefighters and other emergency personnel brought to Atlanta for training before being sent to New Orleans

"The subsequent forays by government forces may have reassured outsiders desperate that help get into the deluged city, but they just pissed off people inside the city. Imagine being rescued and having a fellow American point a gun at you. These are Americans. This is not Iraq."

—Lt. Gen. Russel Honore

UNRAVELING KATRINA

On Sept. 10, 2005 and in subsequent weeks, *"CNN Presents"* aired detailed specials asking whether America was prepared to deal with another national emergency, be it a hurricane, an earthquake, or a terrorist attack. Structured to ask questions of and include quotes from specialists and experts, the programs explored what the nation would do when confronted with several scenarios.

One show began with images of Hurricane Katrina and its effects on New Orleans and the Gulf Coast, including excerpts from interviews with LSU Hurricane Center's Ivor van Heerden and Max Mayfield, director of the National Hurricane Center, both of whom had issued stern warnings about Katrina well in advance of landfall. Said van Heerden, who had foreseen the hurricane's impact and participated in FEMA's mockup disaster plan, called Hurricane Pam: "There is no pride in predicting something like this. It is just a lot of sadness and now a lot of anger, because I personally feel we from academia told everyone it was going to happen. It was based on hard science, good science, and it seems to have been ignored, and as a consequence, probably thousands of people have lost their lives."

Public reassurances by President Bush, Homeland Security Secretary Michael Chertoff, and FEMA director Michael Brown, were juxtaposed with strong statements about the vulnerability of New Orleans and the reality on the ground. Lessons from the Hurricane Pam exercise were noted, and government statements again contradicted its findings.

AP Photo/David J. Phillip

A bulldozer clears debris from Hurricane Katrina in Long Beach, Miss.

Excerpts from *CNN Presents*, "On Lessons Learned"

CNN JEANNE MESERVE: Officials had brainstormed about this kind of catastrophe. Hurricane Pam, a fictional Category 3 hurricane, was the centerpiece of an exercise just last summer.

VAN HEERDEN: It was paid for, it was funded by FEMA. It had a lot of federal agencies participating. There was at least one representative of the White House. They were all there. We discussed it for 12 days. How do we deal with a flooded New Orleans?

MESERVE: The Hurricane Pam exercise involving a storm weaker than Katrina envisioned a million evacuees, a half a million buildings destroyed and flooding, massive flooding. After Pam, officials said they had a search-and-rescue plan. But after Katrina, for days there were not enough boats, helicopters, and amphibious vehicles. After Pam, officials said they had plans to provide medical resources. But after Katrina, there were dire shortages.

After Pam, officials projected a need for 1,000 shelters to hold evacuees for 100 days. And yet after Katrina, the Superdome, the refuge for an estimated 20,000 people, was not well stocked with essentials.

LESSON ONE: Listen to the warnings of experts. Federal officials said they were startled by Katrina's carnage.

MICHAEL CHERTOFF: This is really one which I think was breathtaking in its surprise.

MESERVE: No, it wasn't. Everyone, from journalists to geologists, had long predicted the possible catastrophic effects of a hurricane on New Orleans.

LESSON TWO: Quick response is essential. When the city needed a tourniquet, it got Band-Aids. The result? Frustration, fear, and fatalities.

LESSON THREE: Know what you are dealing with.
It was painfully apparent the president's man on the ground did not know what was already being widely reported.

LESSON FOUR: Figure out who is in charge. Two days after the storm, when local and state officials turned to the president, he said the role of federal officials was only to assist.

LESSON FIVE: Maximize available resources. People and equipment poised to help went untapped. Helicopters used by the federal government to fight fires were ready to move people and supplies but sat unused. Vital equipment sat in boxes.

MESERVE: A $2 million cache of critically needed communications and firefighting gear owned by the federal government was not deployed for a week.

RAY WILKINSON, DHS Pre-positioned Equipment Program: You can't just turn on a light switch and have thousands and thousands of responders showing up. There needs to be an incident-command structure and an organization in place.

MESERVE: The question is, why wasn't that done?

JOHN BREAUX, former La. senator: I think that what you have to learn is how do you coordinate all the great forces we have in this country—local government, state governments, and the federal government. I think there has to be a clearer line on who does what and when.

MESERVE: But even before the investigations and studies, one sad truth is already evident. Hundreds, if not thousands, have lost their lives to floodwaters and to bungling, bickering, and bureaucracy. Why was there no security? Why were officials not ready for civil disorder?

FRANK SESNO, CNN: Chicago. Ripped by a biological terror attack. People dying from plague. New London, Conn., an explosion unleashes mustard gas. Seattle, a radiological device, a dirty bomb. Each scenario, a simulation, gruesome in its implications but an important run-through for officials who might have to deal with the real thing.

MESERVE: But none of these scenarios, none, included the kind of civil unrest we saw in New Orleans or the disappearance of about a third of its police force, events so dramatic that for a time lawlessness and anarchy framed the Katrina story around the world. And of course, in New Orleans itself. It's hard to know how bad and how wide-

spread the unrest was, but this much is clear. It was not predicted, it had not been drilled, and it badly complicated rescue efforts.

ELLEN GORDON, Naval Postgraduate School: Having the disaster victims themselves turn on the first responders isn't necessarily something that we've discussed and talked about in the past at any length. But I believe now that there will be many of us that will say we've got to take time out and discuss this and say, are we prepared to respond to this type of situation in the future.

MESERVE: There will be many investigations into the response to Katrina, but some have already concluded that the primary failure was one of leadership.

MIKE DEAVER, former Reagan advisor: One of the things that's needed in a situation like this is for somebody to sit down with us, and tell us and reassure us, and help us sort of fathom it and tell us that it's going to be all right eventually. That hasn't happened. That's sort of the leadership quotient that we haven't seen yet.

CANDY CROWLEY, CNN: But the president seemed remote from the air, uncomfortable, and out of tune on the ground. Also not seen, the kind of Giuliani command of details that help steady his city. By contrast, the governor of Louisiana has seemed tentative about basics. And where Giuliani brought calm to chaos and poetry to the unspeakable, New Orleans Mayor Ray Nagin had heated frustration. . . . And the sense that comes through the TV screen is of a multi-state, multi-city, multi-government crisis in which everyone is in charge and no one is in control. The truth is the story of Katrina has many heroes. What it's lacked is a leader.

US Coast Guard rescue swimmer preparing to rescue an elderly couple from the flood waters of New Orleans, Wednesday, 7 September, 2005.

EPA/USCG/HO/Landov

A soldier clears the area of high ground for a helicopter to pick up a group of people brought out of their homes in New Orleans. The flooded city is occupied by thousands of National Guardsman and other miliary troops. Officials continued to evacuate residents reluctant to leave the city.

Radhika Chalasani/Getty Images

FACT: Nearly 75 cents of every dollar that the federal government has given to local and state disaster units has been earmarked for terrorism. This leaves only 25 cents to be spent on natural disasters.

The program asked whether the next national emergency meant a new role for the military. In contrast to the National Guard and local first responders, what the military brings to the table, Meserve explained, is sheer manpower—thousands of troops, helicopters, ships, vehicles—and the ability to rapidly move supplies to the stricken area. In Katrina's aftermath, the 82nd was ordered to establish a grid and conduct search-and-rescue house by house, block by block, in cooperation with civilian officials. But FEMA had a different set of maps, and so first, they had to stop and coordinate efforts.

BRIG. GEN. GARY JONES, Louisiana National Guard: We've learned a lot about the things that we have to do to make sure that something like this doesn't happen again. The problem with it, of course, is that a storm like this comes along about once every 180 years. And 180 years is a long time to maintain institutional knowledge.

ANNE MARIE CONROY, San Francisco Office of Emergency Services: I think [Katrina] was a wake-up call for local government.

In another report, several different scenarios are proposed, most of which Homeland Security officials were prepared for; Meserve remarks that even though military and officials with plans on the table have been doing this for years, the actual event is different.

Excerpts from *Security Watch: Is America Prepared?*

Harsh lessons of Katrina are still painfully fresh. Many wonder if America is prepared for the next big disaster, whether it is from nature or man.

A look at response plans for worst-case scenarios.

- A major earthquake plunges the Bay Area into chaos.
- Terrorists contaminate the air with the small pox virus.
- America's milk supply is tainted with a deadly toxin.
- A dirty bomb is detonated, unleashing radiation on the nation's capital.
- Terrorists attack a chemical-filled ship, discharging a toxic cloud.

Each possibility is explored through the eyes of the first responders, the doctors, the experts, and the residents. Each segment ends with a brief summary of the possible solutions to each scenario, beginning with a major earthquake.

MESERVE: The magnitude 7.9 quake of 1906 triggered a ferocious fire. In the end, 3,000 people were dead, half of San Francisco residents, homeless. With two major faults slicing through the Bay Area, seismologists say there is a 62 percent chance of another mega quake by 2032.

MARY LOU ZOBACK, USGS seismologist: The Hayward Fault is the fault we're most concerned about in the Bay

Area. . . . The housing, the density of population, the major freeways crossing it, the water, gas pipelines, all sorts of things. The Bay Area depends on the lifelines that the Hayward Fault crosses.

Tests, and the experience gained from Katrina, have taught San Franciscans some valuable lessons. In addition to courses they've taken on the basics of search and rescue, first aid, and fire fighting, hoping to help themselves and first responders in a crisis, Mayor Jerry Brown says he, too, will get more prepared. Bridges and overpasses have been reinforced, but a new earthquake-resistant Bay Bridge span is uncompleted. The rapid transit system has yet to retrofit its underway tunnel between Oakland and San Francisco, a monumental project.

MESERVE: Though new buildings conform to strict seismic building codes, an estimated 85 percent of San Francisco housing does not. And only nine of 66 hospitals in the immediate Bay Area have been retrofitted to state standards as of 2003.

CONROY: These are big plans. There are big issues, big infrastructure, so it will take some time. And big price tags.

MESERVE: Sixty-five percent of San Francisco's firefighters and an even larger proportion of its police force live outside the city. Can ferries get them to work if roads and bridges buckle?

The scenarios go on, imagining the worst, hoping for the best. Other programs broadcast different approaches, but the number one concern is how to get the jump on these scares. How do you prepare for something when no amount of trial runs can predict all the variables?

In a segment aired Sept. 16, CNN's Tom Foreman concludes that one of the biggest lessons may be the need for self-reliance. With no real certainty about what will be provided, when, or how, says Foreman, "It may be more important to understand the limits of government help."

RICHARD FALKENRATH, former Homeland Security Adviser: People thought with all this attention to first responders and to incident management at the federal level that the federal government was really going to be able to respond instantaneously, or very rapidly to a disaster. And that's just not the case.

So the new leader of FEMA is saying get ready, have water, food, blankets, radios, flashlights, medicine. He says it's not paranoia to be prepared, it's simple prudence. Others put it more bluntly, for cities and their citizens.

RANDALL LARSEN, University of Maryland: In the first 72 to 96 hours after a big disaster, you're probably going to be on your own.

FOREMAN: Just like so many in Katrina's terrible wake.

Kevin Lair (right) assesses the damage to his home with his son Andrew (center) and his other son's girlfriend Meagan Harney (left) in the Lakeview District of New Orleans. The hole in the wall was punched out by the raging water rushing from the 17th Street Canal when the levee broke during Hurricane Katrina.

Many different levels of "What Went Wrong" emerge from those who study the most obvious flaws in the handling to those who criticize, for instance, the desensitization of the public to the dangers of a big hurricane due to daily reports of thunderstorms elevated to "Breaking News." Some focus on how to improve communications and coordination: bury power lines; improve intergovernmental cooperation between city and county; set up a special 311 emergency phone number; create a survivable method of communication that might include lines and antennas impervious to water, wind, and falling debris, and whose electrical power won't fail.

> **"An evacuation plan that consists of telling people to get out on their own is not an evacuation plan."**
> — *Amy Sullivan,* Washington Monthly

Medical responses that rely too heavily on computerized readouts may not survive another Category 4 hurricane; generators kept in basements that soon flood need to be moved upstairs. Doctors must receive training in diagnosing without sophisticated instruments, so that they can measure, as many did during Hurricane Katrina, a patient's IV dose by counting the drips, or ventilating a patient by manually inflating the breathing bag.

Coordination between authorities was probably the biggest lesson learned in 2005, and it included coordination between the lowest end of the responder totem pole all the way to the top. After watching the tension build between Gov. Kathleen Blanco, Mayor Ray Nagin, Sen. Mary Landrieu, and officials from FEMA to the White House, most people generally agreed that better liaisons and relationships need to be established.

Says one top-ten list of Lessons Learned, "Katrina and its after-effects is where 'political bashing' stops being funny. . . . I wonder how many people would be alive if the governor of Louisiana and the president had a good working relationship. When you get all done calling the president every name in the book, you might find you still have to work with the guy and he has to work with you."
— *blog entry from VariFrank, Sept. 10*

As pundits and editors and talk-show hosts debated "The Next Big One," it was already heading straight for Texas. Hurricane Rita, which would make landfall on Sept. 23, less than a month after Katrina, provided a quick exercise in whether or not officials had been paying attention. They had.

By Sept. 21, New Orleans was dry. But Rita was more powerful than Katrina and it was roaring toward land, predicted to hit Houston, within a day. A Category 5 storm, it boasted 165 mph winds and measured 280 miles from end to end. Galveston's 60,000 residents were moving out that day; 250,000 from Corpus Christi were under mandatory evacuation order. President Bush had declared States of Emergency in Texas and again in Louisiana. Rita was 600 miles from New Orleans, moving west and scheduled to hit late Friday or early Saturday. The death toll from Katrina had reached 1,033, and 799 of those were Louisianans. Costs for the storm were by then in the $200 billion dollar range. Galveston had plans to do without outside help, if necessary, for three days at least. All nursing homes and hospitals were emptied, the people bused out. Rita made landfall at 3:30 a.m. Saturday, east of Sabine Pass, Texas, as a Category 4 hurricane, and was 400 miles across, its wind speeds had slightly diminished. Heavy rains prevailed; twisters were spawned. The hurricane wiped out the small Texan town Cameron, pop. 1,900, and left half of Creole, pop 1,500 in splinters. More than a million people escaped before the storm hit. Gov. Rick Perry asked well in advance for 10,000 federal troops, activated 5,000 National Guardsmen, and had 1,000 state troopers on standby.

Did we learn anything about hurricanes themselves? The jury was and is still out on global warming, but recent studies have strongly indicated that it is affecting the severity, if not the frequency, of hurricanes from both the Atlantic and the Pacific.

Even if a second hurricane failed to create the same, or worse, devastation, journalists and the media could not forget the most dramatic and most controversial products of Katrina's rendezvous with New Orleans: pictures, video, and first-hand accounts of the Convention Center and the Superdome, where tens of thousands had been packed together without sufficient food and water, enduring inhuman conditions for day after day while FEMA alternated between claiming to not even know they were there, to promising relief that never came. Yet opinions differed just as dramatically on whether the situation in New Orleans arose from a local public indifference to poverty, and longstanding racial problems. One particularly eloquent and personal account came from the Poynter Institute Dean of Faculty, Keith Woods, who wrote lyrically of his return to Louisiana while driving with his brother Verdun, to gather with their aging father and many relatives, to ensure they were all safe. In particular, Woods zeroed in on the issue of race and poverty as a factor in the failed response to the people of New Orleans.

Rabbi Isaac Leider from the Jewish Zaka volunteers carries a Torah scroll out of the flooded synagogue of Beth Israel in New Orleans on Sept. 13. American volunteers with the Israeli charity rescued seven Torah scrolls from a the synagogue flooded by hurricane Katrina. Many of them were wet. It was uncertain whether they could be salvaged. Four soldiers from a California unit brought Leider and another volunteer to the gate of Beth Israel synagogue by boat, then accompanied them inside through waist-high water to recover the seven scrolls.

Excerpts from *Going Home* by Keith Woods

"Are you a looter or a finder?"

I read the subject line and knew what was in the e-mail. A wave of messages had rolled in on Katrina's heels linking to the same two pictures: A black man pulling a garbage bag full of loot, a white woman towing bread and other food behind her. The black man, one photo caption says, is a looter. The white woman, the other says, found the food she's pulling through the water. Television and print journalists had gotten swept up in the apocalyptic story of a city sinking into anarchy, and now they'd turned on themselves. Wasn't this evidence, many journalists wanted to know, of the media's bigotry?

The argument raged in my inbox. I deleted each one as it arrived.

It was Tuesday. Cheryl's 94-year-old grandmother (they called her Mama Dear) was trapped in her house, awash in rising, putrid water. Fats Domino was missing. People were dying in attics, on rooftops, on the roadsides, and in the Superdome. What the hell did I care whether somebody messed up a caption?

That week, *Slate's* Jack Shafer wrote with glib, liberal superiority that the fear of being called racists cowed white journalists so much that they ignored the most obvious element of the story: that the people who stayed and were now, by the thousands, in harm's way, were overwhelmingly black. Thus, many journalists, their unexamined discomfort with the story's images outed by the widely circulated column, leapt upon the opportunity to add the race of New Orleans' victims to their stories. I wondered if some even felt relieved to have permission finally to state the obvious.

I wish they'd waited for the water to go down low enough for the white people of St. Bernard Parish to start their sorrowful westward sojourn. I wish they'd waited until the Gulf of Mexico had retreated enough to reveal the devastation in Lower Plaquemines Parish and release the bodies of the white people drowned in Buras, Port Sulphur and Boothville and Venice— people who, just like the black people in New Orleans, stayed because they had no options or because they believed this storm, too, would turn, or because they were unwise or because they believed in God but not in Armageddon.

I wish they'd waited until they heard the white president of Washington Parish crying on the radio as he pleaded for help that hadn't come. I wish they'd seen the white president of Jefferson Parish crying on television because he thought help came too late.

continued on next page

I wish they could have seen the white faces of poverty in the Superdome or along the Mississippi Gulf Coast as clearly as they could see the blackness of poor folks in the 9th Ward or the blackness of the mayor who leads New Orleans. Then, maybe, they'd understand how little of this was about race and how much was about a more insidious, long-standing, unconscionable malfeasance of government officials who must have felt secret glee as our eyes diverted from their criminal incompetence. I know rage and racial suspicion. Every time I've cried since the end of August, those tears have been laced with the poisonous fear that we live in such a country where you can die of heat or hunger, drowning or dehydration—on national television—and no one will come to help if your skin is not white.

But I know more. I saw the white people waiting, hurting, dying. I knew they were there even when I didn't see them. I knew that America had also failed them.

As Brother and I neared Baton Rouge, a white woman called in to a radio station from Bogalusa, a devastated victim of Katrina in Washington Parish, just north of the city. They're crying racism in New Orleans, she told the host.

"Now the black people are going to get all the help and we won't get nothing," she said. "So I think we should set up a charity for white people."

"Did you hear about Mama Dear?"

[My sister] Lisa is on the other end of the phone, and I can't listen anymore. My father looks like death. My city is empty. It has been too much. Our trip to Louisiana was mostly symbolic and bordered on an inconvenience for Lisa and her husband, who had other things to do than rescue her older brothers each time we got lost in the back roads of Opelousas. Everything we did to help fell short of finished. Everything we bought or donated felt pitifully inadequate. A week after the storm struck we celebrated Lisa's birthday, kissed my father goodbye, then headed home.

We drove back through Mississippi on the once-impassable Interstate 59. Katrina had come this way. In the darkness, the roadside landscape looked like it had been stomped by giants. A mile south of Poplarville, the trees on either side of the Interstate, many teetering dangerously above us, had been snapped in two, their pine essence hemorrhaging into the night air. On the other side of the highway, dozens of military Jeeps, utility trucks, and ambulances spoke solemnly of what they expected to find as they convoyed south. For miles, we were the only ones on I-59. There were no road signs, no electricity, nothing to point the way home but headlights and memory. The music was back now—soft, saxophone sad, a dirge befitting the birthplace of jazz.

Slowly though, as the dead bobbed to the surface in New Orleans, the living emerged elsewhere. My uncles, aunts, and cousins were with family in Houston, San Antonio, and Baton Rouge. My friend Mario was in Franklin, La. One of my sister-in-law's brothers was in Arkansas, another in North Carolina. Two cousins had gone to Atlanta. Liz's parents and sister were alive in Baton Rouge. The missing reporter surfaced in Gulfport. Fats Domino was pulled from his yellow and black shotgun double in the sodden Lower 9th Ward.

Hope had survived.

Now, Lisa is on the phone, reminding me that this story is not over.

Mama Dear is dead.

She died on Sept. 14, Patrick's birthday. Her 7th Ward house had survived Katrina, but when the levees broke, the water rushed in, and it was nearly two days later that firefighters in a boat plucked her from there. They took her to the nearby Interstate 10 ramp, where she lay on an air mattress for 12 sweltering hours. An ambulance came on the third day and took her to the tarmac of Louis Armstrong airport, where doctors and nurses practiced medicine in the open air, their old and sick patients stacked on luggage carts. She was there for another 12 hours before an airplane came to take her to Houston.

What age and disease couldn't accomplish in 94 years, foolhardiness, dehydration and incompetence did in 16 days.

They buried her in a crypt in Houston just as cars began to flood Texas roads in panicked retreat from Hurricane Rita. She won't stay there, though. They'll bring her back home sometime after the madness recedes and the soldiers go away and, I suppose, when there are enough people around to lay her casket at her husband's side in New Orleans.

How does a city die?

How can it die when cars stream stubbornly back? Some surely come only to carry bleary-eyed family home to pick through the muck of their lives on the way to somewhere else. Some come only to lead a funeral cortege to grieve at the cemetery. But others will stay to rebuild, to pick up the sticks and bricks and trees and, in a few weeks, when it's All Souls Day, to tidy the graves they build above the ground in New Orleans so that no amount of water can totally erase the past upon which my hometown has always built its future.

—October 7, 2005

Entire article: www.poynter.org/column.asp?id=68&aid=90011

The costs of the government's missteps, aired nightly on the news, were also chronicled in a New Orleans paper famous for its enduring coverage of all things New Orleans. The *Times-Picayune*, 168 years old, managed to pick up lock, stock, and barrel and relocate their offices in the journalism building at LSU. Sixty-odd staffers brought out a daily paper in the face of every conceivable obstacle: no advertisers, no money, no cars, no place to sleep—and published a paper every day, online, at their now-famous site NOLA.com. The paper managed to be both timely and newsy; not to mention sustaining the irascible spirit of the town they called home: in one issue, they blasted President Bush not long after his visit to the area.

The media in general turned tough faces toward officials and never backed down. They insisted on seeing the conditions they'd heard rumors about; they carried their cameras and their voices into places that the government insisted were too dangerous, too unstable. They became as much heroes as the firefighters, the police, the Coast Guard, and the emergency technicians who prevailed because they had to, whether they carried the right paperwork or not. The relatively new phenomenon of blogging gave journalism a much-needed shot in the arm, as the man and woman on the street wrote from their cars, flooded apartment buildings, rooftops and bars, telling it like it was. And one article, from the BBC.com, proposed that with Katrina, American journalism had once again found its spine.

Excerpts from "NOLA.com Blogs and Forums Help Save Lives After Katrina," by Mark Glaser, *Online Journalism Review*

As the water finally starts to recede in New Orleans, the watershed for online journalism has been laid bare. Hurricane Katrina brought forth a mature, multi-layered online response that built on the sense of community after 9/11, the amateur video of the Southeast Asian tsunami disaster and July 7 London bombings, and the on-the-scene blogging of the Iraq War.

NOLA.com is known more for its MardiGras.com site and its live webcam, but now has become Exhibit A in the importance of the Internet for newspaper companies during a disaster. When the newspaper couldn't possibly be printed or distributed, the NOLA.com news blog became the source for news on hurricane damage and recovery efforts—including updates from various reporters on the ground and even full columns and news stories.

The blog actually became the paper, and it had to, because the newspaper's readership was in diaspora, spread around the country in shelters and homes of families and friends. The newspaper staff was

---

transformed into citizen journalists, with arts reviewers doing disaster coverage and personal stories running alongside hard-hitting journalism. In a time of tragedy and loss, the raw guts of a news organization were exposed for us to see.

And it wasn't just about news-gathering. NOLA.com editor Jon Donley turned over his NOLA View blog to his readers, who sent in dozens of calls for help. Those calls were relayed onto the blog, which was monitored constantly by rescuers, who then sent in teams to save them. "The site has been fantastic—and quite a lifesaver—and I truly mean a lifesaver," said Eliza Schneller via e-mail. "I listed a friend's mother, who needed rescuing, on the site and between me and the numerous caring people who responded—she and her daughter were picked up by the National Guard. Bless everyone that had a hand in keeping that site up and running!"

"It was weird because we couldn't figure out where these pleas were coming from," Donley told me. "We'd get e-mails from Idaho, there's a guy at this address and he's in the upstairs bedroom of his place in New Orleans. And then we figured out that even in the poorest part of town, people have a cell phone. And it's a text-enabled cell phone. And they were sending out text messages to friends or family, and they were putting it in our forums or sending it in e-mails to us."

Donley said that an aide of Lt. Gen. Russel Honore, the commander of the relief efforts, had tasked a group of people with monitoring the NOLA View blog, and were taking notes and sending out rescue missions based on the postings. "In fact, one time we had some server issues," Donley said, "and [the aide] wrote us frantically saying, 'Get this up as soon as you can, people's lives depend on it. We've already saved a number of lives because of it.'"

But will this renewed vigor in the U.S. press last? Others in the media weighed in and decided it could. Along with the outrage of the press, many hoped that accountability would also survive the storm, and that a different way of looking at government at all levels and even the presidency would be Katrina's legacy. What happened to the Gulf Coast, to New Orleans, and to, in many ways, everyone in the United States and beyond, made the question of accepting responsibility a much less dismissible notion than it had been before the storm.

Brian Williams, NBC anchor: *"I watched Americans die for lack of food and water in my own country, before my very eyes. If this disaster doesn't lead us into a national conversation on the subjects of class, race, urban planning, the environment, Iraq, and oil, then we have failed."*

Melvin Bell looks at a pickup truck that landed on his porch in Biloxi, Miss., during Hurricane Katrina.

Michael Falco/NNS /Landov

Brown said that he did not have the authority to order an evacuation; he also defends the agency's role as a first responder, pointing out that its job was to coordinate.

Sidney H. Schanberg, *Village Voice: "Will the reporters sustain their outrage? Will they reclaim the aggressive portion of their historical role? (Reminder to critics of bold reporting: 'Aggressive' is not synonymous with 'hostile' or 'insulting.') Will the reporters' nervous corporate bosses pass the word to them to cool it? I hope not. But even if such instructions are given, reporters will know that what they saw and lived through in New Orleans and elsewhere on the coast wasn't a one-time event or an exception to the rule."*

On Sept. 27, a House select committee convenes to probe the federal, state, and local response to Hurricane Katrina. Democrats protest the hearings by refusing to appoint members, dismissing what they contend is a too-soft probe of the Bush administration by GOP lawmakers. They demand an independent investigation. Out of four Democrats who are invited to sit in, two attend: Rep. William Jefferson of Louisiana and Rep. Gene Taylor of Mississippi.

"My biggest mistake was not recognizing by Saturday that Louisiana was dysfunctional."
—*Michael Brown*

In more than six hours of testimony, former head of FEMA Michael Brown, says that Mississippi and Alabama had evacuated properly but that New Orleans Mayor Ray Nagin and Gov. Kathleen Blanco were reluctant to order an evacuation. Brown, who resigned on Sept. 12 after two weeks of intense criticism and questions about his qualifications, is still being paid as a consultant (to the end of Oct.) to assess what went wrong.

On Oct. 19, Homeland Security Secretary Michael Chertoff comes before the House committee to answer questions, for the first time, about his own role in the response. Democrats are still absent from the hearings. Chertoff defends his actions before and after Hurricane Katrina, telling lawmakers he relied on FEMA experts with decades of experience in hurricane response.

"I'm not a hurricane expert," Chertoff says several times. When lawmakers grill Chertoff about why he stayed home Saturday before Katrina made landfall on Monday, why he made a previously scheduled trip to Atlanta on Tuesday, and why he didn't act more decisively to speed up the federal response, he says that he relied on former FEMA Director Michael Brown as the "battlefield commander."

Michael Chertoff, Oct. 19: *"You can't plan in a crisis environment. The challenge of dealing with this kind of ultracatastrophe is one that requires a lot of work beforehand—months beforehand. It doesn't require work 48 hours before the event. You're past planning. You've got to be executing."*

Although Brown blamed state and local officials in Louisiana for the slow response to Katrina when he testified before the committee, Chertoff says he does not endorse "those views." He tells the committee that FEMA was overwhelmed by Hurricane Katrina and needs to be retooled to improve preparation and response to natural disasters. FEMA had earlier been an independent agency before it was folded into the Deparment of Homeland Security after the 9/11 attacks.

In what is perhaps the most revealing testimony so far about the failures by FEMA, Marty Bahamonde, a respected regional director and the only FEMA official on the ground in New Orleans at the time Katrina hit told of his fustrations at getting those in charge to understand the severity of situation.

Excerpts from: FEMA Official in New Orleans Blasts Agency's Response—CNN.com, Oct. 20

WASHINGTON (AP)—In the midst of the chaos that followed Hurricane Katrina, a Federal Emergency Management Agency official in New Orleans sent a dire e-mail to Director Michael Brown saying victims had no food and were dying.

No response came from Brown.

Instead, less than three hours later, an aide to Brown sent an e-mail saying her boss wanted to go on a television program that night—after needing at least an hour to eat dinner at a Baton Rouge, La., restaurant.

The e-mails were made public Thursday at a Senate Homeland Security Committee hearing featuring Marty Bahamonde, the first agency official to arrive in New Orleans in advance of the August 29 storm. The hurricane killed more than 1,200 people and forced hundreds of thousands to evacuate.

Bahamonde, who sent the e-mail to Brown two days after the storm struck, said the correspondence illustrates the government's failure to grasp what was happening.

"There was a systematic failure at all levels of government to understand the magnitude of the situation," Bahamonde testified. "The leadership from top down in our agency is unprepared and out of touch."

The 19 pages of internal FEMA e-mails show Bahamonde gave regular updates to people in contact with Brown as early as August 28, the day before Katrina made landfall. They appear to contradict Brown, who has said he was not fully aware of the conditions until days after the storm hit. Brown quit after being recalled from New Orleans amid criticism of his work. Brown had sent Bahamonde, FEMA's regional director in New England, to New Orleans to help coordinate the agency's response. Bahamonde arrived on August 27 and was the only FEMA official at the scene until FEMA disaster teams arrived on August 30.

As Katrina's outer bands began drenching the city August 28, Bahamonde sent an e-mail to Deborah Wing, a FEMA response specialist. He wrote: "Everyone is soaked. This is going to get ugly real fast."

Subsequent e-mails told of an increasingly desperate situation at the New Orleans Superdome, where tens of thousands of evacuees were staying. Bahamonde spent two nights there with the evacuees.

On Aug. 31, he e-mailed Brown from the Superdome to tell him that thousands of evacuees were gathering in the streets outside without food or water and that there were "estimates that many will die within hours."

"Sir, I know that you know the situation is past critical," he wrote.

A short time later, Brown's press secretary, Sharon Worthy, wrote colleagues to complain that the FEMA director needed more time to eat dinner at a Baton Rouge restaurant that evening.

"He needs much more than [sic] 20 or 30 minutes," Worthy wrote.

"Restaurants are getting busy," she said. "We now have traffic to encounter to go to and from a location of his choise [sic], followed by wait service from the restaurant staff, eating, etc. Thank you."

In an August 29 phone call to Brown informing him that the first levee had failed, Bahamonde said he asked for guidance but did not get a response.

"He just said, 'Thank you,' and that he was going to call the White House," Bahamonde said.

Senators on the committee were dismayed.

"We will examine further why critical information provided by Mr. Bahamonde was either discounted, misunderstood, or simply not acted upon," said GOP Sen. Susan Collins of Maine, who heads the committee. She decried the "complete disconnect between senior officials and the reality of the situation."

In e-mails, Bahamonde described to his bosses a chaotic situation at the Superdome. Bahamonde noted also that local officials were asking for toilet paper, a sign that supplies were lacking at the shelter.

"Issues developing at the Superdome. The medical staff at the dome says they will run out of oxygen in about two hours and are looking for alternative oxygen," Bahamonde wrote Regional Director David Passey on August 28.

Bahamonde said he was stunned that FEMA officials responded by continuing to send truckloads of evacuees to the Superdome for two more days even though they knew supplies were in short supply.

"I thought it amazing," he said. "I believed at the time and still do today, that I was confirming the worst-case scenario that everyone had always talked about regarding New Orleans."

Rebuilding the city of New Orleans is now added to a growing list of outstanding problems facing the country. Most believe there is no question that it must be done, but *how* is something that will take careful and extensive planning. It's a task that will take years and transform economies and it faces a host of hurdles from questions about financing and environmental damage to more intractable problems of race and poverty. The private Insurance Services Office, which provides industry data, estimated $34.4 billion in insured property losses from Katrina, dwarfing the inflation-adjusted $20.8 billion from Hurricane Andrew. Many of New Orleans houses are on the National Register of Historic Places. Architects and planners will discuss the need to preserve historic regions and revitalize high-poverty neighborhoods. More than half the housing destroyed by Katrina were rentals, about 70 percent of which were affordable to low-income renters.

Singer Harry Connick, Jr., addressed lawmakers on behalf of Habitat for Humanity, urging them to help remedy the housing crisis in New Orleans and other hurricane-affected areas of the Gulf Coast. "During my three trips to New Orleans after the storm," he said, "I experienced humanity as I never thought I would. From horrifying, nameless death to clinging, new life. From relentless suffering to inspirational heroism . . . working with Habitat for Humanity as the honorary chair of Operation Home Delivery, Connick went on to say it had given him "an avenue to channel this incredible sadness that has devoured my soul. This program is getting people back into homes, back on their feet, and on with their lives." Connick asked that the 300,000 families in need of homes and work be part of the rebuilding, given training and priority, and said that it would in part restore their dignity. Their input was, he said, "the meaningful voice of its citizens at the table." Anxious for the poor not to be "priced out" of their own city, Connick also requested lower and moderately priced homes. "New Orleans is my essence, my soul, my muse," he said. "I have no doubt that the government of this great nation will work with its people to lead New Orleans and the Gulf Coast back to an enlightened, proud, safe, part of the world."

New Orleans resident Cynthia Allen, and her son, Anthony, wait at the evacuation staging area on Interstate 10 in Metaire, La..

Reginald Banks pulls his uncle's tool box through foot-high mud in Violet, La., in St. Bernard Parish.

INTERVIEW

Aaron Brown

Walter Isaacson,
CEO, Aspen Institute

BROWN: Eventually a new city will arise from the Mississippi Delta. Joining us to discuss the future of New Orleans—and we believe it has a future—one of its native sons, Walter Isaacson, who now runs the Aspen Institute, and used to run this network and this anchorman. Nice to see you, Walter. Your heart broken?

ISAACSON: I'm definitely heartbroken. It's very, very sad. But as you said, I do think the city will come back. And there are lots of us who are expatriates from that city, love that city very much. And they'll plan to rally around the city and do what we can to help it come back.

BROWN: We talked a bit about this last night, and I suspect will for a long time to come. You can come up with a plan to build buildings. That's sort of easy, actually. I mean, it takes money and time and the rest. But rebuilding the soul of New Orleans is a complicated piece of business.

ISAACSON: It is. In fact, the stories next week and the week after will be how easy it will be for the buildings. Because most of the buildings in the French Quarter and in the central business district and in the warehouse district, they're pretty much OK. They're there. The parts of New Orleans that most people know and most people, visitors go see, those buildings are OK. And that's not going to be the problem.

As you said, what's going to be the problem is recreating the magic of the city. And the even more complex thing is taking what was magical and beautiful about one of the world's greatest cities and restoring that, but maybe getting rid of some of the things, or many of the things, that were not good about the city—the sort of torn social fabric that we saw.

BROWN: That's where I wanted to go next. This was going to be one of those wandering questions you used to chide me about. But in all of this there was peeled back something about New Orleans that was really quite unpleasant—an abject poverty in the city. You look at some of these pictures, you can't imagine how people lived that way. In that sense, I wonder if there is any magic left at all.

ISAACSON: Oh, I think there's magic to the city. And I think everybody who lived in that city, you know, from various parts of the city, from the Lower Ninth Ward to Uptown, all had a special feel for New Orleans and I think still do.

I think you saw some social pathologies there. But, you know, you have segregation and racism and problems in any major American city. I think the ones in New Orleans came to the surface because of the flood.

But maybe—and I hate using bad metaphors. Maybe you should—I chided you for that as well, but you didn't do it as often—but it might flush out some of the pathologies. It rises it to the surface. And we can say, let's build, let's take this as an opportunity to build this city, where we get the social fabric right, where we get some opportunities for all.

We have a city that can really work and that can restore the magic of being what was and will be, you know, one of the world's great places for creativity, for music, for art, and one of the great ports of the world.

Something—you know, New Orleans has given a lot to the world and a lot to this nation. It's given its port, its economy. It's helped ship the grain out and ship the oil in and refine the oil, but also created jazz and created great music and created great food.

And that came from a magical mix of people in the City of New Orleans. It came from the fact that you couldn't just have a homogenous group. You had to sometimes have a very complex layers of society there.

And the question is, can you get a city back that can be as creative and as good? And I'm sure you can, and do it where you have a better education system, where you have less crime, where you have less corruption and you have a better social fabric.

BROWN: One more, and not a whole lot of time either. Is there in the city, do you believe, the leadership—the political leadership, the leadership in the business community and the tourist community, whatever you call that—to rebuild the special New Orleans?

ISAACSON: You know, that's what we've talked about for the past week, those of us who love New Orleans. It's not a place where a lot of Rudy Giulaiani's march forward, take charge, roll up their sleeves. You don't see the great leadership. But you do have the passion, you do have the love, you do have the sensitivity. And I suspect the leadership will emerge.

"People talk about this [rebuilding] being an opportunity. . . . It's more than an opportunity: It's an obligation to fix the housing problems that were here."

—Sheila Crowley, president of the National Low-Income Housing Coalition

---

E-mail responses to CNN Question: Should New Orleans be rebuilt? If so, how?

We can't throw away almost 400 years of American history! Would anyone abandon Boston, Philadelphia, Chicago, or San Francisco because of a disaster? Both Chicago and San Francisco, in previous disasters, were destroyed as well.

—David Aeschliman, Corona, Calif.

New Orleans was never just another town. It represented a certain state of mind. It wasn't for everyone, and most of the time in the summer was like a steam room. For some going to Mardi Gras was a youthful rite of passage, and for others just another reason to let off steam. What other town represents that kind of spirit? Has that kind of history? Las Vegas comes close, but its glass and steel glitz and glamour pale in comparison to the wood buildings and urban legends of New Orleans. Clearly, those old levees must be improved. Made higher, stronger, and it will take time. Eventually the city will come back and Katrina will be part of the legend that will continue. Just like the great fire of Chicago. The big earthquake of San Francisco. . . .but look at those cities today. They hardly packed up and moved away. Why should the people of New Orleans?

—Stephen Martin, Los Angeles

Being a proud native of Louisiana, there is absolutely no doubt in my mind that New Orleans should be rebuilt and will be rebuilt. Cajun people have two things instilled in them at a very young age. Never give up in what you believe in (we are survivors) and when you have hit your lowest (rock bottom) come back bigger and better with a sense with a whole lot of wisdom.

—Eva L. Broussard, Perry, Fla.

The most important thing that needs to be saved (and rebuilt) is lower- and middle-income housing,

shotguns, double shotguns, corner stores, creole cottages and camelbacks all combine to make an urban fabric that does not exist in any other city. Residential areas constitute the bulk of the character and spirit of New Orleans. What visitors see—the famous spots —remain largely intact. Rebuilding should be a combination of salvaging and reconstructing with a keen eye focused on the vernacular. For this to happen, native New Orleanians need to be employed on all levels—urban planners, architects, designers, historians, contractors. It would be a shame to see a national panel of designers without any sort of deep and personal knowledge of New Orleans import suburban-type housing. New Orleans' spirit is unique among American cities—we have an opportunity to keep it that way.

—Erin Rensink, New Orleans

Yes, they should rebuild New Orleans. N'awlins is a unique place historically and ethnically and should not be abandoned. Instead, take a page from Galveston's book, a city demolished by the 1900 "perfect storm," and raise the level of the city at least three feet, possibly more, and build a sandbar or breakwater with some of the concrete and brick rubble left behind by Katrina. Make sure the breakwater or sandbar is navigable so that essential shipping can still get in and out of the great port and harbor. Residents of the lowest ground should just get a land swap for a lot on higher ground, and make the lowest ground a nature sanctuary or leave it as a floodplain. Take heart, N'awliners, from Galveston and San Francisco and Atlanta and many other cities devastated by natural disasters or wars, they all were rebuilt.

—Laura Sosnowski, Milwaukee, Wis.

Yes, New Orleans can evolve and its spirit thrive if it does not throw out its family jewels: its rare scale for humans rather than for cars; its wisdom that we work to live, not live to work; its *joie de vivre* and architecture. We'll need Dutch help for stronger levees; otherwise, New Orleans got it right in so many ways in its past. Architecturally, I would rather be poor in New Orleans than rich in Dallas, Houston, or Atlanta. Rebuild in New Orleans style.

—Jamie Rein, San Francisco

As families searched out and found each other, remarkable stories unfolded of how long-separated members had survived. They suggest the resilience and backbone of the people of New Orleans, who will in the days to come participate in their city's rebirth. And within a month after the storm that practically shut down the city, beignets are back, and so are 24-hour cafes. Some will return to the only place they can ever imagine as home. Some will stay in the state that welcomed them after Katrina. Many have not made up their minds.

Mobile homes for evacuees from Hurricane Katrina are seen at a FEMA staging area near Baton Rouge, La.

"Living in Camp Cemetery"
by Christy Oglesby, CNN.com, Oct. 17

When Hurricane Katrina struck New Orleans, dozens of people stayed alive by setting up camp among the graves of a cemetery, where they lived for days with no sign that help would come. Nellie Francis, 77, was one of the residents of the makeshift camp at Mt. Olivet Cemetery, where mausoleums served as shelters and people set up their own emergency government, running rescue efforts, tending to the sick, and feeding the hungry—in short, filling the void left by the lack of a noticeable official response to the disaster.

Francis came to the cemetery from her one-story Pauger Street home, where she spent the day after Katrina struck in knee-deep water, trying to save what she could. "I took my birds and raised them up high," she said. Tank, her big black Akita, had a dry spot on the flowered living room sofa.

Then hope docked at her door. Men from her neighborhood had launched their fishing boats and one was there for Francis. The boat dropped her off three blocks away at the highest, and only dry section, of the community—Mt. Olivet Cemetery.

"Nobody else was coming. It wasn't no Coast Guard or nothing," said Russell Plessy, who put Francis and Tank in his boat. "We all know each other around here so we just started helping people."

The helping went on for almost a week. In Katrina's aftermath and the absence of city, state, or federal attention, neighbor saved neighbor. Among the white tombs and slick marble crypts, the cemetery's living residents had full bellies, soft bedding, shelter and security.

They came together, as people have across the country in the aftermath of Katrina. With governments and agencies seemingly overwhelmed by the depth and breadth of hurricane destruction, assistance has ranged from frustratingly slow to fatally nonexistent.

"There was a guy in the group, I think he was retired Navy, a Vietnam veteran. He oversaw everything," Francis said. Another man named Lawrence, she said, "made the decision about where to go—it was the coolest and cleanest place in the mausoleum.

"They rescued us. They took care of us from Monday to Friday. They had a Family Dollar right across the street, and these guys went in there and got food and made sure everybody had food. . . . One man who lived across the street still had gas, and he went home and fried chicken for us. . . I couldn't have asked for no better treatment."

Francis's only anxiety, she said, was over her second oldest son, Walter. He lived about seven blocks from her on Jasmine Street, and once she decided not to evacuate, he stayed behind too-in case his momma would need him."

Walter Francis, 57, couldn't reach his mother's house on August 29, because of flooding on Gentilly Boulevard. It took him two and a half days before he was able to break down the door of her home, where he found waist-deep black water full of his mother's belongings. It terrified him to discover her dresses.

"I was panicking. I could hear the fear in my voice. I was just shouting, 'Momma! Momma!' Her clothes were floating around, and I didn't know whether the clothes had her in it." Finally, Walter emerged from the house. Neighbors in a boat told him his mother was safe at a cemetery, where she was being taken care of. The next day, he found her sitting on a bench.

"There was a crowd of people around the bench, but when they stepped back, I could see that was her sitting on the bench. I dropped my stick, and ran to her. She has trouble standing up. But I just grabbed her and pulled her to me and I cried like a baby."

Walter said he was impressed with the Mt. Olivet operation. "These people were very innovative. I was living like a caveman, and she had the best amenities right there." On Friday, a helicopter had lifted his mother, and a few others, out of Mt. Olivet. Walter decided not to evacuate, and nearly a week after Katrina roared through, he and a small caravan of neighbors drove their SUVs out of the city.

Now, he's in Napoleonville, La., where he remains in a rental with his wife, Tank, and his momma.

When it comes to rebuilding, one of the main concerns is, of course, the levees. Having almost taken on an identity of their own, even their names have become household words: 17th Street, Industrial Canal, London. Their fate is much discussed, and how to repair, improve, and strengthen them has preoccupied almost every facet of the recovery issues facing New Orleans. But the funding and plans that should have been in place before Hurricane Katrina are still in short supply, and construction on the levees begins the first week of October to rebuild them to withstand a Category 3 storm.

Anderson Cooper: "*The mayor of New Orleans said again today that he is just not thinking about rebuilding his city, but is thinking big, he said. He called on others to do the same, which brings us to the levees that surround the city. They weren't strong enough to withstand Katrina. We all know that by now. And remember, after the storm, how everyone said the levees were going to be rebuilt bigger and stronger and safer? Well, apparently not everyone got the memo, because, right now, the levees are being rebuilt exactly the same. CNN's Dan Simon investigates.*"

DAN SIMON: These bulldozers in St. Bernard Parish are moving dirt to rebuild what nature destroyed. Hard to believe, but this is where levees that once rose 17 feet in the air were washed flat, and with it, much of this parish.

COL. LEWIS SETLIFF, Army Corps of Engineers: What's exciting today is we came out here this week and started our initial construction aimed at long-term recovery of the hurricane-protection system.

SIMON: The plan, is to rebuild that hurricane-protection system like it was, just sufficient to withstand a Category 3 storm. The excitement here is hardly universal.

UNIDENTIFIED MALE: Get the job done right, to where you won't have to worry about having a problem like this again.

SIMON: In a community in which house after house was destroyed by the floodwaters from a Category 4 storm, many residents unable to hide their frustration.

UNIDENTIFIED MALE: They need to rebuild them high, in my opinion, to the proper level, where they could handle a Category 5 or 4, instead of just a Category 3.

SIMON: But the Army Corps of Engineers says it doesn't have the funding, nor the resources, to rebuild bigger and better and still have the levees finished by next summer. It says it could strengthen them further at a later date—still not a good plan, says Louisiana Republican Sen. David Vitter.

VITTER: I'm tired of living by the old Corps standard and the old Corps schedule. This is an emergency situation.

SIMON: I know you don't make those decisions, but you're aware that that sentiment is out there.

SETLIFF: We are intimately aware that that sentiment exists. Again, authority to act rests solely to restore what was here before the storm.

SIMON: Touring the parish, as we did today, the magnitude of rebuilding the levees become clear. Mile after mile will have to be rebuilt. Everywhere, there are examples of the powerful storm surge.

And this right here is pretty striking, when you consider that, before the storm, you could not even see that pipe. That's because it went right through the levee. The Corps says even getting the levees back to pre-Katrina strength by next year will be difficult.

KEVIN WAGNER, Army Corps of Engineers: We are very committed to actually getting the work done. We know a lot of people are not going to rebuild until we have these levees in place, because that—provides the protection for them from the hurricanes' storm surges.

SIMON: Kevin Wagner, who is overseeing the levee rebuilding in St. Bernard Parish, knows what's at stake. He, too, lost his home. The planned replacement levees, he says, will be enough for him to rebuild his house.

WAGNER: Forty years, the system worked very well. And I think you can have complete confidence that, once we finish with this, people will have a level of protection that they'll feel comfortable with.

SIMON: The Corps concedes a stronger, bigger levee system would be preferable, but there's no money, no plans, and no time to build before the start of next year's hurricane season.

Mayor Ray Nagin, Sept. 14: *"New Orleans is coming back. We're bringing New Orleans back. We're bringing this culture back. We're bringing this music back. I'm tired of hearing these helicopters. I want to hear some jazz. And we're bringing these people back. And we're going to bring the spirit that makes New Orleans one of the greatest, unique cultural cities in the world."*

Carol Costello Interview with Stephen Perry, New Orleans Convention and Visitors Bureau, Sept. 14.

COSTELLO: Let's talk about those areas of New Orleans, because I know that city leaders, including you, have gotten together to talk about building a new New Orleans. I want to read you a quote from one businessman in New Orleans, taken from the *Wall Street Journal.*

This man says his name is James Reiss. He says: "Those who want to see the city rebuilt want to see it done in a completely different way demographically, geographically, and politically. I'm not just speaking for myself here. The way we've been living is not going to happen again, or we're out."

PERRY: Well, Jimmy is head of the Business Council, and he's looking at this from a business

Anja Niedringhaus/AP

Work continues on the 17th Street Canal levee in New Orleans on Sept. 15, 2005. The Army Corps of Engineers plans to rebuild the levees to the same specifications as before Katrina (Category 3) has generated a lot of controversy, especially in St. Bernard Parish where 15-foot levees were leveled by the storm. The Corps for its part says it does not have the funding to do it better.

perspective. And certainly the recovery of the business sector is absolutely critical.

But there's really almost a more important opportunity here. We have a historic opportunity in the United States in policy development to create a living urban laboratory for revitalization. This is an opportunity to rethink the social ills that beset nearly every major urban environment in America, to think about how do you build—rebuild real neighborhoods with the right kind of schools for all people, not just for people with means.

COSTELLO: Well, I was just going to ask you that, because by this statement, some would think that the poor and disenfranchised will not be welcome back to the city.

PERRY: Well, that doesn't reflect my view or the views of those in the tourism industry nor the views of the governmental leaders that I've talked to, because what they're envisioning is a New Orleans that is new and revitalized for every people, for all persons, regardless of race or economic sector. Because the reality is in New Orleans, there's no loyalty here. The culture bubbles up from the street. And what makes New Orleans great, it's French and Spanish and African and Caribbean culture, this multicultural melting pot, comes because of the nature and character of all of the people. And remember, in New Orleans, it's all about opportunity.

COSTELLO: Yes.

PERRY: The people coming out of poor neighborhoods are the ones who grow up to be incredible saxophone players, thoracic surgeons, business entrepreneurs. This is—if we miss this opportunity to rebuild every sector of our society and to create the kind of urban environment that is critical to good lives, we'll have missed the greatest opportunity in American history.

"New Orleans Easing Back into Business" by John King, October 19

The scene at Café du Monde on Tuesday was frenetic: employees polishing the counters and wiping the windows, contractors installing new equipment in the kitchen and applying one last coat of paint inside and around the landmark's outside seating area.

Early Wednesday morning, the hard work paid off, as the cafe's trademark beignets and coffee were once again available to the public. More than seven weeks after Katrina, the reopening of Café du Monde is helping New Orleans project a "back in business" image.

"There are many jobs to be had here right now in the city of New Orleans," Café du Monde Vice-President Burt Benrud said. "If you come to the city of New Orleans and you don't have a job, you're not looking."

Despite his optimism about New Orleans' economic climate, Benrud acknowledges a fair amount of uncertainty. In his case, he wonders what will happen to a 142-year-old business that operates around the clock when the city's curfew kicks in.

"[Are] the cops going to show up over here and say it is midnight—you guys need to close? It is my hope that that situation gets resolved shortly, so we can go back to business as usual: 24 hours a day, 364 days a year." Café du Monde gives its workers Christmas Day off.

On St. Claude Avenue in the predominantly black neighborhood of Bywater, banks, restaurants, fast-food establishments, and corner groceries remain shuttered, many of them heavily damaged.

But count Joseph Peters among the optimists there. Peters reopened his tire-repair shop within a week of Katrina passing, when there was still water in the

streets. His business is bustling because of all the damage to cars caused by the debris-strewn streets, and Peters says cleanup crews have been showing up in recent days at a seafood restaurant across the street from his shop.

As Peters spoke to CNN on Tuesday, a man with a wheelbarrow made more than a dozen trips in and out of a small mom-and-pop grocery store nearby, dumping debris on the median of what once was a busy thoroughfare from the working-class neighborhood to the central city.

"I don't think it is being unfair. It's just the way it works," Peters said between repairs when asked if he believed more help was going first to downtown and richer neighborhoods.

"You come back in six months you are going to see this up and running," Peters said. "Those people are going back into business. Trust me, they will be back. This is home."

In the final analysis, much of what Hurricane Katrina taught us was how Americans had not lost their ability to rely on each other, to reach out to each other, to depend on neighbors, communities, local newspapers, police force, firefighters, even volunteers from the Fish and Wildlife agency. Though it would have been far better to have the federal government swing into force, maybe there was a lesson to be learned in having to reach out, even in being able to see the kind of sorrow and anger that developed all over the Gulf Coast when no help came. Because it touched all of us. With luck, it also touched every official at every level of government. If it didn't, it is our obligation to make sure that it does.

Whether it was a sympathetic neighbor taking in households of people and serving dinner, or a reporter who listened and tried to help, the real silver lining wasn't that New Orleans could rebuild again better, without its poverty or feeble infrastructure, or hard lessons were learned about survival and preparation. The real silver lining in the aftermath of Hurricane Katrina was in people reconnecting with each other, minus the cell phones, the closed doors, the office cubicles, and the isolation of cars and SUVs. What was taken from the tragedy in New Orleans was some of the spirit of the Big Easy itself: the community, the fragile openness of a poor neighborhood that also allows bonds to develop; the outrage of its citizens at being neglected and unprotected; the connectedness of its families and history and love for the city. We were all there. Because of a revitalized press that allowed us inside, we were there. And we are all the better for it. The lessons really learned from this are ones few will ever forget. They remain in the heart, a place which only very recently got a whole lot bigger.

Sharon Morrow left and Nita Hemeter pause to dance for a moment to the sounds of Al "Carnival" Johnson playing from Nita's car as they clean up on Wilson Drive after Hurricane Katrina in New Orleans on Friday, Sept. 30.

Alex Brandon/NNS/Landov

173

Anderson Cooper: Reporter's Notebook

I've been coming to New Orleans since I was a kid. My dad used to live here, and his heart always did. This gritty gumbo city, its hot humid streets, seeing it like this, well, it's hard to explain. Blink and you're in Baghdad. Black water, guys with guns, rubble-strewn streets, Black Hawks in the sky.

That sound, that sound, crushing and comforting, the cavalry's come, help has arrived, urgent seconds ticking by. Street signs are down, new signs are up. Hand-drawn, heartfelt, be thankful God loves you. Looters will be shot. This one's my favorite: "Don't try. I'm sleeping inside with a big dog, an ugly woman, two shotguns, and a claw hammer."

Working here, it's unlike any story I've ever been on. I've never been prouder of the people I stand by. You shoot and you edit. You do live shots and shows. You're always in motion, slamming sodas and candy. It just doesn't stop.

Last week we were living in trailers packed tight, poorly stocked. No one complained. There was no need to explain. Compared to everyone else, we had it good. The phones didn't work. We still clung to our blackberries, our heads always down. Now we've got an office set up with food and supplies, at night a hotel where we disinfect our feet.

We're all taking something—Cipro, a whole bunch of shots. Some have conjunctivitis and cuts. You have to be careful. What's happened here has been a story about failure, of governments and officials and systems and places. But it's also a story about kindness, of strangers helping strangers and neighbors in need.

There have been moments, I think for a lot of us working here, where we all feel very much alone. We're surrounded by ruin and rubble. You feel like you're on the edge of the world. I guess in a way you get used to seeing all this destruction, but you never get used to seeing the people it's affected.

In the shelters it really hits you. The babies are oblivious, thank God, their parents' arms the only home they have. The young and the old have little but doubts and questions. What will I do? How can I rebuild? What will happen tomorrow?

Governments can help, but they can't do this. Holding, hugging, human connections were strengthened by the storm. I know sometime soon viewers are going to move on from this story. The water level is falling. The tide is ebbing and so will the interest. I know it's going to happen. I just don't know when. I don't think we should forget what we've seen. I know those of us who were here never will.

Well, that's what we've been seeing these last few weeks here. We wanted you to see kind of a behind-the-scenes look at what we've been doing. And we all feel honored to be here.

I know that New Orleans will win its fight in the end. I was born in the city and lived there for many years. It shaped who and what I am. Never have I experienced a place where people knew more about love, about family, about loyalty and about getting along than the people of New Orleans. It is perhaps their very gentleness that gives them their endurance.

They will rebuild as they have after storms of the past; and they will stay in New Orleans because it is where they have always lived, where their mothers and their fathers lived, where their churches were built by their ancestors, where their family graves carry names that go back 200 years. They will stay in New Orleans where they can enjoy a sweetness of family life that other communities lost long ago.

San Antonio Express-News, Edward A. Ornelas/AP photo

The Numbers

(as of Oct. 20, 2005)

Whether it was foreign aid or how many MREs were dropped during the aftermath of the hurricane, the totals never failed to be a reminder of just what it takes to deal with a disaster of these proportions. [At press time, Katrina's "numbers" were still climbing.]

- Official death toll: **1,277**
- Official cost of damage to entire Gulf Coast area: **$200+ billion**
- Federal aid: **$62.3 billion**
- People in New Orleans without privately owned transportation: **120,000**
- Poverty rate in New Orleans: **38 percent**
- Miles covered by national disaster declarations: **90,000**
- American Red Cross shelters across 27 states: **1,150**
- People that American Red Cross has provided financial assistance for: **1.2 million families**
- American Red Cross workers who provided relief aid: **190,000**
- Names registered online at the American Red Cross "Family Links Registry": **285,983**
- Animals that the Humane Society of the United States rescued and sheltered at the Lamar-Dixon facility in Gonzales, La.: **6,036**
- Animals that the Humane Society of the United States rescued and sheltered at Hattiesburg, Miss.: **2,385**
- Donations received by the Humane Society: **$15 million**
- Fish that died at the New Orleans Aquarium of the Americas: **10,000**
- Evacuees in Texas: **230,000**
- Evacuees in Tennessee: **12,000**
- Evacuees in Arkansas: **50,000**
- Total Katrina evacuees across the country in shelters, homes, hotels and other housing: **374,000**
- Total number of evacuees: **1+ million**
- Percentage of evacuees who say they'll return to New Orleans: **45–50 percent**
- Percentage of evacuees in Texas who plan to stay there: **40 percent**
- Percentage of evacuees who say they'll move anywhere but Louisiana: **15 percent**
- People who left the Great Plains states during the Dust Bowl migration in 1930s: **300,000**
- National Guard personnel deployed to hard-hit areas: **50,000**
- Total active-duty troops deployed to hard-hit areas: **22,000**

- Lives saved by Coast Guard: **33,000**
- Reports to National Center for Missing and Exploited Children of children separated from their families due to Hurricanes Katrina and Rita: **4,724**
- Families reunited: **2,526+**
- Amount of sand dropped by Coast Guard to repair levees: **350 tons**
- Emergency response teams from FEMA: **61**
- Tons of water, ice, and ready to eat meals (MREs) brought in as of Oct. 20: **125 tons**
- Total liters of water delivered to Gulf Coast as of Oct. 20: **24.2 million**
- Liters of water delivered to Gulf Coast as of Sept. 3: **13.4 million**
- Liters of water delivered to New Orleans as of Sept. 3: **7 million**
- Total (Oct. 20) MREs delivered to affected areas: **13.6 million**
- MREs delivered to Gulf Coast as of Sept. 3: **5.4 million**
- MREs delivered to New Orleans as of Sept. 3: **2 million**
- Total pounds of ice delivered to Gulf Coast: **67 million**
- Households that received a portion of $3.51 billion in disaster assistance: **1,189,000**
- Feet of levee breach repaired as of Sept. 3: **200 with 600 remaining**
- People inside Houston Astrodome by Sept. 3: **16,000**
- People still to be evacuated from New Orleans hospitals on Sept. 3: **1,700**
- People still at Superdome on Sept. 3: **2,000**
- Meals served outside the New Orleans Convention Center from Sept. 2–3: **more than 75,000**
- Estimated insurance claims as a result of Hurricane Katrina: **$25 billion**
- Amount of national-emergency grant: **$62 million** to Louisiana, **$50 million** to Mississippi
- E-mails CNN received from people searching for their relatives as of Sept. 3: **15,000**
- Amount of oil spilled from Bass Enterprises South Facility in Cox Bay, La.: **3.8 million gallons**
- Amount of oil spilled from Sundown Energy East in Potash, La.: **18,900 gallons**

List compiled from CNN transcripts, Department of Homeland Security Web site, American Red Cross Web site, the National Center for Missing and Exploited Children Web site, the Associated Press, CBS News, and Wikipedia the Free Encyclopedia.